PLEASE CHECK FOR CD

SCHOLASTIC

D0245587

100 SCIENCE LESSONS

NEW EDITION

TERMS AND CONDITIONS

IMPORTANT - PERMITTED USE AND WARNINGS - READ CAREFULLY BEFORE USING

Licence

SCOTTISH PRIMARY 7

YEAR 6

Minimum specification:
- PC with a CD-ROM drive and 512 Mb RAM (recommended)
- Windows 98SE or above/Mac OSX.1 or above
- Recommended minimum processor speed: 1 GHz

0
507
ONE

WS 2252794 X

5-2008

Clifford Hibbard, Karen Mallison-Yates and Tom Rugg

Authors
Clifford Hibbard
Karen Mallinson-Yates
Tom Rugg

Series Editor
Peter Riley

Editors
Tracy Kewley
Kate Pedlar

Project Editor
Fabia Lewis

Illustrators
Tony O'Donnell, Sarah Wimperis

Series Designers
Catherine Perera and Joy Monkhouse

Designer
Catherine Perera

CD-ROM developed in association with
Vivid Interactive

Published by Scholastic Ltd
Villiers House
Clarendon Avenue
Leamington Spa
Warwickshire CV32 5PR

www.scholastic.co.uk

Designed using Adobe InDesign.

Printed by Bell and Bain Ltd, Glasgow

1 2 3 4 5 6 7 8 9   7 8 9 0 1 2 3 4 5 6

Revised Text © 2007 Clifford Hibbard, Karen Mallinson-Yates and Tom Rugg © 2007 Scholastic Ltd

British Library Cataloguing-in-Publication Data
A catalogue record for this book is available from the British Library.

ISBN 978-0439-94508-0

ACKNOWLEDGEMENTS

With thanks to Louise Petheram for the use of some lessons in Chapter 7 of this book, taken from *100 Science Lessons – Year 5*, by David Glover, Ian Mitchell, Louise Petheram and Peter Riley © 2001, David Glover, Ian Mitchell, Louise Petheram and Peter Riley (2001, Scholastic Ltd) revised by Louise Petheram, for this edition.

With thanks to Kendra McMahon for use of some lessons in Chapter 7 of this book, taken from *100 Science Lessons – Year 4*, by Kendra McMahon © 2001 Kendra McMahon (2001, Scholastic Ltd) revised by Kendra McMahon, for this edition.

All Flash activities developed by Vivid Interactive.

Material from the National Curriculum © Crown copyright. Reproduced under the terms of the Click Use Licence.

Extracts from the QCA Scheme of Work © Qualifications and Curriculum Authority.

Extracts from the Primary School Curriculum for Ireland, www.ncca.ie, National Council for Curriculum and Assessment.

Every effort has been made to trace copyright holders for the works reproduced in this book, and the publishers apologise for any inadvertent omissions.

This new edition of *100 Science Lessons* follows the QCA Science Scheme of Work and also meets many of the demands of the curricula for England, Wales, Scotland, Northern Ireland and Eire. The book is divided into eight units – one unit to match each unit of the QCA scheme for Year 6, and one enrichment unit.

The planning grid at the start of each unit shows the objectives and outcomes of each lesson, and gives a quick overview of the lesson content (starter, main activity, group activities and plenary). The QCA objectives for Year 6 provide the basis for the lesson objectives used throughout the book.

After the planning grid is a short section on Scientific Enquiry. It is based on a QCA activity and provides a context for children to develop certain enquiry skills and for you to assess them. The section ends by showing where the activity can be embedded within one of the lessons.

Each unit is divided into a number of key lessons, which closely support the QCA scheme and all units end with an assessment lesson which is based on those key lessons. In addition to the key lessons, a unit may also contain one or more enrichment lessons to provide greater depth or a broader perspective. They may follow on from a key lesson or form a whole section, near the end of the unit, before the assessment lesson. The lesson objectives are based on the statements of the national curricula for England, Wales, Scotland, Northern Ireland and Eire, which are provided, in grid format, on the CD-ROM.

Lesson plans

There are detailed and short lesson plans for the key and enrichment lessons. About 60 per cent of the lesson plans in this book are detailed lesson plans. The short lesson plans are closely related to them and cover similar topics and concepts. They contain the essential features of the detailed lesson plans, allowing you to plan for progression and assessment. The detailed lesson plans have the following structure:

OBJECTIVES

The objectives are stated in a way that helps to focus on each lesson plan. At least one objective is related to content knowledge and there may be one or more relating to Scientific Enquiry. When you have read through the lesson you may wish to add your own objectives. You can find out how these objectives relate to those of the various national curricula by looking at the relevant grids on the CD-ROM. You can also edit the planning grids to fit with your own objectives (for more information see 'How to use the CD-ROM' on page 6).

RESOURCES AND PREPARATION

The Resources section provides a list of everything you will need to deliver the lesson, including any photocopiables presented in this book. The Preparation section describes anything that needs to be done in advance of the lesson, such as collecting environmental data.

As part of the preparation of all practical work, you should consult your school's policies on practical work and select activities for which you are confident to take responsibility. The ASE publication *Be Safe!* gives very useful guidance on health and safety issues in primary science.

BACKGROUND

This section may briefly refer to the science concepts which underpin the teaching of individual lessons. It may also highlight specific concepts which children tend to find difficult and gives some ideas on how to address these during the lesson. Suggestions may be given for classroom displays as well as useful tips for obtaining resources. Safety points and sensitive issues may also be addressed in this sections, where appropriate.

VOCABULARY

There is a vocabulary list of science words associated with the lesson which children should use in discussing and presenting their work. Time should be spent defining each word at an appropriate point in the lesson.

STARTER

This introductory section contains ideas to build up interest at the beginning of the lesson and set the scene.

MAIN TEACHING ACTIVITY

This section presents a direct, whole-class (or occasionally group) teaching session that will help you deliver the content knowledge outlined in the lesson objectives before group activities begin. It may include guidance on discussion, or on performing one or more demonstrations or class investigations to help the children understand the work ahead.

The relative proportions of the lesson given to the starter, main teaching activity and group activities vary. If you are reminding the children of their previous work and getting them onto their own investigations, the group work may dominate the lesson time; if you are introducing a new topic or concept, you might wish to spend all or most of the lesson engaged in whole-class teaching.

GROUP ACTIVITIES

The group activities are very flexible. Some may be best suited to individual work, while others may be suitable for work in pairs or larger groupings. There are usually two group activities provided for each lesson. You may wish to use one after the other; use both together (to reduce demand on resources and your attention); or, where one is a practical activity, use the other for children who successfully complete their practical work early. You may even wish to use activities as follow-up homework tasks.

Some of the group activities are supported by a photocopiable sheet. These sheets can be found in the book as well as on the CD-ROM. For some activities, there are also accompanying differentiated ideas, interactive activities and diagrams – all available on the CD-ROM (for more information, see 'How to use the CD-ROM' on page 6).

The group activities may include some writing. These activities are also aimed at strengthening the children's science literacy and supporting their English literacy skills. They may involve writing labels and captions, developing scientific vocabulary, writing about or recording investigations, presenting data, explaining what they have observed, or using appropriate secondary sources. The children's mathematical skills are also developed through number and data handling work in the context of science investigations.

ICT LINKS
Many lessons have this section in which suggestions for incorporating ICT are given. ICT links might include: using the internet and CD-ROMs for research; preparing graphs and tables using a computer; using the graphing tool, interactive activities and worksheets from the CD-ROM.

DIFFERENTIATION
Where appropriate, there are suggestions for differentiated work to support less able learners or extend more able learners in your class. Some of the photocopiable sheets are also differentiated into less able support, core ability, and more able extension to support you in this work. The book contains the worksheets for the core ability while the differentiated worksheets are found on the accompanying CD-ROM.

ASSESSMENT
This section includes advice on how to assess the children's learning against the lesson objectives. This may include suggestions for questioning or observation opportunities, to help you build up a picture of the children's developing ideas and guide your future planning. A separate summative assessment lesson is provided at the end of each unit of work. One may also be provided for a group of enrichment lessons if they form a section towards the end of a unit.

PLENARY
Suggestions are given for drawing together the various strands of the lesson in this section. The lesson objectives and outcomes may be reviewed and key learning points may be highlighted. The scene may also be set for another lesson.

HOMEWORK
On occasions, tasks may be suggested for the children to do at home. These may involve using photocopiables or the setting of a research project, perhaps involving the use the books on display (as suggested in the background section) to broaden the knowledge of the topic being studied.

OUTCOMES
These are statements related to the objectives; they describe what the children should have achieved by the end of the lesson.

LINKS
These are included where appropriate. They may refer to subjects closely related to science, such as technology or maths, or to content and skills from subjects such as art, history or geography.

ASSESSMENT LESSONS
The last lesson in every unit focuses on summative assessment. This assessment samples the content of the unit, focusing on its key theme(s); its results should be used in conjunction with other assessments you have made during the teaching of the unit. The lesson usually comprises of two assessment activities, which may take the form of photocopiable sheets to complete or practical activities with suggested assessment questions for you to use while you are observing the children. These activities may include a mark scheme, but this will not be related directly to curriculum attainment targets and level descriptors. These tasks are intended to provide you with a guide to assessing the children's performance.

PHOTOCOPIABLE SHEETS
These are an integral part of many of the lessons. They may provide resources such as quizzes, instructions for practical work, worksheets to complete whilst undertaking a task, information, guidance for written assignments and so on.

Photocopiable sheets printed in the book are suitable for most children. The CD-ROM includes differentiated versions of many photocopiables to support less confident learners and stretch more confident learners.

How to use the CD-ROM

SYSTEM REQUIREMENTS
Minimum specifications:
- PC or Mac with CD-ROM drive and at least 512 MB RAM (recommended)
- Microsoft Windows 98SE or above/Mac OSX.1 or above
- Recommended minimum processor speed: 1GHz

GETTING STARTED
The accompanying CD-ROM includes a range of lesson and planning resources. The first screen requires the user to select the relevant country (England, Scotland, Wales, Northern Ireland, Eire). There are then several menus enabling the user to search the material according to various criteria, including lesson name, QCA unit, National Curriculum topic and resource type.

Searching by lesson name enables the user to see all resources associated with that particular lesson. The coloured tabs on the left-hand side of this screen indicate the differentiated worksheets; the tabs at the top of the page lead to different *types* of resource (diagram, interactive or photocopiable).

PHOTOCOPIABLES
The photocopiables that are printed in the book are also provided on the CD-ROM, as PDF files. In addition, differentiated versions of the photocopiables are provided where relevant:
- green indicates a support worksheet for less confident children;
- red indicates the core photocopiable, as printed in the book;
- blue indicates an extension worksheet for more confident children.

There are no differentiated photocopiables for assessment activities.

The PDF files can be annotated on screen using the panel tool provided (see below). The tools allow the user to add notes, highlight items and draw lines and boxes.

PDF files of photocopiables can be printed from the CD-ROM and there is also an option to print the full screen, including any drawings and annotations that have been added using the tools. (NB where PDF files are landscape, printer settings may need to be adjusted.)

INTERACTIVE ACTIVITIES
The CD-ROM includes twelve activities for children to complete using an interactive whiteboard or individual computers. Most activities are based on one of the photocopiables taken from across the units. Activities include: typing headings to create an animal branching key; clicking on objects, in the home, to identify those which need energy; dragging and dropping arrows to label force diagrams.

GRAPHING TOOL
The graphing tool supports lessons where the children are asked to gather and record data. The tool enables children to enter data into a table, which can then be used to create a block graph, pie chart or line graph.

When inserting data into the table, the left-hand column should be used for labels for charts; the right-hand column is for numeric data only (see example below). The pop-up keypad can be used to enter numbers into the table.

DIAGRAMS
Where appropriate, diagrams printed in the book have been included as separate files on the CD-ROM. These include examples of tables and diagrams for children to refer to when undertaking experiments or building objects, such as a home-made filter in 'More about dissolving'. These can be displayed on an interactive whiteboard.

GENERAL RESOURCES
In addition to lesson resources, the CD-ROM also includes the planning grids for each unit, as printed in the book, and the relevant curriculum grid for England, Scotland, Wales, Northern Ireland and Eire. The curriculum grids indicate how elements of each country's National Curriculum are addressed by lessons in the book. The planning grids are supplied as editable Word files; the curriculum grids are supplied as Word and PDF files. Selection of a planning grid leads to a link, which opens the document in a separate window; this then needs to be saved to the computer or network before editing.

CHAPTER 1 Interdependence and adaptation

Lesson	Objectives	Main activity	Group activities	Plenary	Outcomes
Enrichment Lesson 1 Grouping objects	• To sort objects into groups based on observable features.	Sorting of objects according to their features.	Complete two sorting tasks involving observation and logic.	Discuss problems encountered and the need for classification of living things.	• Have experience of placing objects into groups based on observable features.
Enrichment Lesson 2 Animal kingdoms	• To know that living things can be grouped according to observable features. • To know that these groups can help in identifying unknown living things.	Explain that living things are divided into kingdoms. Break down the animal kingdom into invertebrates and the five classes of vertebrates.	Sort pictures of living things into their correct vertebrate groups.	Discuss the classification of the duck-billed platypus.	• Can Identify an animal as a vertebrate or an invertebrate. • Can classify a vertebrate using external characteristics.
Lesson 3 Investigation	• To know that plants need light, water and warmth to grow well. • To design a fair experiment and make predictions that they can test.	Revise that plants needs to grow healthily.	Use cress seeds to plan and set up an investigation into factors that affect plant growth.	Share plans and ideas to be tested. Discuss fair testing and make predictions.	• Know the importance of water, light and warmth for healthy plant growth.
Lesson 4 Leaf investigation	• To know that plants use air to create new material. • To know that plants need leaves.	Class discussion of photosynthesis; including the study of a potato. Discuss how to test whether leaves are important in growth of seedlings.	Use seedlings to plan and carry out an investigation into how the number of leaves affects plant growth.	Share predictions about possible results.	• Know that leaves enable plants to grow.
Lesson 5 Healthy plants	• To know that plants need nutrients from the soil for healthy growth. • To know that farmers and gardeners often add nutrients to the soil in the form of fertiliser.	Discuss the need for fertilisers in gardening. List the main nutrients needed by plants, and the symptoms of deficiency.	Assess the nutrient deficiencies of some unhealthy plants. Design an advertisement for a fertiliser.	Discuss hydroponic cultivation and crop rotation.	• Know that plants need nutrients for healthy growth, and that fertilisers can provide these. • Can recognise unhealthy plants.
Lesson 6 Using keys	• To use branching and numbered keys to identify an organism.	Introduce the idea of keys and work through an example of a branching key and a numbered key.	Collect various leaves and make a key for them in order to identify plants. Make a key for pictures for bug specimens.	Discuss the children's keys.	• Can use a key to identify an organism.
Lesson 7 Variation	• To know that plants and animals of the same species vary.	Discuss variations between individuals in the class. Introduce the ideas of continuous and discontinuous variation.	Complete a table of variations within their group. Draw a bar graph of grouped height data.	Discuss the results recorded, and whether the variations are continuous or discontinuous.	• Recognise how living things of the same species vary.
Lesson 8 Plant species	• To use their knowledge of keys to identify plant species in the field.	Carry out fieldwork. Identify tree species using guide keys.		Discuss the need to conserve trees and wild flowers.	• Can use keys to identify plant species in the field.
Lesson 9 Hedgerow habitats	• To know that animals and plants in a habitat depend on each other in a variety of ways.	Discuss the hedgerow as an example of a habitat in which many different plants and animals coexist.	Study of a hedgerow – the children link the different living species of the hedgerow habitat. Build pitfall traps.	Consider the environmental value of hedgerows and the damaging effects of their removal.	• Can describe ways in which plants and animals in a habitat depend on each other. • Have some awareness of the environmental value of hedgerows.
Lesson 10 Food chains	• To know that food chains are used to describe feeding relationships in a habitat.	Introduce the key terms. Show the children how to construct a food chain.	Construct food chains. Make mobiles of food chains.	Introduce the role of decomposers in the food chain.	• Know that the sun provides the energy for food chains. • Can construct food chains.
Lesson 11 Soil conditions	• To know that different plants grow better in different soil conditions.	Demonstrate preparation of dandelion roots for examination under a microscope. Discuss plants that live in difficult conditions.	Examine the fine structure of dandelion roots and record their observations. Solve some gardening problems.	Consider the impact of acid rain on plant life and the use of lichens as indicators of air quality.	• Know that different plants are adapted to living in different types of soil. • Can describe the functions of roots.

Lesson	Objectives	Main activity	Group activities	Plenary	Outcomes
Lesson 12 Comparing soils	• To know that different soils can be compared.	Explain the main soil types and their drainage characteristics.	In pairs, examine the settling of soil into layers.	Discuss ways of maintaining soil drainage.	• Can compare features of different soil types. • Can interpret a model of the soil.
Enrichment Lesson 13 The busy world of soil	• To be aware of the variety of animal life found in soil.	Introduce techniques for looking at animals which live in the soil.	The children collect and identify soil invertebrates and draw a cross-section of life in the soil.	Consider the roles of animals and plants in maintaining the soil, and the need to protect soil from erosion.	• Can describe different methods for collecting invertebrates. • Are aware that soils support a variety of life.
Lesson 14 Arctic habitats	• To know that unfamiliar habitats can be studied in the same way as familiar habitats.	Shared reading of a text about an Arctic habitat. Complete the related comprehension exercise.	Construct an illustration of the feeding relationships in an Arctic environment.	Consider the threats posed by industry to a fragile ecosystem such as the Antarctic..	• Can describe the features of an unfamiliar habitat. • Can construct food chains from information about an unfamiliar habitat.
Lesson 15 Adaptation	• To know that plants and animals have special features that help them to survive in a habitat.	Brainstorm how a cactus is suited to life in the desert. Introduce the concept of adaptation.	Choose a picture of an animal or plant and label the special adaptations that it possesses.	Introduce the idea of behavioural adaptation in relation to humans.	• Recognise the features of a plant and a animal species that help them to survive in their habitats.
Enrichment Lesson 16 Surveying techniques	• To use simple environmental surveying techniques.	Introduce using quadrat and line transect to estimate the abundance of plant species.	Set up their own line transects and carry out quadrat studies .	Consider other data could be collected along a line transect.	• Can use quadrats and line transects to collect environmental data.
Enrichment Lesson 17 Environmental survey	• To develop their investigative skills. • To develop their understanding of environmental survey techniques.	Plan and carry out an investigation, using surveying techniques.		Discuss the need to carry out environmental surveys to be carried out before new roads are built.	• Can carry out a line transect and quadrat study. • Recognise the usefulness of environmental surveying techniques.
Lesson 18 Woodland habitats	• To gather information about woodland and forest habitats using ICT, maps and other secondary sources.	Describe woodland habitats in the British Isles. Discuss why woodlands are important.	Using computers and atlases, work in pairs to locate woodlands and forests from different parts of the world.	Present findings to the rest of the class. Discuss deforestation.	• Can describe the importance of woodlands as habitats.and understand the pressures that forests are under. • Can use the internet to retrieve information.
Lesson 19 Freshwater habitats	• To know the importance of freshwater habitats.	Identify surface water in the local area. Draw phytoplankton as seen under a microscope.	Find our about producers and consumers in a pond food web.	Present findings. Reveal answers to research questions.	• Can name species found in fresh water habitats. • Understand the value of conserving freshwater habitats for wildlife.
Lesson 20 Seashore habitats	• To describe the features of a seashore habitat. • To understand why seashore organisms need special adaptations.	Discuss the features of a seashore habitat.	Research different beach zones and answer questions on specific organisms.	Present findings. Discuss possible food chains.	• Understand the rich variety of life found in a coastal habitat.
Enrichment Lesson 21 Global issues	• To understand that the Earth's habitats are under threat from human activity. •To learn why conservation is important.	Discuss the affect of humans on the planet.	In groups research a conservation topic such as global warming. Create a multi-media presentation.	Present findings to class 'delegates'.	• Are aware of the threats caused by poor management of the planet. • Can discuss the major environmental issues facing the planet.

Assessment	Objectives	Activity 1	Activity 2
Lesson 22	• To assess the children's understanding of branching keys.. • To assess the children's understanding of food chains and adaptations.	Answer questions on variation.	Answer questions on food chains and adaptation.

SC1 SCIENTIFIC ENQUIRY

What are the features of different types of soil?

LEARNING OBJECTIVES AND OUTCOMES
- Decide how to answer the question.
- Make observations.
- Compare results.
- Draw conclusions.

ACTIVITY
The children work in pairs to examine the settling of soil into layers and discuss ways of maintaining soil drainage.

LESSON LINKS
This Sc1 activity forms an integral part of Lesson 12, Comparing soils.

ENRICHMENT
Lesson 1 ▪ Grouping objects

Objective
- To sort objects into groups based on observable features.

Vocabulary
classification, groups, classes, features

RESOURCES
Main activity: Assorted objects including a plant, a rock, iron nails, shells, woodlice (in a pot).
Group activities: 1 Paper; writing materials. **2** One tray for each table containing a variety of objects such as: a knife, a spoon, a fork, a paper clip, staples, paper fasteners, a glue stick, a roll of sticky tape, two sea shells, two pebbles, some gravel, a pencil sharpener, two coloured crayons, a ball-point pen, two potted plants, some dead leaves and petals, water (in sealed, transparent containers), some coins (10p, 5p,1p), a screwdriver, a pair of pliers, five playing cards, two dice, a chess piece, a battery, a bulb. (These are just ideas and you may wish to adapt items, as long as a variety of materials are provided).

BACKGROUND
Many criteria can be used for organising objects. This lesson requires the children to decide on a sensible way of sorting a wide variety of materials into groups or classes. They may wish to use formal criteria such as 'living' and 'non-living', or 'solid', 'liquid' or less formal criteria such as colour, size or shape. Whichever criteria they choose, the activity will start them thinking about alternative ways of classifying objects. This will lead nicely into the next few lessons, which go on to look at the classification of organisms in the living world.

STARTER
Gather the children together. Ask them to imagine that they are moving house and that a lorry has turned up, ready to remove everything. *Imagine if all the cupboards, drawers and wardrobes were just emptied out and everything was tipped into the back of the lorry, along with the contents of the fridge and the freezer, the toolbox, the goldfish bowl... what a mess! We wouldn't really do this – but why not? (Because of the confusion* it would cause.) Explain to the children that to prevent confusion, it is useful to sort items, before they are loaded onto the lorry.

MAIN ACTIVITY
Explain that this lesson is about sorting things into groups: making

Differentiation
Group activity 1
Support children by asking whether they could group things according to how they are used: things we wear, things we eat and so on.
Group activity 2
Some children will need additional guidance to organise the groups they place objects into. You may want to prompt them with questions such as: *Is this object useful as a tool? Are any of the others?*

decisions about what should go with what, and being able to explain how they have been organised. Then explain that organising objects, based on their features, is common in science, and is known as classification. Explain the group activities to the class. The first task will be to imagine they are moving house. They will need to sort out how to pack each item by deciding which box to put them into. The second task will be to sort the objects, on the trays, into groups, based on their characteristics (what they look like or the type of object they are).

GROUP ACTIVITIES

1 Each table group should spread five sheets of A4 paper on their table. Explain that each sheet of paper represents a box. They have 15 minutes to decide and write on each 'box' what it will contain when they move house. At the top of each sheet, they should write 'Box containing...' and add a short description of the contents such as 'electrical things'. Ask the children to keep their ideas secret from the other groups. Stop the class after 15 minutes and ask each group, in turn, to explain the decisions they have made. The children will offer a wide range of solutions – all valid although some may be more practical than others. It will be interesting to see how the children explain their ideas.

2 In the same groups, ask the children to look through the contents of the trays on each of their tables and decide how to sort the objects into groups. Try not to guide the children: just prompt them to explain to how they are making their decisions. They can place the objects on separate sheets of A4 paper and write the name of the group at the top of each for example, 'Objects that are used as tools'. Give them another 15 minutes to do this, then ask each group to share their ideas with the class.

ASSESSMENT

The feedback from each group will serve as a useful reference in gauging the children's ability to take logical steps in their organisation of the objects.

PLENARY

Draw out the different approaches that the children have used in sorting the objects and ask them to share the problems that they encountered. Explain that deciding how to sort things into groups has been a common problem for scientists over the ages – particularly for biologists who have had to sort living organisms into groups. Ask the children to find out the special name for a biologist who studies the groups into which organisms are placed. (A taxonomist.)

OUTCOMES

● Have experience of placing objects into groups based on observable characteristics.
● Understand that trying to sort things into groups can cause problems.

ENRICHMENT
Lesson 2 ▸ Animal kingdoms

Objective
● To know that living things can be arranged into groups according to observable features.
● To know that these groups can help in identifying unknown living things.

Vocabulary
classification, kingdom, vertebrate, invertebrate, species, mammal, reptile, amphibian, bird, fish

RESOURCES ⊙
Main activity: A non-fiction book from a local library.
Group activity: One copy per group or pair of photocopiable page 41 (also 'Animal kingdoms' (red) available on the CD-ROM), enlarged to A3; scissors; adhesive; A3 paper.
ICT link: 'Animal kingdoms' or 'Vertebrate or invertebrate' interactive activities, on the CD-ROM.

BACKGROUND
The living world is divided into five main groups or 'kingdoms', the most familiar of which are the animal and plant kingdoms. This lesson gives the children some experience of looking at the features of different organisms and placing them in their correct kingdom. The plant kingdom can be divided into flowering and non-flowering plants (non-flowering plants include mosses and ferns; flowering plants include most of the rest). The animal kingdom is divided into vertebrates and invertebrates. A vertebrate is an animal with a backbone. There are five vertebrate groups (classes): mammals, reptiles, amphibians, birds and fish. There are five major invertebrate groups (phyla): molluscs, jellyfish, arthropods, worms and starfish. (The children don't need to know these.)

STARTER
Show the class the spine of the non-fiction book. Explain that libraries use something called 'classification' to decide what goes where. Ask what 'classification' means. *You are in a 'class' – what does that mean?* Explain that biologists need to sort living things into groups which everyone can recognise and agree on, and that this is known as 'classification'.

MAIN ACTIVITY
Ask the class for ideas about how living things should be sorted. It may be useful to write the names of some organisms on the board for example: 'oak tree', 'daffodil', 'ant', 'elephant', 'slug', 'crocodile', 'dolphin', 'kestrel', 'frog', 'shark'. *What groups can these living things be put into?* Hopefully, the classification as either 'plant' or 'animal' will be suggested.

Explain that living things are divided into five kingdoms and that the class will be looking at two of these: the plant and the animal kingdoms. Explain that the plant kingdom includes living things that make their own food and is divided into 'flowering plants' (such as roses and apple trees) and 'non-flowering plants' (such as mosses and ferns). You may want to point out that mushrooms cannot make their own food and so are not plants. (They belong to the fungus kingdom). Ask the children to suggest the names of the two main parts of the animal kingdom. *Aristotle, an Ancient Greek philosopher, suggested that animals should be grouped according to whether they live on land or in water. Was this a good idea?* Introduce the names 'vertebrate' and 'invertebrate' and explain their meaning. Some of the children may already be aware of the terms.

Tell the children that vertebrates belong to five main groups. Draw a table on the board:

The animal kingdom		
Vertebrates		
Name of group	Special features	Examples

Differentiation
Group activity

Some groups may need further help deciding how to classify organisms. You could guide them with questions such as: *Do you think the organism is a plant or an animal?* (Animal.) *Do you think it has a backbone?* (Yes.) *OK, so it must be a vertebrate. Which one?* You could leave the names of the five main groups on the board, with one key clue for each group as a guide (for example, 'Birds: feathers').

To extend children, give them 'Animal kingdoms' (blue) from the CD-ROM, which asks them to explain what the mammals have in common.

Brainstorm the class to see whether they can name these groups and fill in appropriate details. (Birds have feathers; mammals provide milk for their young and usually have hair or fur; amphibians have moist skin and lay eggs in water; reptiles have scales and lay eggs on land; fish have gills and scales.)

GROUP ACTIVITY

Give each group or pair a copy of page 41, preferably enlarged to A3 size. Ask them to cut out the animals and arrange them into the five vertebrate groups on an A3 sheet of paper, giving each group its correct name. Underneath each group, they must write down what the animals in that group have in common. Can they spot the odd ones out that don't belong to any vertebrate group? The answers are:

Mammals - humpback whale, giraffe, human, duck-billed platypus.
Reptiles - python, iguana, crocodile, turtle.
Fish - hammerhead shark, plaice, stickleback, salmon.
Birds - golden eagle, sparrow, swallow, heron.
Amphibians - common frog, salamander, great crested newt, natterjack toad.
Odd ones out - Portuguese man o' war (jellyfish - invertebrate), tarantula (arthropod - invertebrate), oak tree (flowering plant), bumble bee (arthropod - invertebrate), fern (non-flowering plant).

ICT LINK

Children can use the 'Animal kingdoms' or 'Vertebrate or invertebrate' interactives to sort animals into different groups.

ASSESSMENT

Check the accuracy with which each group has sorted the vertebrates. Did they spot the odd ones out? Can they explain why these are not vertebrate animals?

PLENARY

Look at a picture of a duck-billed platypus. Point out that it has a bill (a rounded beak), webbed feet and fur. It lays eggs on land but also provides milk for its young. Explain that when biologists first saw a platypus (in the form of a dead specimen), they thought it was a hoax: parts of different animals stitched together. *How would you have decided which group to place it in?* (It is a mammal.) Ask the children to explain their reasons.

OUTCOMES

● Can identify an animal appropriately as a vertebrate or an invertebrate.
● Can classify a vertebrate accurately as a bird, amphibian, reptile, mammal or fish using external characteristics.

LINKS

Unit 6a, Lesson 8, Plant species.

Lesson 3 ▪ Investigation

Objective
● To know that plants need light, water and warmth to grow well.
● To design a fair experiment and make predictions that they can test.

RESOURCES

One copy per group of photocopiable page 42 (also 'Investigation' (red) available on the CD-ROM); cotton wool; cress seeds; petri dishes; sticky labels; measuring cylinders; storage sites (cupboard, fridge, window sill).

MAIN ACTIVITY

Explain that the lesson will be about revising what plants need in order to

Differentiation
Group activity
Some children may need additional guidance in planning their ideas; adapt the prompt statements provided if required.

Other children could be asked to find out more about why plants need light and water to grow. (Light provides the energy used to make food by photosynthesis.

Water is one of the raw materials that plants use to make sugars in this reaction, and is also necessary to keep plant cells firm and enable the plant to stand upright.)

grow healthily. Write the phrase 'Healthy growth' on the board or a flipchart and brainstorm the children for suggestions. From these ideas, pick 'light', 'water' and 'warmth' (or 'the right temperature') as three conditions for the children to investigate, using the cress seeds.

GROUP ACTIVITY
Ask the children to work in groups to plan their ideas for the investigation, using photocopiable page 42 as a guide. Each group may choose to investigate just one factor (such as how well the seedlings grow at different temperatures) or more than one factor – but they must remember to keep their tests fair.

ASSESSMENT
Use the guide sheet as a reference to check that the children are able to take logical steps in forming the process of enquiry and in reviewing their observations.

PLENARY
At the end of the investigation, all the groups should share their results. Was a common trend observed? Ask the children why it is important for scientists to share their observations and results. (It allows them to reach a greater understanding of the topic being researched.)

OUTCOME
● Know the importance of water, light and warmth for healthy plant growth.

Lesson 4 ▪ Leaf investigation

Objective
● To know that plants use air to create new material
● To know that plants need leaves.

Vocabulary
chlorophyll, photosynthesis, autotroph, carbon dioxide

RESOURCES
Starter: A variety of different types of leaf; granulated sugar; a sheet of green paper; a sealed jam jar; a beaker of water; a potted plant.
Main activity: A potato; a vegetable knife (for adult use only); sticky tape, microscope slides of leaf pores (prepared or unprepared, as appropriate); a microscope/ class set of microscopes; eight questions- one set for each group (see Preparation).
Group activity: A selection of broad or runner bean seedlings; measuring cylinders; sticky labels; beakers or jars; paper clips; tin foil. You will also need somewhere warm and sunny to place the beans while they grow.

PREPARATION
You will need to begin growing seedlings (runner beans or broad beans are ideal) one- to two weeks before you begin this investigation. The seedlings need to have grown at least two open leaves. You will also need to prepare copies of the questions below, for each group to answer during the Group activity:

1. What are we trying to find out?
2. What are we planning to do?
3. How long will we continue the investigation for?
4. What measurements will we make?
5. What do we think will happen?
6. Why do we think this?
7. How will we make the test fair?
8. How will we record the results?

BACKGROUND

After the formation of the planet Earth, plants were the first form of life to colonise the land. Plants are technically known as 'autotrophs', which simply means they can feed themselves ('auto' = self and 'troph' = feeding). In food chains we call plants producers because they make materials that provide energy for the animals which feed on them. Plants contain a green chemical called chlorophyll which fills their leaves and with it, they take the simple materials (water and carbon dioxide) and, using the sun's energy, turn these into sugars (glucose or sucrose) The plants can also store these sugars as starch for later use. Potatoes are in fact stores of starch in the potato's roots. They can also add other materials to these sugars in order to make new tissue as they grow.

Plants take in gases through tiny pores in their leaves. Leaves are the food-making organs and so they need to be able to obtain the raw materials (ingredients) for making sugar. What they need is shown by this equation:

$$\text{Carbon dioxide} + \text{water} \longrightarrow \text{sugars} + \text{oxygen}$$

The plant takes in carbon dioxide through the pores in its leaves and releases the oxygen in the same way. The plant takes in water through tiny root hair cells and this is carried up to the leaves through a network of tiny tubes, which eventually branch out to form the veins in the leaf. In this lesson the children will find out if leaves really are important for plants.

STARTER

Gather the children so that they are facing you and give them each a leaf to hold. Elicit from them why plants have leaves. Ask if they know why the leaves are green. Then ask them what plants need to survive.

Place a potted plant in front of you. Explain that the plant is making food while it is in the light. Show them the sugar. Pour it out onto a green piece of paper (representing the leaf) and explain that the plant makes this sugar using two simple ingredients - carbon dioxide (show them the sealed jar to imply a colourless, odourless gas) and water (put down the beaker of water). Ask them what the special name for this process is - hopefully they will remember the term photosynthesis.

MAIN ACTIVITY

Explain that in plants like the potato the sugar is stored in the roots as starch. Cut a potato in half to demonstrate this. Ask them to look at the leaf that they are holding and to suggest how the leaf gains the carbon dioxide it needs and then how the leaf gains the water that it needs.

Explain the role of the roots and the pores in the leaves. To support your explanation you could place sticky tape on the underside of a leaf. Once removed, the tape is left with the impressions of the stomata (the leaf pores which take in and let out gases). Place the sticky tape on a slide and the stomata can then be identified under the microscope. To save time you may want to set up some sample slides in advance of the lesson, or, if this is the first time your group have used microscopes, you may want to extend this activity as an introduction to microscope skills.

Next, explain to the group that they are going to be investigating the importance of leaves for the survival of the plant. Take out the bean seedlings (which hopefully will have at least two fully-opened leaves). Share ideas about how you could see if leaves make a difference to the growth of the seedlings.

GROUP ACTIVITY

Arrange the class into groups and tell them they will have three bean seedlings to work with. Give each group copies of the questions (see Preparation) to discuss and agree on.

Hopefully each group will decide to grow one seedling with both leaves intact, one with a leaf removed (or covered with tin foil) and one with both leaves removed (or covered with tin foil).

The fair test should include ideas about treating the plants in the same way - watering using the same measured amount, placing the plants in conditions of equal light/temperature and so on. They may decide to measure the change in stem length/girth in mm, over a number of days.

The children should then set up their investigation, ensuring that their pots are clearly labelled, before leaving them in a suitable location.

ASSESSMENT
Use the prompt questions from the Group activity to check that the children are able to form a clear plan and follow the process of enquiry.

PLENARY
Ask each group to share their plans and ideas for fair testing. Check that they have agreed on their predictions and can give reasons for these. Make sure that the groups have organised a clear rota, in order to take and record measurements, over the next few days. The results can be compared and the methods evaluated in subsequent lessons.

OUTCOME
- Know that leaves enable plants to grow.

Differentiation
Group activity
Less confident learners could work with two seedlings instead of three.
Mixed ability groups could enable more confident learners to assist those who are less confident.

Lesson 5 ▪ Healthy plants

Objective
- To know that plants need nutrients from the soil for healthy growth.
- To know that farmers and gardeners often add nutrients to the soil in the form of fertiliser.

RESOURCES
Main activity: An empty bottle of children's multivitamins; a pot plant with food colouring added to the soil; a glass beaker big enough to hold the plant pot.
Group activities: 1 Labelled empty bottles of indoor plant fertilisers; a range of unhealthy pot plants (three for each group); copies of a prepared chart-enough for each pair (see diagram on page 16); paper; pencils.
2 Paper; colouring pencils.

PREPARATION
Ask at a garden centre for some unhealthy pot plants. You will need to collect the empty bottles of indoor plant fertiliser in advance of the lesson. For safety, do not allow children to handle fertilisers.

BACKGROUND
Green plants use the energy of sunlight to combine simple materials (water and carbon dioxide) to make sugar in their leaves (photosynthesis). However, there are other nutrients that plants need in order to grow healthily (just as we need vitamins and minerals in our diet). Sometimes the plants require only tiny quantities of particular chemical elements - these are known as 'trace' elements. The three main substances needed by plants are 'nitrates' (used for making proteins), 'phosphates' (used for a number of purposes, including an important role in photosynthesis) and 'potassium' (also involved in photosynthesis). 'Iron' and 'magnesium' are also needed as trace elements in order for plants to grow healthily. These minerals are used in the formation of the essential green pigment 'chlorophyll' in the leaves.

Nutrient	Symptom of deficiency
Nitrates	Stunted growth, older leaves turn yellow
Phosphates	Poor root growth, purple younger leaves
Potassium	Yellow leaves with dead spots

STARTER

Show the children the empty bottle of children's multivitamins. Ask whether any of them have ever taken vitamin tablets. *Why did they take them?* Explain that if we lack a particular vitamin, we are said to be deficient in it (we have a deficiency) and that we need the correct balance of vitamins, in our diet, in order to stay healthy.

MAIN ACTIVITY

Ask the children where plants get their nutrients from. Hopefully some will suggest 'the soil'. If they suggest 'photosynthesis', explain that this process only makes sugars in the leaves. *Does anyone know what farmers and gardeners do to help improve the growth of their crops?* (Add compost, manure or fertiliser.) Place the pot plant, with food colouring in its soil, inside the large glass beaker and pour water into the pot. As the water drains through, it will wash out the colouring. Explain that rain will wash or 'leach out' nutrients from the soil in this way.

Explain that sometimes house plants also need to be given extra nutrients to stay healthy. Write on the board the names of the main nutrients that plants need for healthy growth and explain how the plants show particular symptoms if they are lacking any of these. The children will need to refer to this list of visible symptoms when carrying out the Group activities.

GROUP ACTIVITIES

1 Ask the children to examine the labels of some liquid fertiliser bottles and find and list the nutrients that they each contain. They should then work in pairs to assess the health of the three unhealthy plants on their table, referring to the deficiency symptoms on the board, and then complete a chart like the one shown below. Pairs on the same table can check to see whether they agree with the another pairs' observations.

Plant	Observation	Treatment needed
Geranium	No purple leaves. Some dead spots on leaves.	Might need more potassium.

2 The children can work individually to design an advertisement for a fertiliser, explaining why their product is the best for healthy plant growth and showing what plants might look like without it. Alternatively, they could make an information booklet called *Look After Your Plants!* to instruct plant owners how to check whether their plants are healthy and what to do if they are not.

ASSESSMENT

At the start of the Plenary session, show the children examples of plants that appear to be suffering from a lack of one or more of the nutrients discussed. Check to see whether there is general agreement between the children in their assessment of these plants.

PLENARY

Tell the children that in many greenhouses, tomato plants are grown using water that has all the essential nutrients added to it; the tomato roots are trailed directly into this water solution. Growing crops in this way is called hydroponic cultivation. Ask: *Where else have you heard the prefix 'hydro'? What might it mean?* (Water.) *What are the advantages of growing the plants in this way?* (It is possible to check the nutrient levels in the water continually and so make sure that all the plants are getting exactly what they need – this is not so easy if they are all in individual pots.) *Are there any disadvantages?* (The growers need to make sure that they get the

Differentiation
Group activity
Some children may benefit from working in mixed ability pairs.

levels right, or else the whole crop suffers.)

Explain that the farmers, who grow the same crop on their land year after year, eventually find that the quality (yield) of their crop starts to fall. *Why is this?* (The plants are using up the same nutrients year after year, so the crop begins to suffer from nutrient deficiencies.) *What might the solution be?* (The farmer can add fertilisers to the soil.) Explain that although the farmers usually do this, leaching of these fertilisers into rivers and streams caused by rainfall, can harm the environment. Another solution is to change (rotate) the type of crops grown – bean and pea plants actually add nitrates to the soil, because of special microbes living in their roots.

OUTCOMES
● Know that plants need nutrients for healthy growth and that fertilisers can provide these.
● Can recognise unhealthy plants.

LINKS
Unit 6b, Lesson 4, Decay.

Lesson 6 ● Using keys

Objective
● To use branching and numbered keys to identify an organism.

Vocabulary
branching key, numbered key, identification

RESOURCES
Main activity: A copy of photocopiable page 43 (also 'Using keys' (red), available on the CD-ROM) enlarged to A3 size or viewed on an interactive whiteboard.
Group activities: 1 Access to plants in the local environment; plain paper; pencils; reference books on plants. **2** Plain A4 paper; rulers; pencils; colouring pencils.
ICT link: 'Branching keys' interactive activity, on the CD-ROM.

PREPARATION
Collect a range of leaves from common British trees.

BACKGROUND
Two different types of key are commonly used by biologists to work out the identity of an organism: branching keys and number keys. The children should be aware of both methods. Branching keys are useful for identifying organisms from a limited selection. Numbered keys (also known as 'dichotomous', 'word' or 'go to' keys) are useful when a larger number of organisms are being studied- most field reference keys are of this type. Simple examples of each type of key are shown here and on page 18.

Branching key
Animal
vertebrate   invertebrate
legs   no legs   legs   no legs
A   **B**   **C**   **D**

STARTER
Explain to the children that scientists in rainforests around the world, are working hard to identify the rich variety of colourful plants and animals that they find. Keys guide them, step by step, towards classifying a specimen and finding its name (or being able to give it a name if it is a new discovery).

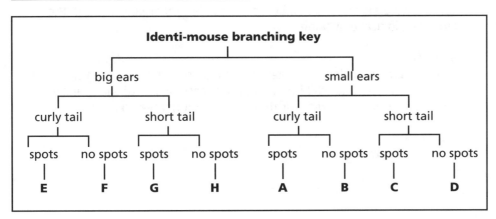

Identi-mouse branching key
big ears   small ears
curly tail   short tail   curly tail   short tail
spots no spots spots no spots   spots no spots spots no spots
E   **F**   **G**   **H**   **A**   **B**   **C**   **D**

Tell the children that they are going to find out about two different types of key and learn how use them to identify animals.

MAIN ACTIVITY

Display the enlarged version of photocopiable page 43, initially revealing the mice only. (Giving the mice the names of children may make the activity more fun!) Ask the children to suggest how a stranger would be able to tell the mice apart. Hopefully they will identify mice with straight and curly tails, big and small ears, spots and no spots. Reveal the branching key and explain each of its branches. Model using the key to identify one of the mice, filling in a blank box with the appropriate letter (A-H) or child's name. Practise further examples with the children if needed. Give out copies of photocopiable page 43 and ask the children to complete section 1. Then show the class how to set out a 'Go to' or numbered key:

Identi-mouse numbered key

1. Does the mouse have big ears?	Yes No	Go to 2. Go to 5.
2. Does the mouse have spots?	Yes No	Go to 3. Go to 4.
3. Does the mouse have a curly tail?	Yes No	It's E. It's G.
4. Does the mouse have a curly tail?	Yes No	It's F. It's H.

Talk the class through using this key. The children may have difficulty in making their own key of this kind, as fairly logical sequencing is needed.

GROUP ACTIVITIES

1 Take children out, (groups at a time), to collect leaves from up to eight different trees. Ask them to make rubbings or drawings of the leaves. They will then use reference books to name the plant that each leaf comes from. Ask the children to then make a plant key to distinguish these plants, so that other children will be able to identify them, from their leaves.
2 Ask the children to practise making their own keys for the bug specimens, on the bottom of photocopiable page 43. You may want them to work in pairs as they organise their ideas and draw out the keys.

ICT LINK 💿

The children could use the 'Branching keys' interactive to identify mice to make a mouse branching key.

ASSESSMENT

Can the children follow a numbered key to identify organisms? Can they produce a logical branching key?

PLENARY

Talk through examples of the keys the children have drawn, and check for any problems. Ask the children to draw a branching key of their family (including pets if they wish) or their friends, for homework.

OUTCOME

● Can use a key to identify an organism.

Lesson 7 ▪ Variation

Objective
● To know that plants and animals of the same species vary.

Vocabulary
species, variation, continuous, discontinuous

RESOURCES 💿
Group activities: 1 and **2** Rulers; graph (or squared) paper; colouring pencils; a height chart (see diagram on the CD-ROM); a computer and data-handling software; reference books with details about blood groups.
ICT link: Use the 'graphing tool', from the CD-ROM.

BACKGROUND
Classification of living things starts with the main divisions into kingdoms and eventually sub-divides into the smallest categories, which scientists call 'species'. A species is a group of living things that can successfully reproduce together. Differences between organisms of the same species are called 'variations'. As humans, we have all (with the exception of identical twins) inherited different combinations of genes from our parents: we show genetic variation. Differences in experience and lifestyle contribute to physical variation between people. There are two main types of variation: continuous variation (differences that are difficult to place in distinct groups, such as hand span, height, body mass or foot length) and discontinuous variation (differences that are easy to group people by, such as blood group, gender or ability to roll your tongue).

STARTER
Ask the class: *Can you roll your tongue from the sides inward? Can everyone?* Explain that this is an example of variation between individuals, and that the lesson is about such variations.

MAIN ACTIVITY
Ask: *What do you think 'variation' means?* Agree on a definition and then ask the children what variations they can see within the group (ask for

Name of child	Height (cm)	Sex (male/female)	Shoe size	Roll tongue?	Handspan (cm)
Mary					
Joe					
Kulvinder					
Andy					
Zaidi					
Liz					
C or D?					

Height class (cm)	No. of children
110–114.9	
115–119.9	
120–124.9	
125–129.9	
130–134.9	
135–139.9	
140–144.9	
145–149.9	
150–154.9	

general observations rather than individual differences). Brainstorm suggestions on the board around the title 'Variations in our class'.
   Explain the two types of variation. Ask the group to look at the board and to decide which type of variation each is (you may want to treat eye colour as discontinuous, though there are subtle variations between shades). To demonstrate that height is an example of continuous variation, get the class to stand in order from shortest to the tallest. Then stand them in two groups: males on the left, females on the right. *What kind of variation is this?* (Discontinuous.)

GROUP ACTIVITIES
1 Ask the children, working in groups of six or more, to complete a table like the one shown above (draw the chart on the board or a flipchart or print off copies, from the CD-ROM, for the children to complete). For each variable, they should also note whether it is continuous (C) or discontinuous (D).

Differentiation
Group activities

Support children by giving them blanks of the two tables. Those who complete the tasks quickly could calculate the average height of the children in the class (this is easy if the results are in a spreadsheet).

These children could also use reference books to find out the names of the different blood groups. *What kind of variation is this?* Ask them to find out their own blood group. This data can be added to the chart for the next lesson.

Ask the children to then plot a bar chart, showing all of the discontinuous variations in their class.

2 Write some height categories on the board in intervals which span the entire height range of the class –from the shortest to the tallest child (see the example height chart on page 19 or use the blank chart from the CD-ROM). Ask each child to put a tally mark in the height class that he or she belongs to. Once complete the children should then draw a bar chart of the class data and label this as 'Continuous variations in our class …'. If possible, challenge some children to input this data into a spreadsheet so that they can plot graphs of the results.

ICT LINK
The children may want to use the graphing tool, from the CD-ROM, to plot their graphs.

ASSESSMENT
See Plenary.

PLENARY
Talk through the charts and check that there is common agreement as to which variations are continuous.

OUTCOME
● Recognise how living things of the same species vary.

LINKS
Maths: discrete and continuous data.

Lesson 8 ▸ Plant species

Objective
● To use their knowledge of keys to identify plant species in the field.

RESOURCES
Copies (one per pair) of photocopiable page 44 (also 'Plant species' (red) available on the CD-ROM); a field reference guide to trees of the British Isles; a photograph of a car from a magazine.

MAIN ACTIVITY
If your school grounds are not suitable for field work, you may wish to organise a trip to a local park, canal or the hedgerows on nearby farmland. Warn the children that they may need wet weather clothing. You will need to organise the work with the children's safety in mind. Additional support, from another teacher may be required, to help with supervision. Remind the children to always treat the living things with respect- '*Take nothing but photographs, leave nothing but footprints*'. Taking a single leaf from a large tree is acceptable but uprooting or picking wild flowers is against the law.

Remind the children of their previous work on keys. Check if they remember the names of the two types of key (branching and numbered). Tell them that the kind most commonly used 'in the field' (the phrase researchers use for outdoor work) is the numbered key. Explain that they will be working in pairs, using a type of key to identify common trees. Hold up a picture of a car from a magazine and ask the children to identify its make and model. Some may be able to answer immediately. Point out that makes and models of cars change every year but that the plants they will be identifying have been around for hundreds of thousands of years – so we should be able to identify them!

Give each pair the guide key copied from photocopiable page 44 and take them to an appropriate site. They should use the guide key to identify as many tree species as possible.

Differentiation 💿
If children need support you may want to provide a sample of leaves (from common British trees) for them to fit to the examples given on the sheet.
   To extend children, give them 'Plant species' (blue), which includes a range of additional tasks.

ASSESSMENT

Back in class, describe the various plants you have found to the children. Use their responses to judge how easily they recognise the most common species in their local environment. Alternatively, play a game using the guide keys: the children are only allowed to ask you four questions to work out the identity of a tree you have thought of. This will require them to use the keys as a reference. Allow each table one question in turn (they will need to confer) and disqualify teams who shout out.

PLENARY

Why do the class think picking wild flowers is against the law? In Britain, many trees have Tree Preservation Orders put on them so that permission from the county council is needed before they are cut down. *Is this a good idea? Why?* Herbicides (sprays used to kill unwanted plants) are used by farmers on their crops. *Why might this be bad news for wild flowers?*

OUTCOME

● Can use keys to identify plant species in the field.

Lesson 9 ▪ Hedgerow habitats

Objective
● To know that animals and plants in a habitat depend on each other in a variety of ways.

Vocabulary
habitat, organisms, relationships, pollinate, oxygen, predators

RESOURCES 💿
Main activity: A picture of a song thrush.
Group activities: 1 Plant/bird identification guides or keys; hand lenses; clipboards or notebooks; pencils. **2** Photocopiable page 45 (also 'Hedgerow habitats' (red) available on the CD-ROM); trowels; plastic cups; an insect identification guide; hand lenses. **3** Photocopiable page 45; paper; pencils.

BACKGROUND
Ideally, you should teach this topic in the late spring or early summer, when the hedgerows are in bloom.
   The place where a living thing (organism) is found is called its habitat. A habitat is often named after the type of plants that are found there – for example, woodland, hedgerow, grassland, rainforest. The animals depend on the plants for shelter, nesting sites and food. The plants benefit from the activity of the animals which pollinate their flowers and disperse their seeds. Most animals breathe in oxygen, and this gas is produced by green plants when they make their food via the process of photosynthesis. So the relationship between plants and animals is a very close one and the children need to appreciate this.
   Hedgerows provide a habitat for a rich web of life. They are also vital 'corridors' of movement for many species, which use the cover of hedgerows to move between woodlands and other habitats. Removing the hedgerows leaves some animals and plants isolated, which can lead to their local extinction.

STARTER
Tell the class that the next few lessons are about the environment, the relationships between living things in an environment and how living things get the energy they need to survive. Explain that in this lesson, you will be looking at how the animals and plants in a habitat depend on each other.

MAIN ACTIVITY
Ask: *What is a habitat?* Ask the children to name some examples. Elicit the idea that different habitats are home to various animals and plants, which all need certain things to survive. *What do all living things need to survive?* Hopefully, the children will suggest that animals need food, water, the right

temperature and shelter and that plants need light, water and nutrients from the soil.

Explain that the class are going to look at hedgerows as an example of a habitat and that many birds are found living in hedgerows. Show a picture of a song thrush. *Why is the hedge a good habitat for a thrush?* (It provides somewhere to nest; it contains insects, snails and berries to eat; it gives shelter from predators.) *The thrush benefits in many ways from the plants – but does anyone know whether the thrush helps the plants?* Explain that the thrush feeds on invertebrates that could harm the plants and that it also carries away fruit seeds, such as blackberries, in its gut and so helps to disperse them. *Do other animals help these plants?* Guide the children towards thinking about the role of bees and other insects in pollinating flowers (see Unit 5b of *100 Science Lessons: Year 5/Primary 6* for more details on this topic including information on the song thrush as an endangered species).

GROUP ACTIVITIES

1 If possible, organise a trip to a nearby hedgerow. Ask the children to find and name four species of plant found there, using keys or guide books to help. Ask them to also note any bird and insects which they see.
2 Let each group build their own pitfall trap, using the guidance given on photocopiable page 45. They should check the trap's contents each day for several days, identify any insects caught, using reference materials, and then release the insects.
3 Each group can use the information on photocopiable page 45 to make a 'web of life' diagram by showing the links between the animals and plants in the picture (see example opposite- note that this is not a 'food web'.)

ASSESSMENT

As a whole class, check through the photocopiable sheet and note whether the children have identified the key relationships between the organisms. Check whether the children can suggest other relationships that are not shown in the picture.

PLENARY

Explain to the class that thousands of miles of hedgerow are torn up by farmers each year. Ask the class why this is a problem for wildlife. Explain that hedgerows are both habitats and 'corridors' for many species (see Background). Ask them to imagine that a hedgerow, near the school, is being torn up. Ask the children to design a poster (perhaps as homework) telling local people why they should try to protect it, or construct a joint letter to the local newspaper.

OUTCOMES

● Can describe ways in which plants and animals in a habitat depend on each other.
● Have some awareness of the environmental value of hedgerows.

LINKS

History: changes in local land-use.

Lesson 10 ▪ Food chains

Objective
● To know that food chains are used to describe feeding relationships in a habitat.

RESOURCES
Main activity: A pot plant; a worksheet (see Preparation); an OHP or interactive whiteboard (optional).
Group activities: 1 A3 paper; colouring pens. **2** Cotton thread; wire coat-

Vocabulary
food chains, producer, primary consumer, secondary consumer, top predator, prey, herbivore, carnivore, omnivore, energy

hangers; card; scissors; coloured pens; wildlife magazines or reference books
ICT link: 'Food chains' interactive activity, on the CD-ROM.

PREPARATION
Write the following on the board or display it on an OHT or interactive whiteboard. Prepare it as a worksheet with a word bank of the missing words for the support activity or alternatively, you could use the interactive activity, 'Food chains', from the CD-ROM.

Food chains
All green plants use energy from the _____ to make food in their leaves. Plants are called _____ because they can make food for themselves. Animals cannot make food for themselves: they have to eat plants or other animals to get the energy they need for life. Animals are called _____. An animal that eats only plants is called a _____. An animal that eats only other animals is called a _____. In a food chain, arrows are used to show which way the _____ is going.

BACKGROUND
The energy from the sun is harnessed in a complex reaction called 'photosynthesis', that takes place in the leaves of plants. Using sunlight, water and carbon dioxide gas, plants make their own sugars. Green plants are called 'producers' because they can make their own food. Animals cannot make their own food and so are known as 'consumers'. They obtain their energy by eating other animals or plants. Almost all life on Earth depends on the producers.

Food chains are used to show feeding relationships or 'what eats what'. The producer (plant) is always the first step in the food chain. Next come the consumers:

Producer ⟶ primary consumer ⟶ secondary consumer (predator) ⟶ tertiary consumer (top predator)

The tertiary consumer is often the 'top predator' as nothing else preys on it. Not all food chains are this long, however; producers might be eaten by the top predator – for example, brown bears sometimes eat berries. The arrows are very important: they show the direction of flow of energy through the food chain. (The sun is not usually included as part of the food chain.)

An animal that eats only plants is called a 'herbivore'. Herbivores are often eaten by (are the prey of) other animals or 'predators'. Animals that only eat other animals are called 'carnivores'. Some animals (such as pigs and humans) eat plants and animals. They are called 'omnivores'.

STARTER
Tell the children that this lesson links the work they have done on the interdependence of plants and animals in their habitats to understanding how energy is passed through living communities. They have already looked at how the living things in a hedgerow rely on each other for survival – but how do all living things get the energy they need to survive?

Explain that almost all life on Earth depends on energy that has come from the sun. Invite the children to prove you wrong. For example, a child might say that a chocolate bar doesn't contain energy from the sun – but explain that the chocolate bar contains sugar that was produced by a plant called the sugar cane, which got its energy from the sun. If a child suggests that he or she got energy from a bacon sandwich at lunchtime, explain that bacon comes from pigs, and that pigs eat plants that got their energy from the sun.

Differentiation

Main activity
Support children by giving them a worksheet with the paragraph and a word bank to choose answers from or you could use the 'Food chains' interactive from the CD-ROM.
Group activity 1
Support children by suggesting some food chains, but leave them to draw the arrows in the correct direction.

MAIN ACTIVITY

Hold up a plant and ask the children: *What do most plants have in common? What colour is most of the countryside when seen from above?* The idea that plants are mostly green should emerge. *Why green? Why is green so important?* Explain that it is because of the green chemical in plants that we are alive. This green chemical or 'chlorophyll', is used by plants to catch the sun's energy and turn simple materials into sugars, in their leaves. This energy is passed on to animals when they eat the plant. Explain that we call plants 'producers' because they can make their own food and we call animals 'consumers' because they have to eat other organisms to stay alive.

Write the word 'sun' in a circle in the middle of the board. On one side of this, write 'grass'. Then ask the children to name an animal that eats grass (such as a 'rabbit'). Write the animal's name next to 'Grass' and draw an arrow going from the grass to this animal. Ask for the name of a 'predator' of this animal (if they are unfamiliar with this word, explain that a predator is an animal that hunts other animals for its food – the animal it hunts is called its prey). Write down the name of this animal (such as 'Fox'). Now draw an arrow going from the prey to the predator. Explain that this is called a food chain. Explain that the arrows show the direction the energy is going in through the food chain. *Do you know which animal is a herbivore?* Check that the children know what 'herbivore' means. *Can you name a carnivore in this food chain?* Check that they know what 'carnivore' and 'omnivore' mean.

Talk through the paragraph on the board, or ask the children to copy it and fill in the blanks. The missing key words are: sun, producers, consumers, herbivore, carnivore, energy.

ICT LINK

The children could use the 'Food chains' interactive activity, from the CD-ROM, to complete sentences about food chains.

GROUP ACTIVITIES

1 Ask the children, working in groups, to draw a circle in the middle of a sheet of A3 paper and write the word 'Sun' in it, then copy the example of a food chain that you have done as a class. Now ask the groups to each think of five more food chains and add these, radiating outward from the Sun. They should write 'P' next to each producer and 'C' next to each consumer. Who can make the longest sensible food chain?
2 Ask the children to make mobiles of food chains, using cards (with words, drawings or pictures cut from magazines) hung from coat-hangers on cotton threads, or just linked together with cotton and hung on the wall.

ASSESSMENT

Can the children identify a producer and a consumer? Can they draw arrows appropriately to show the flow of energy through the food chain?

PLENARY

Ask the children to read out examples of their food chains. Check to see whether everyone agrees. *What happens to top predators when they die?* Explain that their bodies are broken down by decomposers, such as fungi and bacteria. These form the start of a new food chain. Decomposers are covered in more detail, later in this unit.

OUTCOMES

- Know that the sun provides the energy for food chains.
- Can construct food chains.
- Can use the words 'producer', 'consumer', 'herbivore', 'carnivore', 'predator' and 'prey' correctly.

Lesson 11 ◾ Soil conditions

Objective
● To know that different plants grow better in different soil conditions.

Vocabulary
surface area, absorb, root hairs, acid, alkaline, minerals, anchor

RESOURCES

Main activity: A dandelion (pulled up with roots intact); a Venus fly-trap; a cactus; heather; marram grass; some lichen (from a stone surface); some moss; a bag of peat; a beaker of sand; a bag of lime.
Group activities: 1 Slides of dandelion roots; tiles; knives and slides; hand lenses and/or microscopes; paper; pencils. **2** Paper and pens or a computer and DTP software.

PREPARATION

Collect the plants, peat, sand and lime from a garden centre. The scientific equipment could be borrowed from your local secondary school. If possible, prepare a number of microscope slides with dandelion roots. Make sure the children take care when handling knives or slides; they will need close supervision. Warn them never to reflect the image of the sun in a microscope mirror.

BACKGROUND

The roots of plants provide anchorage and a large surface area over which plants can absorb water and essential nutrients. The swollen roots of some plants are used as food storage depots.

Plants have different tolerances of soil conditions. Lichens grow on bare rock (though strictly speaking, they are not true plants but a fungus and an alga in partnership). Marram grass grows well in sand. Cacti survive in drought-stricken landscapes. Willows grow on waterlogged riverbanks. The Venus fly-trap thrives in nutrient-poor soils, obtaining the nutrients it needs from invertebrate snacks. Mosses can only survive in damp conditions. Heather grows well in acid soils, which are unsuitable for many other species. Plants are as varied as animals in their needs.

The factors that vary between soils include pH (how acid or alkaline they are), temperature, water content, humus content and texture (size of grains). The pH can be found by adding a sample of soil to a test tube, adding water, shaking it and then adding drops of universal indicator. Peaty soils are acid; soils rich in lime are alkaline. Find out the pH of the soil around the school. If you have any hydrangea plants, find out whether these are also good indicators of the pH of a soil. *Do the petals grow red or pink in acid soils and blue in alkaline soils?*

STARTER

You may want to divide this into two lessons if time is short. Show or remind the children how to set up a microscope, ready to view a specimen.

MAIN ACTIVITY - PART 1

Ask the children: *How do plants take in the water and nutrients they need?* (Hopefully, they will refer to the roots). *Plants use their roots to absorb what they need from the soil, but the roots do another job - what is this?* (They anchor the plant to the ground and can act as a storage site for food.) Show the children the dandelion with its roots intact. Explain that the branches give the roots a large surface area to absorb water and minerals. Show the children how to cut off one of the fine branches of the roots on a tile and then sandwich it between two slides, ready to be viewed under a microscope.

A simple way to explain surface area is to ask the children to hold out their hands in front of them– palms and fingers together. Ask them: *how much of their hands would be covered if they dipped them in paint? How much would be covered if they opened their hands and dipped them in the paint? What would happen if they opened up their fingers and dipped*

Differentiation
Support children by giving them a list of soil types and asking them to name one plant that is adapted to each soil type (for example, 'Nutrient-poor soil – Venus fly-trap').

again? The roots of plants need as large a surface area as possible to take in water and dissolved minerals, so they divide into fine branches.

GROUP ACTIVITY 1

Let the children view the prepared microscope slides, make and view their own slides and/or use hand lenses to look at the roots close up. They should draw what they see. Ask: *What do you notice about the roots?* (They are covered in hairs, which further increase the surface area.)

MAIN ACTIVITY – PART 2

Gather the children together and remind them of the work they have done on soils. Explain that plants are sensitive to soil conditions, and that different plants grow in different soils. One way that soils vary is in their pH (how acid or alkaline they are). To demonstrate this, add some peaty soil to a beaker of water and give it a swirl. Then do the same to a sample of soil from the school grounds. Add universal indicator and match the colour formed to the indicator colour chart. What does it show? Explain that a pH of 1-6 is acidic, 7 is neutral and 8-14 is alkaline. Add some lime to a separate beaker of water and test this with the indicator. *What does it show? Why do you think gardeners add lime to acidic soils?* (The lime neutralises the acidity of the soil, making it more favourable to plants.)

Show an example of each plant as you explain the following: Some plants (such as heather) thrive in acidic soils, but many others cannot survive there. *Cacti survive in dry conditions – how is this possible?* (Long roots, spines instead of leaves to reduce water loss and a fleshy stem to store water.) Venus fly-traps can survive in soils that are very poor in nutrients because of their ability to trap and consume insects. Lichens grow on bare rock, absorbing minerals from dissolved rock and moisture from the air. Mosses tend only to grow in damp conditions. Marram grass has a curled leaf to reduce water loss and strong roots that bind sand together.

GROUP ACTIVITY 2

Let the children pretend that they are responding to questions from a problem page of a gardening magazine, such as: '*My soil is very sandy. What plants could I grow?*' They should invent and answer a question, about each of the soil types, covered during the lesson. They could use a DTP program to present their work in a magazine format.

ASSESSMENT

Assess whether the children can describe ways in which soils may vary. Can they name a plant that may suit a particular soil type and explain clearly why plants have roots?

PLENARY

Explain that fumes from burning fossil fuels (coal, oil and natural gas) combine with rainwater to make it more acidic. Rainwater is naturally slightly acidic because carbon dioxide from the air dissolves in it. *Why might this 'acid rain' cause problems for plants?*

As an extension, the children could find out how many different types of lichen are growing on old stonework around the school. Lichens are good indicators of local air quality: the cleaner the air is, the greater the number of different types of lichen there will usually be.

OUTCOMES
- Know that different plants are adapted to living in different types of soil.
- Can describe the functions of roots.

Lesson 12 ▪ Comparing soils

Objective
● To know that different soils can be compared.

Vocabulary
rock, fragments, air spaces, particles, sandy, clay, humus, nutrients, texture, loam

RESOURCES
Main activity: A piece of rock (sandstone would be ideal); a hammer; a bucket of clay-rich soil (labelled A); a bucket of sandy soil (labelled B); a bag of compost material (such as a growbag) or peat; 1p and 2p coins; sand; dry peas; a bag of flour; two beakers; newspaper; rubber gloves; an apron; spatulas or spoons; water.
Group activity: A bucket of loamy soil (labelled C); boiling tubes (ideally) or test tubes, test tube racks, spatulas (these may be borrowed from your local secondary school); water in beakers (or access to taps); hand lenses (one per pair); a bucket; paper; writing materials.

PREPARATION
Draw a copy of the soil settling diagram (see page 28) on the board without labels, or view the diagram on the CD-ROM, using an interactive whiteboard, Cover desks and tables with newspaper.

BACKGROUND
Soils are made from weathered rock fragments, decayed plants and animal remains (humus). In between the grains or particles of soil are air spaces.

Water is an additional and very important component of soils. The texture of a soil depends on the size of the grains. Sand is made from large grains and holds little water. Sandy soils feel dry and gritty. Silt is the name given to smaller mineral particles found in soils. The smallest kind of soil particles are clay. When they are dry, the particles in clay soils clump together, making it feel lumpy. When they are wet, they make the soil feel sticky. In water, clay particles make the water cloudy and take time to settle (they are called suspended particles). Clay is important in helping a soil to keep some of its water, and so helping plants to grow after rains have passed. Ideal soils are a combination of sand, clay, silt and humus, with spaces for air to enter the soil. This type of soil is called 'loam' and there are different types. Small invertebrates play an essential role in giving soil its structure and in recycling nutrients (this process will be looked at in more detail later).

The children should not to handle the soil if they have open cuts on their hands. They must wash their hands at the end of the lesson. Also, make sure that the children don't flush waste soil down the sinks, at the end of the investigation.

STARTER
Gather the children around a table that has been covered with newspaper and on which there is a piece of rock and a container filled with sand. Explain that you are going to look at soil. Ask: *What is soil?* If the children suggest that it is just dirt or mud, explain that some of the bits in soil come from rocks that have been broken up by ice and water; the small bits are carried by the wind or water until they settle in layers. If you have a piece of sandstone, tap it gently with a hammer to show particles crumbling off. Now display the sand. *This is made out of bits of rock – but is it soil?* Explain that soils contain humus – the name given to bits of plant remains, such as rotting leaves. If you have a growbag handy, take some out and show it to the children, explaining that the peat is made from partially decomposed plant remains that are full of the nutrients plants need to survive. Mix some sand and peat, and ask the class whether now you have made soil. Explain that the missing final ingredient is water, which is vital for all plant and animal life. Air trapped in the larger spaces in the soil is also needed to support life. Check that the children know the main ingredients of soils: rock particles, humus, water and air.

Differentiation
Support children by giving them a copy of the soil diagram with some labels provided and some blanks left for them to complete or you may wish to you the diagram from the CD-ROM.

Alternatively, you may want to set up a larger version of the soil experiment so that you can point out the layering. Arrange 1p and 2p coins on a desk to illustrate the air gaps between soil particles.

MAIN ACTIVITY

Lift up two buckets: one labelled A (sandy soil) and another labelled B (clay soil). Explain that there are different types of soil. The different sizes of particles mean that the soils look and feel very different. For the next part, you may need an apron or lab coat (and gloves if you have any open cuts.) Lift some soil out of bucket A and ask what the children notice. (It is grainy.) Say that the feel of a soil is called its texture. Add some water to it and try to roll it into a ball. *Does it hold its shape?* Now lift some dry soil out of bucket B and crumble it in your fingers. At first, it appears to be made from bigger particles than the other soil but you should then wet it and show the children what it looks like in your hands. Try to mould the wet soil into a ball shape. Tell the children that one of the soils is a clay soil and one is a sandy soil. *Which do you think is which?* Explain that the clay soil is made from microscopic particles that clump together when the soil is dry, but when wet, make the soil very heavy and sticky. *Have they ever walked in a clay soil and nearly lost their wellies in the mud?*

Now show the class two beakers: one full of peas and the other full of flour. Pour some water into each. *Which lets the water drain through more easily?* (The peas.) *Why?* (There are bigger gaps between the particles.) *Which holds more water?* (The flour.) *Which do you think behaves more like a sandy soil?* (The peas.) *Why?* (Sandy soils drain quickly.)

Explain that to farmers, the texture of a soil is very important: clay soils can become waterlogged, whereas soils that are too sandy dry out quickly. Ideal soils are a mixture of sand and clay, and are called loams. Show the class bucket C (a loamy soil). Tell them that they will now look at this soil.

GROUP ACTIVITY

Working in pairs, ask the children to quarter-fill a test tube with loam using a spatula. They should then fill the test tube up to about the three-quarters mark with water. With the palm of one hand (or a thumb) over the end of the tube, they should shake it a few times and then leave it to stand in a test tube rack. When they have done this, they can use what they observe and what has been discussed in the lesson to copy the diagram from the board and fill in the labels (working in pairs or individually). The diagram below shows what they will observe.

At the end of the session, remind the children to tip the contents of their test tubes into a spare bucket – not down the drain. Remind them to wash their hands.

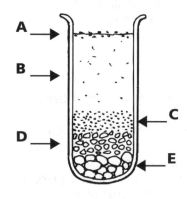

Settling of soil
A - floating humus (plant and animal remains)
B - suspended clay particles
C - fine silt
D - sand particles
E - small stones

ASSESSMENT

Look at the children's labelled diagrams, correcting any mistakes or misunderstandings as they arise.

PLENARY

Explain that heavy machinery or trampling can squash the soil, reducing the number of air spaces. Ask why this might cause a problem. (It makes it more difficult for the water to drain away, and there is less air available to support soil organisms that are essential for the breakdown of plant material. This is one reason why farmers use tractors with wide back wheels, so that the soil is less compressed.) Ask what a gardener should do if he/she has a heavy clay based soil which is poor at letting water drain away. (Add some sand.)

OUTCOMES
- Can compare features of different soil types.
- Can interpret a model of the soil.

LINKS
Unit 6a, Lesson 5, Healthy plants.

ENRICHMENT
Lesson 13 ▪ The busy world of soil

Objective
- To be aware of the variety of animal life found in soil.

RESOURCES
A clamp and stand; a gardening sieve; a lamp on a stand; a funnel; a beaker; leaf litter; freshly collected soil; a 'wormery' (made from a glass tank at least 30cm in depth, containing soil interspersed with layers of chalk and sand, with leaves on the top); hand lenses; brushes; petri dishes; an invertebrate identification guide; insect pitfall traps (see Lesson 9); plastic margarine tubs; trays; white paper; a microscope; fresh topsoil.

MAIN ACTIVITY
This lesson gives children an opportunity to explore the rich variety of life found on and within soils. Take the children outside with margarine tubs (one per pair) to collect leaf litter and soil. (Make sure they have no open cuts on their hands, and that they wash their hands afterwards.) If possible, encourage them to explore underneath stones or rotten wood for larger invertebrates. They could use pitfall traps to collect larger insects living on the soil. Back in the classroom, they can spread the leaf litter and soil onto white paper in a tray and brush any small invertebrates into a petri dish. They can use an identification guide to name their specimens, draw a sketch of each one and explain where it was found. Ask them to try to find out which are herbivores and which are carnivores.

As a class demonstration, set up a 'Tullgren funnel' to collect small invertebrates. Place topsoil and leaf litter in a gardening sieve and clamp it with a funnel underneath leading to a glass beaker. Set up a lamp above the sieve. The heat and light produced by the lamp should cause the animals in the soil to move downwards until they fall through the sieve, down the funnel and into the beaker. The children can attempt to identify them later.

Set up a wormery (see Resources). This will enable the class to observe over the following weeks the important role of worms as mixers and fertilisers of the soil: they pull leaves down into their burrows to feed. To collect worms, add 50ml of washing-up liquid to 10 litres of water and pour it gradually onto 1m² of soil. As the worms come up to the surface, rinse them in water and place them in the wormery.

Leave a microscope set up with a fresh sample of topsoil in view. Ask the children to look and try to spot more soil organisms. Ask them to draw a cross-section picture of 'The busy world of the soil'.

ASSESSMENT
Each child should be able to describe three ways of collecting invertebrates. Can they name an example of an invertebrate found using each method?

PLENARY
Ask the children to give you a summary of the different invertebrates they have found. Explain that along with decomposers, they play a vital role in recycling nutrients. Plants also play a vital role in binding the soil and protecting it from erosion (being washed or blown away). Ask the children to suggest why it is so important for farmers to try to reduce soil erosion.

Differentiation
Support children by asking them to name and sketch just one example of an animal that lives on or in the soil, and add this to their cross-section.

Other children could use library reference books or CD-ROMs to find out more about earthworms: *How do they feed, move through the soil, reproduce? Why do farmers and gardeners think they are vital for a healthy soil?*

- Can describe different methods for collecting invertebrates.
- Are aware that soils support a variety of life.

Lesson 14 ◗ Arctic habitats

Objective
- To know that unfamiliar habitats can be studied in the same way as familiar habitats.

Vocabulary
arctic, habitat, predator, prey, producer, consumer, temperature

RESOURCES 💿
Main activity: Copies of photocopiable page 46 (also 'Arctic habitats' (red) available on the CD-ROM); paper; pencils.
Group activity: Coloured A2 sugar paper (blue and white); adhesive; scissors; coloured pens; rulers; an encyclopedia CD-ROM, such as Encarta®.

PREPARATION
You may want to carry out this exercise as a comprehension quiz with groups in competition, in which case the children could be arranged in mixed-ability groups for a more even distribution of ability. Alternatively, you may prefer to distribute copies of page 46 for the children to complete individually.

BACKGROUND
All habitats on Earth share basic features: an energy source (usually, but not always, the Sun), producers and consumers. This lesson deals with the Arctic environment and the feeding relationships between species that inhabit it.
   Did you know? Many people mistakenly believe that polar bears eat penguins. They don't – not just because they can't get the wrappers off, but because polar bears are found in the Arctic (near the North Pole) and penguins are found in the Antarctic (near the South Pole).

STARTER
Ask the children to remind you of the name given to organisms who are able to make their own food (producers). Ask them where most producers get their energy from (the sun). Explain that almost all habitats on Earth share certain features. Explain that they are going to hear a description of an unfamiliar habitat. They will need to be detectives: to listen to the details of the habitat and try to spot the different parts of a food chain. Explain that you will be quizzing the class at the end to see which group can get the most questions right. (You may want to regroup the children into mixed-ability teams before you begin.)

MAIN ACTIVITY
Read out the information on page 46. Ask each table group a question on which to confer before their spokesperson answers, or distribute copies of the page so that the children can work through them at their own pace. The answers are: 1. tundra; 2. heather, lichen; 3. deer, arctic hares; 4. polar bear; 5. thick coat for warmth, white for camouflage, claws to grip ice, powerful jaws to kill prey, broad legs to use like paddles when swimming, small ears to reduce heat loss, hibernating during the coldest months; 6. ringed seals, walrus; 7. from the sun; 8. plankton ⟶ fish or crabs ⟶ ringed seal or walrus ⟶ polar bear.

Differentiation 💿
Main activity
To support children, give them 'Arctic habitats' (green) from the CD-ROM, which highlights key words in bold.
   To extend children, give them 'Arctic habitats' (blue), which includes some additional questions.

GROUP ACTIVITY
Ask each group to produce an illustration of the habitat, the different species found there and the food chain (using arrows to show the flow of energy). They can use blue and white sugar paper as backgrounds. They may wish to find out more about each species by referring to encyclopedia CD-ROMs, such as Encarta®. Ask them to label the energy source, producer, consumers, herbivores, carnivores and top predator on their drawings.

ASSESSMENT
Check that the children have successfully identified a producer, a primary consumer and a predator in the Arctic habitat. Can they construct an appropriate food chain, using arrows to indicate the flow of energy?

PLENARY
Explain to the class that many Arctic regions have oil reserves which could possibly be developed in the future. Ask: *What problems could building and using oil rigs cause for this habitat?* Many people believe that the Antarctic should be preserved as an unspoiled sanctuary for wildlife – do the class agree?

OUTCOMES
- Can describe the features of an unfamiliar habitat.
- Can construct food chains from information about an unfamiliar habitat.

LINKS
Geography: polar regions.

Lesson 15 ▪ Adaptation

Objective
● To know that plants and animals have special features that help them to survive in a habitat.

Vocabulary
survive, adaptation, adapt, environment, habitat

RESOURCES
Main activity: A cactus and a geranium (or similar).
Group activity: Sugar or A3 paper; colouring pencils; scissors; adhesive; a tray of wildlife pictures (see Preparation); reference books and CD-ROMs on world wildlife; sources of wildlife pictures (such as exotic plant catalogues, old infant reference books, wildlife park visitor resources).

PREPARATION
Prepare a resource tray with pictures of animals (such as a camel, lion, shark, eagle, owl, crocodile, jellyfish, mosquito, polar bear, hedgehog, seal) and plants (such as a cactus, Venus fly-trap, water lily). The pictures can be stuck on card and laminated.

BACKGROUND
To survive, every living thing must possess features that make it suited to its environment. For example, a seal has a streamlined body and powerful flippers to help it move quickly through the water, sharp teeth for grasping and eating its prey (fish, crabs and so on), blubber to keep it warm, and a clear skin (membrane) that covers its eyes when it is swimming. When a living thing has developed a special feature to help it survive, this feature is called an 'adaptation' as it enables the organism to adapt to its environment.

STARTER
Ask the children to imagine that they are going scuba diving off a coral reef in the Caribbean. *What will they need?* They will probably mention air cylinders for breathing, a wetsuit to keep them warm, flippers for swimming, goggles to protect their eyes, and perhaps a knife to use for protection or as a tool. Now ask them to think of a shark living in the same ocean. *How does it survive?* Humans need special equipment to prepare themselves for new environments, but the animals already living there have their own special adaptations.

MAIN ACTIVITY
Explain that this lesson is about surviving in the wild. Show the group a cactus and a geranium (or similar plant). Ask them which they think would survive better in a desert. Write the word 'Cactus' in the middle of the board,

Support children by giving them prompts such as: *How does the animal feed/move/defend itself?* Challenge children with a brain-teaser: *Which animal is responsible for the greatest number of human deaths on Earth?*

Perhaps they will be surprised when you tell them that it is the mosquito. *What special features does it have?* Leave them to find this out, using reference books or a CD-ROM, such as Encarta®.

and ask them to suggest what features make it suited to a life in the desert. Write the suggestions as a brainstorm around the word 'Cactus'. Ideas might include: no true leaves (the leaves of cacti have changed to become spines which reduces water loss); a thick fleshy stem for storing water; long roots that can reach down to water trapped in the rocks; furrows in the stem to channel water and hold the tiny breathing pores; spines to ward off grazing animals. Tell the children that all the special features that they have mentioned are called adaptations and these help a plant or animal to survive in its habitat. Write the word 'Adaptations' under the cactus brainstorm.

Now suggest a seal as another example of an organism that is suited to its environment. Ask the children to tell you what special adaptations the seal displays (see Background for ideas.)

GROUP ACTIVITY
The children should work in pairs to choose an animal or plant from the resource cards. On a sheet of A3 or sugar paper, they should draw a picture (or cut out and stick pictures from an old book or magazine) of the animal or plant they have chosen. Make this more fun by including dangerous animals such as a great white shark, a piranha fish, a golden eagle or a Portuguese man o' war. Among the plants, include a Venus fly-trap or another 'carnivorous' plant – if you have specimens available, so much the better! Around each drawing, the children should label the special adaptations.

ASSESSMENT
You may want to ask each pair to present their chosen example to the group. Check that they can name appropriate adaptations and explain how these help the organism to survive.

PLENARY
Ask the class: *Humans are relatively defenceless as they lack claws and sharp teeth, so why have we been quite successful as hunters?* (Because of our behavioural adaptations: we can work and communicate in teams, and invent weapons. Our hands are physically suited to holding and using tools.)

Discuss how 'carnivorous' plants such as the Venus fly-trap, sundew and bladderwort are able to survive in nutrient-poor soils. They still make their own food by photosynthesis; but by snacking on small insects, they obtain the additional nitrates they need for healthy growth.

OUTCOME
● Recognise features of a plant and an animal species that help them to survive in their habitats.

LINKS
History: early humans.

ENRICHMENT
Lesson 16 ▪ Surveying techniques

Objective
● To use simple environmental surveying techniques.

Vocabulary
quadrat, line transect, abundance, distribution, vegetation, estimate

RESOURCES
Main activity: Samples of the leaves of the most common plant species found in your study area; a quadrat frame (see Background); photocopiable page 47 (also 'Surveying techniques' (red) available on the CD-ROM).
Group activity: Quadrat frames (one per pair, ideally 25cm × 25cm); record sheets (one per pair) with six 5 × 5 squares drawn on squared paper; long tape measures; field identification guides for wild flowers; squared paper; clipboards.

Differentiation 💿
Group activity
Support children by giving
them 'Surveying techniques'
(green), which asks them to
count the total number of
plant species inside their
quadrats and then to work out
the average number of
different plants in their study
area, instead of calculating
percentages.
 Extend children by asking
them to draw bar charts,
showing the abundance of
different species.

PREPARATION

Before going into 'the field', you may want to familiarise yourself with the most common plant species the children are likely to encounter. It would be useful to photocopy page 47, which provides space for children to record their observations, and also shows how to make percentage calculations). The children will need to be suitably dressed for outdoors.

BACKGROUND

A quadrat is a square frame (which can be a wire coat-hanger bent into a square, approximately 25cm × 25cm) that is placed on the ground. The observer has a sheet of squared paper with boxes drawn on it (for example, a 5 × 5 square), and on this draws a sketch of the ground inside the quadrat, showing the proportion covered by each type of vegetation. For example, out of 25 squares, 5 might be bare ground, 9 moss, 7 broad-leafed plantain and 4 grass. It is now possible to estimate the percentage of the quadrat covered by each type of vegetation. If your grid on the paper is 5 × 5, then each square is 4% of the total (since 4 × 25 = 100). So, in our example, bare ground occupies 5 × 4 = 20% of the total. Children can design a key for their quadrat sketches, using symbols to represent each type of plant found. Quadrats are widely used for habitat surveys. Ecologists use quadrats to study the ocean floor and researchers have dropped huge frames onto the rainforest canopy from hot air balloons.

 Quadrats can be used in a number of ways. They can be thrown randomly onto the ground to take a 'sample', or they can be used along a line (which is called a line transect). Line transects are useful for looking at trends in vegetation for example, how the plant species change as you move from a sand dune into adjacent heathland, or from a meadow into a nearby woodland. A tape measure can be laid on the ground, along the line to be studied. At regular intervals (such as every 2m), a quadrat is laid on the ground and the vegetation is recorded. The changes in the abundance and distribution of species can then be studied.

STARTER

Ask the children to imagine hot air balloons above the Amazon rainforest, lowering a huge square frame onto the trees. Explain that scientists have done this to study small sections of the rainforest in detail, in order to learn more about its fragile habitat. Say that these frames are called quadrats, and that smaller quadrats can be used to study the habitats around the school.

MAIN ACTIVITY

Show the children one of the quadrats and explain how it is used. Draw a 5 × 5 grid on the board and explain that when they look down on the quadrat, they will have to use this grid to help them sketch the quadrat, showing the areas covered by different types of plant. Talk them through making a key and using different degrees of shading to indicate the different plant species. Explain how the use of quadrats along a line (making a line transect) can be useful in learning about changes in vegetation between different areas. Perhaps the children will be able to suggest reasons why the plants found on the ground might differ according to their location (changes in soil type, level of acidity or alkalinity, water content, degree of sunlight or shade, whether the plants are regularly cut by a lawnmower or grazed by sheep and so on).

GROUP ACTIVITY

Give each pair a record sheet and ask them to carry out a line transect, placing a tape measure across the field (you will probably need different pairs to use the same length of tape measure, perhaps starting at either end). They will need to place the quadrat at 2m intervals. Ask them to try to identify the plant species that they find, using reference guides.

Ask the children to work out the percentage of ground covered by each plant species in each quadrat. They can do this by counting each of the 25 squares as 4% of the total – so they multiply the number of squares covered by 4. If only half a square is covered, it can be counted as 2%. If more than half a square is covered, it is usually rounded up as being a whole square.

The children should check that their total for each quadrat is 100%. Give each pair a copy of page 47 to help them with their calculations. Ask: *Which type of plant is the most common? Which is the least common?* The children should draw a sketch of the leaves and/or flower of the most common species they find. On a school field, the grass species will be difficult to identify, but it may be possible on the uncut margins.

ASSESSMENT

Check that the children have understood how to estimate the abundance of different plants by using their quadrat work as a reference.

PLENARY

What other information could be collected along a line transect? Elicit suggestions such as: soil samples for analysis, water content or variety of invertebrates (caught in pitfall traps).

OUTCOME

● Can use quadrats and line transects as a way of collecting environmental data.

LINKS

Maths: estimates; percentages.

ENRICHMENT

Lesson 17 ▫ Environmental survey

Objectives
● To develop their investigative skills.
● To develop their understanding of environmental surveying techniques.

RESOURCES

Wildflower identification guides or keys; long tape measures; quadrats; photocopiable page 47 (also 'Surveying techniques' (red) available on the CD-ROM).

MAIN ACTIVITY

There are a number of possible options for this lesson; the investigation you choose will depend on the environment around the school. If you have access to an area of land where the grass is often allowed to grow to full height, the children can carry out a transect from the trampled ground near a path to the uncut grass. Two common types of plantain are found in grassland. The ribwort plantain (Plantago lanceolata) has thin leaves and grows tall in long grass; it competes well for light and is not easily outshaded. The greater plantain (Plantago major) has shorter, broader, rounded leaves that grow flat to the ground. It is very resistant to trampling and thrives near footpaths but in long grass it is soon out-shaded due to its flat leaves, and so is far less common. The children could develop an investigation and predict how the frequency of each species will change as they move from short trampled grass to longer grass, along a line transect.

Alternatively, they could carry out a line transect from an open area of a field into the shade and see how the abundance of moss changes. You will need to check whether the children can they explain their observations. If it is possible to organise (perhaps by contacting an outdoor education centre), the children could investigate how plant species change as you travel from meadowland to woodland or from marshland to forest.

ASSESSMENT
Can they make predictions and draw conclusions from their fieldwork?

PLENARY
Tell the class that before the construction of a new road takes place, a number of possible routes are considered. Ask them why environmental surveys are needed to help in the decision-making process. (They provide data on the abundance and distribution of plant and animal species in an area, so that its conservation value can be assessed.) Important sites in terms of conservation value are called 'Sites of Special Scientific Interest' (SSSIs). Ask whether they know of any of these sites, in the local area?

OUTCOMES
- Can carry out a line transect and quadrat study.
- Are aware of the use of the usefulness as environmental surveying techniques.

Lesson 18 ▪ Woodland habitats

Objective
- To gather information about woodland and forest habitats using ICT, maps and other secondary sources.

RESOURCES
Starter: An Ordnance Survey map of the local area
Group activity: An outline map of the world (one copy per pupil); atlases; colouring pencils and access to the internet.

STARTER
Explain to the pupils that the variety of types (species) of plants and animals in an area is called its biodiversity. Having a high biodiversity is usually a sign of a thriving habitat. Explain that over the next three lessons you will be looking at three habitats– woodlands, wetlands (places with a lot of freshwater) and the seashore.

Show the children an Ordnance Survey map of the local area. Ask them to identify which parts show woodland. Distinguish between coniferous trees (mostly pine species which keep their leaves throughout the year), deciduous trees (which shed their leaves in the autumn), ancient woodlands and plantations. Tell the pupils that it is thought that it was once possible for a squirrel to travel the entire length of the British Isles without ever having to set foot on the ground!

You could also tell the pupils that Britain was once nearer the equator and covered in tropical woodland and that we know this from the enormous coal deposits which were left behind from the layers of compressed wood.

MAIN ACTIVITY
Ask the children why woodlands and forests are important and make a 'mind map' of their ideas on the board. Ideas might include: they are sources of timber for construction, fruits for food, fibres for making cloth. They are also habitats for medicinal plants, refuges for native wildlife as well as sites for human recreation (walking the dog, mountain biking).

GROUP ACTIVITY
Give the children an outline map of the world showing the outlines of each country. Ask them to work in pairs to locate forests and woodlands in different parts of the world (including tropical rainforest). These can then be added to the map in green. Alpine (coniferous), temperate (deciduous) and tropical woodland can be shaded in three different colours showing examples of where they are found on the planet. Pupils then describe a food chain for one of the woodland/forest areas they have located They can then select and describe how at least one species is adapted to life in this

Differentiation
Group activity
Allow children to work in mixed ability pairs so that they can support each other and use atlases to help locate forests and woodlands.
   You could also support children by giving them the beginning of a food chain to develop.

habitat. Some of the children may wish to use the internet or use CD-ROMs to further research about the habitat of their chosen woodland/forest.

PLENARY

The pupils present their research to the rest of the group, using the world map as a reference during their presentation.

Compare global maps of forest. Explain that although statistics vary, it is clear that the rate of deforestation is increasing every year. Ask the pupils why forests are cut down and *why it matters if we cut down the forests? What could be done to reduce the rate of deforestation?* (Forest clearance.)

OUTCOMES

● Can describe the importance of woodlands as habitats and understand the pressures forests are under.
● Can use the internet to retrieve information.

Lesson 19 ◘ Freshwater habitats

Objective
● To know the importance of freshwater habitats.

RESOURCES
Starter: An Ordnance Survey map of the local area.
Main activity: Microscopes; slides; drops of pond water; plain paper and pencils for drawing.
Group activity: Access to the internet; sheets of A2 paper.

STARTER
Show the map of the local area used for the lesson on woodlands. Now ask the children to pick out surface water (streams, rivers, lakes, ponds, reservoirs etc.) You can explain to the children that water meadows (which are regularly flooded) and marshland are now far less common than they were as the land has been drained for farming. We have lost many precious habitats for wildlife. Explain that in this lesson you want them to find out about some of the species found in freshwater and why it is so important to protect wetland habitats.

Ask the pupils to explain how the water got onto the land in the first place – this will remind them of work they have completed on the water cycle.

MAIN ACTIVITY
After checking that the pupils are all familiar with and can safely use a microscope, ask them to look at a drop of pond water on a slide. Tell them that any green objects they can see are types of pond plankton. There are two main types of plankton – phytoplankton (plant plankton) and zoo plankton (animal plankton), though some types are difficult to group. Phytoplankton starts the pond food webs and is the producer in the pond. Ask the children to draw one example of phytoplankton as they see it (this will improve their observation skills) and one example of zoo plankton.

If you are lucky enough to have your own school pond, or if you can visit your local wildlife trust's pond, you will be able to find bigger specimens like dragon fly nymphs. Failing this, the pupils can go online to www.naturegrid.org.uk/pondexplorer/pond3.html and carry out a virtual pond-dipping exercise.

Differentiation
Group activity
Pupils can work in pairs or small groups of mixed ability.
   Extend children by asking them to undertake further research to find out:
What percentage of the Earth's fresh (non-salty) water makes up the snow and ice of the Arctic and Antarctic? Which is the longest river in the world? Which lake is the deepest? Which river releases the most water into the world's oceans?

GROUP ACTIVITY
Using www.naturegrid.org.uk/pondexplorer/pond3.html or following a real pond-dipping exercise, ask the children to find out about one type of producer and four different consumers in a pond food web, explaining how each one is adapted for life in a pond. They should then draw and label their

pond food web on a sheet of A2 paper for display and for sharing in the plenary.

PLENARY
Invite groups to present their findings from the Group activity and ask children who carried out further research to feedback answers.

OUTCOMES
● Can name species found in freshwater habitats and describe their adaptations.
● Understand the value of conserving freshwater habitats for wildlife.

Lesson 20 ▪ Seashore habitats

Objective
● To describe the features of a seashore habitat.
● To understand why seashore habitats require special adaptations of the organisms found there.

Differentiation
Group activities
Let children work in mixed ability groups so that they can support each other.

RESOURCES
Starter: An Ordnance Survey map of the local area.
Group activities: 1 Access to the internet; drawing and writing materials.
2 Access to the internet; secondary sources of information.

STARTER
If you are fortunate enough to live near a coastline, this topic represents an excellent opportunity to explore! On a map (projected onto the whiteboard if possible) follow the flow of a local river to where it eventually joins the sea.

MAIN ACTIVITY
Remind the pupils of their last lesson on freshwater habitats and ask them what the coastal area where the freshwater flows into the sea is called. Explain that estuaries (the part of the river where the salt water and freshwater merge) are very rich habitats for wildlife – thousands of wading birds feed on shellfish and worms in the thick mud which becomes deposited on the banks. Explain that as you move further along the coast you are on the seashore, where the land and the sea meet. Ask the group to describe some of the changes that happen on a seashore during one day.

Hopefully their suggestions will include changes in sea level (as a result of the tides) and temperature changes (in the summer it is much warmer out of the water and in the winter it can be warmer in the water). The organisms on the shore also have to put up with the battering effects of the waves and the danger of being exposed to predators when the sea retreats.

The shore can be divided into four zones. Turn one wall of the class room into a profile of the beach and divide it into four zones: Splash Zone – the area above the high tide point, Upper Shore, Lower Shore and Sub-littoral Zone (rarely exposed to the air).

GROUP ACTIVITY 1
Divide the children into groups of four. Within each group, the children should select one beach zone each and find out about an organism living there. Ask them to draw a picture of their organism and to write four accompanying facts. Each group could look at a temperate shore ecosystem (such as the UK coast line) or perhaps a tropical or arctic shore.

GROUP ACTIVITY 2
Ask the children to use reference books and the internet to find the answers to questions such as: *How do crabs breathe? Do limpets move? Why? What is an oystercatcher and how does it feed? Why does bladder wrack have bubbles in its leaves? What is a weaver fish and why should you tread carefully near one? How do barnacles feed?*

PLENARY
Invite each group to present their facts about the organisms found on the shore. Once each group had added their contribution, ask the class to suggest possible food chains. Give them adhesive arrows to make links, building up a food web if possible. *Which organisms would be most affected by an oil spill reaching the coastline?*

OUTCOME
● Understand the rich variety of life found in a coastal habitat.

ENRICHMENT
Lesson 21 ◖ Global issues

Objective
● To understand that Earth's habitats are under threat from human activity.
● To learn why conservation is important.

RESOURCES
Group activity: Reference books on the topic about rainforests/woodlands and conservation; access to computers and presentational software; access to the internet.

STARTER
'We do not inherit the Earth from our Ancestors, we borrow it from our children'. Ask the children what is meant by this saying? Ecologists talk about the impact we have upon the planet as being our 'footprint'. *What type of changes do we cause to the planet in our lives? What has happened as humans have developed more technology, such as the motor car? What has happened to the Earth's resources (for example forests and coal and oil reserves)? Which countries consume the most?*

MAIN ACTIVITY
Every few years there is a meeting of the nations of the world at an Earth Summit. Tell your pupils that this year the class have been invited to a conference and that they will be representing the scientific and environmental organisations around the world. They will need to explain why humans have to change their behaviour to prevent further damage to the planet. Discuss some initial ideas as a class: *How do humans damage the environment? Why is it a problem if humans chop down forests and burn oil?*

GROUP ACTIVITY
Divide the class into groups of four and ask each group to select a conservation topic that they will become specialists in. Suggested topics include: global warming, acid rain, deforestation, ozone destruction, over fishing. Explain to the children that they should research the topic and then prepare a multi-media presentation explaining what the particular issue is, how it affects the planet (using statistics if possible), then suggesting what the governments of the countries at the Earth Summit should do. Encourage role play and the use of titles (Professor Nozone, Dr TooLittleTooLate and so on!). A useful website is www.yptenc.org, which provides fact sheets on environmental issues.

Differentiation
Group activity
Allow pupils to work in mixed ability groups so that they can support each other. You can also support children by giving them some focus questions to help them structure their work: *What is deforestation? Where does this take place? Why should we stop it? What can we do to solve the problem?* Each question could form one slide of a multi-media presentation.

PLENARY
Invite the groups to present their research to the class 'delegates'. Encourage the 'delegates' to ask questions and take brief notes.

OUTCOMES
● Are aware of the threats caused by poor management of the planet.
● Can participate in a discussion about the major environmental issues facing the planet.

Lesson 22 ▪ Assessment

Objective
● To assess the children's understanding of branching keys.
● To assess the children's understanding of food chains and adaptations.

RESOURCES
Photocopiable pages 48 and 49 (also 'Assessment – 1' and 'Assessment – 2' available on the CD-ROM); writing materials.

STARTER
Before carrying out the assessment activities, you may wish to remind children of the work they have covered on keys and variation. Encourage them to think about the quadrat method they used in fieldwork for looking at vegetation.

You may also want to go through the terms covered in this unit that relate to food chains, adaptations and the environment. A word wall containing these terms would form a useful focus for the start of the lesson. You could give each group a selection of the vocabulary and ask them to share their understanding of each word.

ASSESSMENT ACTIVITY 1
Give the children a copy each of photocopiable page 48 and let them complete it individually.

ANSWERS
A = spots; B = no spots; C = legs; D = no legs; E = legs; F = no legs; G = Fip; H = Zy; I = Chuck; J = Zak; K = Peep; L = Vodo; M = Teepee; N = Dibble.

1. Antennae?	Yes	Go to 2.
	No	Go to 3.
2. Spots?	Yes	Go to 4.
	No	Go to 5.
3. Spots?	Yes	Go to 6.
	No	Go to 7.
4. Legs?	Yes	It's Peep.
	No	It's Vodo.

LOOKING FOR LEVELS
All the children should be able to identify the missing alien names in the branching key. Most children should be able to add the missing labels to the branches of the key. Some children will be able to devise a logical numbered (Go to) key to help people identify the aliens.

ASSESSMENT ACTIVITY 2
Give the children a copy each of photocopiable page 49 and let them work through it individually.

ANSWERS
1. wheat ⟶ greenfly ⟶ carnivorous beetle ⟶ vole ⟶ hawk
2. P = wheat, H = greenfly.
3. The Sun provides energy for the producers to make food.
4. Powerful wings to hover and swoop, sharp eyesight for spotting prey, claws for grasping prey, hooked beak for tearing flesh.
5= E
6= C
7=B
8=A
9=D

LOOKING FOR LEVELS

All the children should set out the organisms into a food chain, identifying the sun as the source of energy. They should all identify at least two adaptations of the hawk.

Most children should orientate the arrows in the food chain correctly to show the flow of energy through the chain, and should be able to identify the producer. Most children should name four adaptations of the hawk.

Some children might be able to identify the consumers – the top predator, carnivores or herbivores. Most pupils should be able to match one or two environmental problems, to their effects, correctly.

PLENARY

You may wish to go over the answers to the tests with the children after you have collected the work in for marking. There may be a question that many pupils get wrong. If this is the case it is advisable to go over the concepts that relate to this question.

Animal kingdoms

■ Cut out the pictures below and sort them into these groups:

Mammals	Reptiles
Amphibians	Fish
Birds	Odd ones out

■ Why do the 'Odd ones out' not fit into any of your other groups?

Illustrations © Tony O'Donnell © Sarah Wimperis

PHOTOCOPIABLE

Investigation

What I aim to find out: _____

_____

How I plan to do this: _____

_____

_____

Measurements I will need to take: _____

_____

What I need to keep the same to make the test fair: _____

_____

What I think will happen and why: _____

_____

How I will make sure the test is SAFE: _____

_____

Results (tables and graphs can be attached on a separate sheet of paper):

Do my results show a pattern or trend? What is it? _____

_____

Do my results support my prediction? _____

_____

Can I trust my results? Why? _____

_____

What I have learned from this investigation: _____

_____

If I were to carry out this investigation again, how would I change it to make the results more reliable?

_____

Other ideas I could investigate are: _____

_____

■ SCHOLASTIC

Using keys

A   B   C   D   E   F   G   H

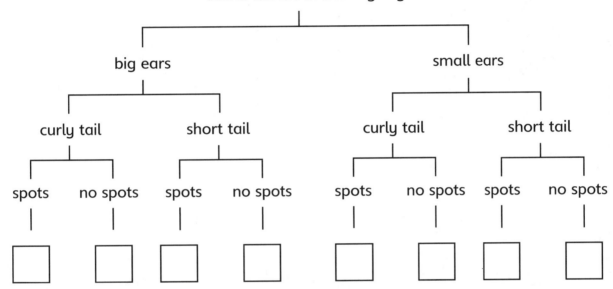

Identi-mouse branching key

big ears — small ears

curly tail — short tail — curly tail — short tail

spots — no spots — spots — no spots — spots — no spots — spots — no spots

1. Write the correct letter, for each mouse, in the blank boxes at the bottom of the key.

2. Look at these bugs and make your own branching key to help identify them.
a) Start by spotting the differences.

b) Now make a numbered 'Go to' key for the bugs.

Illustrations © Tony O'Donnell © Sarah Wimperis

PHOTOCOPIABLE

Plant species

- Use this sheet to help you identify trees around your school.
- See how many types of tree you can learn to recognise in one week.

Horse chestnut

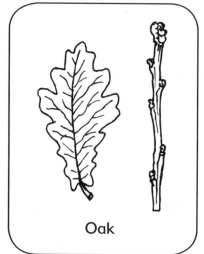

Oak

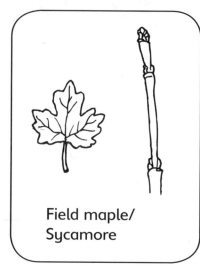

Field maple/
Sycamore

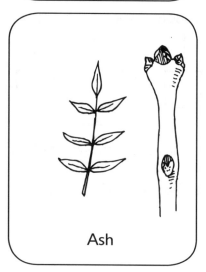

Ash

Beech

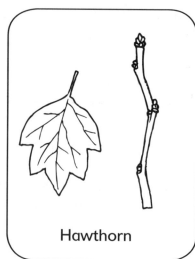

Hawthorn

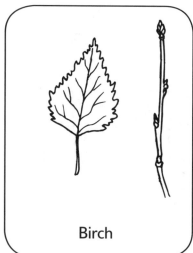

Birch

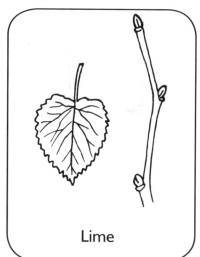

Lime

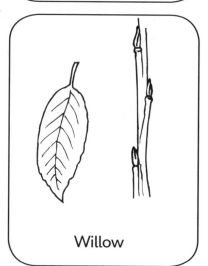

Willow

Illustrations © Tony O'Donnell © Sarah Wimperis

■SCHOLASTIC

Hedgerow habitats

📖 Read the information below. Draw lines on the picture to show how the living things are linked together.

Most British hedgerows are very old and are made from hawthorn – its spiky stems being a useful barrier against livestock. The song thrush uses the cover of the hedgerow to build its nest, so it is hidden from predators. The song thrush feeds on slugs and snails. Slugs and snails are herbivores that feed on the leaves of plants in the hedgerow. The thrush also eats the blackberries growing on the bramble bushes and carries the seeds away in its belly. These seeds pass out in the thrush's droppings, giving them the chance to germinate in a new location. The hedgehog nests in hollows and old burrows, between the roots of the hedge. It eats slugs, snails, beetles and fruits. Bumble bees feed on the nectar of wild flowers. They pollinate the flowers as they move between them, and so play a vital role in the life of the hedgerow.

📖 Make a pitfall trap leaving space for bugs to crawl under.
a) Make sure you check the trap every day and record what you find using a key or guide book. Collect the bugs and try to identify them. Draw three examples.
b) When you have finished, remove the cup and fill in the pit. Why do you think litter (like empty plastic bottles) can cause the death of small animals?

I. Dig a hole with a trowel.

2. Put a plastic cup in the hole (top level with soil).

3. Put three stones around the cup.
4. Place a flat rock on top of the stones.

Illustrations © Tony O'Donnell © Sarah Wimperis

PHOTOCOPIABLE

Arctic habitats

The most northern part of Canada extends into the Arctic Circle. The summers here are brief but beautiful, with a landscape that is bathed in light for all 24 hours of the day. The melted snow clears to reveal the Arctic tundra – a special landscape of lichens and small shrubs, like heathers, that grow slowly but are tough enough to withstand the fiercest bite of the

Arctic cold. For a few short months flowers bloom, are pollinated and then shed their seeds. Arctic hares and grazing deer feed on the new growth of the plants. The summer melting of the sea ice allows walruses and ringed seals to pull up onto the rocky coastline to have their pups, always looking out for polar bears – the fierce top predators of the Arctic landscape. The seals feed on kelp (a type of seaweed), fish and crustaceans (such as crabs). The fish feed on plankton (tiny plants that float on the currents of the ocean and make food by using the energy from the sun). Very small animals also feed on plankton and these animals are the first consumers in the food chain of the Arctic seas.

Once summer has passed, the chill of winter returns. The light fades and the days rapidly become shorter. Temperatures drop to below -30°C, and the sea once more begins to freeze as the tundra is buried beneath a blanket of snow and ice. Polar bears move onto the ice to hunt for food. They wait by the breathing holes made in the ice by seals, ready to ambush them as they surface for air. The polar bear is well adapted to survive in the Arctic landscape, with its thick camouflaged coat, claws for gripping the ice, broad legs (which it uses as paddles when it swims) and tiny ears (to reduce the amount of heat lost from them). As well as these physical adaptations, the polar bear has another survival technique: through the coldest months of the

winter it hibernates, in a den beneath the snow and it is here that the mother bear eventually gives birth to her young in the spring.

With the return of the sun and the onset of spring, the sea ice melts to reveal a thawing tundra landscape that is flourishing with life.

Comprehension questions
1. What is the special name given to the land inside the Arctic Circle?
2. Name a producer that grows there.
3. Name a herbivore that feeds on the plants there.
4. What is the top predator in this habitat?
5. Name three ways in which this animal has adapted to survive in the Arctic environment.
6. Name one prey of the top predator.
7. How do the tiny plants called plankton get the energy they need to survive?
8. Write out a food chain for this habitat.

Illustrations © Tony O'Donnell © Sarah Wimperis

■SCHOLASTIC

Surveying techniques

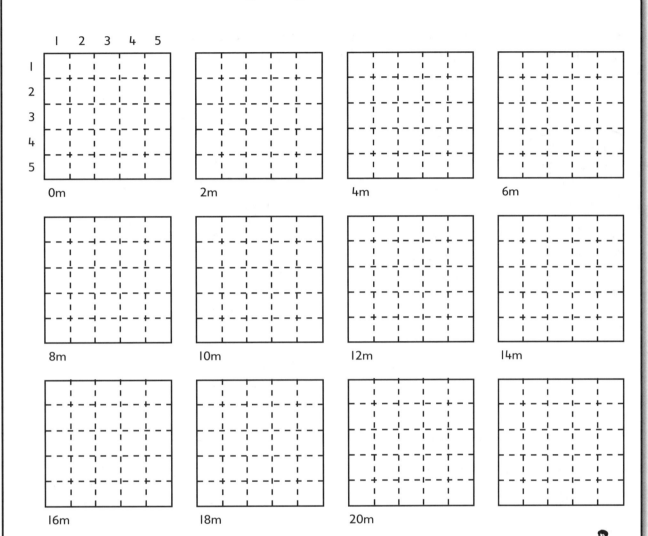

Use a tape measure to make a line transect.

Place your quadrat along the tape every 2m.

Key

= bare ground
= grass
=
=
=
=
=
=

To work out percentages

1. Look at your grid for each quadrat. Count up the number of squares covered by each type of plant. If most of a square is covered, count it as a whole square.

2. There are 25 squares, so each square covers 4% of the total area. Multiply the number of squares covered by each type of plant by 4%. So if 5 squares are grass, the area covered = 5 × 4% = 20%.

3. Try to list the plant species found along the transect from the most common to the least common.

Illustrations © Tony O'Donnell © Sarah Wimperis

Assessment – 1

■ This branching key has not had all its branches labelled. Fill in the blanks (A–F). Now use the key to fill in the names of the aliens in boxes G–N.

Peep   Fip   Teepee   Chuck

Vodo   Zy   Dibble   Zak

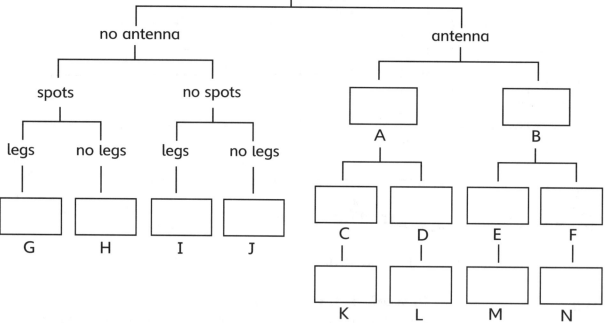

Identi-alien branching key

■ Now make a 'Go to' (numbered) key to help someone recognise these aliens. The first part has been done for you.

1. Antenna?   Yes   Go to 2.
              No   Go to 3.

2. Spots?   Yes   Go to _____.

                   No   Go to _____.

■SCHOLASTIC

Illustrations © Tony O'Donnell © Sarah Wimperis

Assessment – 2

wheat

hawk

greenfly

vole

carnivorous beetle

◀ Write your answers on a separate sheet.

1. Write out a food chain using the organisms above.

2. Put a P above the producer and an H next to a herbivore.

3. Why is the Sun so important to food chains?

4. Write down the special adaptations that the hawk has for hunting.

◀ Match up the environmental problems with the harm they cause.

5. Over fishing	A. Causes trees to die and wildlife in lakes to be harmed.
6. Global warming	B. Allows more harmful UV rays from the Sun to hit the Earth.
7. Ozone destruction	C. Could cause ice caps to melt and global climate change.
8. Acid rain	D. Leads to the loss of rich habitats for wildlife and the extinction of rare species.
9. Deforestation	E. Can destroy marine food webs.

Illustrations © Tony O'Donnell © Sarah Wimperis

CHAPTER 2 Micro-organisms

Lesson	Objectives	Main activity	Group activities	Plenary	Outcomes
Lesson 1 Germs and disease	• To know that micro-organisms cause many diseases.	Explain the idea that some microbes cause communicable diseases.	Work in groups to dramatise discoveries about the prevention of diseases. Perform the sketches to the class.	Place events on a timeline. Discuss the need for scientists to share their findings.	• Know that many diseases are caused by micro-organisms. • Can describe how a scientific theory is based on evidence.
Lesson 2 Microbes and illnesses	• To know about the range of diseases caused by micro-organisms.	Use models to explain the nature of bacteria, viruses and fungi and the diseases that they cause.	Complete a table listing types of microbes and diseases they cause. Complete a chart showing the growth of a bacterial population.	Briefly introduce the idea of the body's specific defence system.	• Can describe some diseases and identify their causes.
Lesson 3 Investigation: mouldy food	• To know that mould on food is caused by micro-organisms. • To plan and carry out a fair test.	Brainstorm ideas for an investigation into the conditions that favour mould. The children set up an investigation.		Review the children's findings. Discuss food preservation techniques.	• Can describe good practice for food hygiene. • Can explain why food hygiene is necessary. • Can plan and carry out a fair test.
Lesson 4 Decay	• To know that the decay caused by micro-organisms is useful in the environment.	Introduce the term 'decomposers' and explain their role in the recycling of organic materials.	Label a flow a diagram to show how decomposers return nutrients to the soil. Label a diagram of a compost heap and answer questions about it.	Consider biodegradable and non-biodegradable materials and the need for recycling.	• Understand that the decay caused by micro-organisms allows nutrients to be recycled.
Lesson 5 Finding out about yeast	• To know that yeast is a useful organism.	Explain the nature of yeast. Describe the experiment the children will carry out.	Carry out an experiment with yeast and record their observations.	Consider the role of yeast in the baking of bread.	• Can identify the conditions needed for yeast to grow and reproduce. • Know the function of yeast in bread-making.
Lesson 6 Micro-organisms in food production	• To know that micro-organisms are used in food production.	Explain the use of microbes to produce a variety of foods.	The children use facts about microbes to complete a summary grid and make a poster about the ways in which microbes are useful in food production.	Link this lesson to the role of microbes in causing decay and the recycling of nutrients.	• Can describe how micro-organisms are used in food production.

Assessment	Objective	Activity
Lesson 7	• To assess the children's understanding of micro-organisms and their functions.	Answer questions about micro-organisms and their functions.

SC1 SCIENTIFIC ENQUIRY

What causes mould on food?

LEARNING OBJECTIVES AND OUTCOMES
- Decide how to answer the question.
- Plan an investigation.
- Make a fair test.
- Evaluate results.
- Draw conclusions.

ACTIVITY
The children plan and carry out an investigation into the conditions that favour mould.

LESSON LINKS
This Sc1 activity forms an integral part of Lesson 3, Investigation: mouldy food.

Lesson 1 ▪ Germs and disease

Objective
- To know that micro-organisms cause many diseases.

Vocabulary
microbes, disease, quarantine, vaccine, immunisation, sterile, antiseptic, antibiotic, virus, bacteria.

RESOURCES
Group activity: Photocopiable page 60 (also 'Germs and disease' (red) available on the CD-ROM) photocopied onto card and cut into sections (one section per group); paper; writing materials. The books, *Horrible Science: Deadly Diseases and Suffering Scientists' and 'Horrible History: The Measly Middle Ages* (published by Scholastic), will be entertaining and useful sources of reference material for yourself and the children.

BACKGROUND
Micro-organisms are often called 'microbes' – a convenient name for any living thing that is too small to be seen clearly by the human eye. The category is huge, and the children need only be aware that it includes fungi, bacteria and viruses. Before micro-organisms could be seen under a microscope, the causes of many diseases remained a mystery and were the basis of many superstitions. The first bacteria observed under a microscope were seen in 1676 by a Dutch scientist called Leeuwenhoek, who was looking at food samples taken from between his teeth. A combination of microscopic observation and experiment enabled scientists to demonstrate and explain how contagious illnesses spread. This lesson will help the children to see how ideas about microbes and diseases have developed through history.

STARTER
Ask the children: *Why is it considered a good thing to cover your mouth when you cough?* You may wish to ask them why we are taught to wash our hands after going to the toilet. Both questions should lead to the idea of germs. *What are germs?* Make it clear that germs are too small to be seen by the human eye, and so they are known scientifically as micro-organisms. They can also be called microbes. Our hair, skin, mouths and even intestines have microbes living inside them – most cause us no harm, and many are helpful to us. However, some microbes can cause illness and even death.

MAIN ACTIVITY
Explain that people haven't always known about microbes. People were once very superstitious about the causes of diseases – for example, 'flu is short for influenza, which is derived from the old belief that the illness was

Differentiation
Some groups will need help with reading through the text and dramatising it. Prompt them with questions such as: *What was the idea? How was it tried out? Did it work?*

caused by sleeping outside under the influence of the stars! Today, we know about how diseases spread and how to reduce the harmful effects of certain microbes.

Tell the children that they are going to work in groups to find out something about the history of our knowledge of microbes and diseases. You may wish to read through the whole factfile on photocopiable page 60 as a class, before you begin, or to keep the paragraphs separate until the children present their sketches.

GROUP ACTIVITY
Divide the children into seven groups and give each group a card copied from photocopiable page 60. Each group should develop a role-play sketch to show one of the discoveries that have helped us to understand microbes and how diseases are spread. Encourage them to take roles and to make their sketch entertaining. When they are ready (after 20 minutes, or however long you feel they need), call each group in order of date to present their sketch. They may want to prepare scripts.

ASSESSMENT
At the start of the Plenary session, ask the children to place the key events in the understanding of diseases on a timeline. Note whether they understand and can sum up these events.

PLENARY
Explain that our understanding of diseases is based on the research and evidence accumulated by scientists over hundreds of years. This process has enabled scientists to develop ideas that we call 'theories', which may explain what is known. Once a theory has been put forward, scientists try to prove or disprove it.

OUTCOMES
● Know that many diseases are caused by micro-organisms.
● Can describe how a scientific theory is based on evidence.

LINKS
History: *the Black Death.*
PSHE: *immunisation.*

Lesson 2 ▪ Microbes and illnesses

Objective
● To know about the range of diseases caused by micro-organisms.

Vocabulary
virus, bacteria, fungus, disease

RESOURCES ◉
Main activity: A red balloon; split pins; beads; cotton wool; a football.
Group activities: 1 A worksheet (see Preparation); writing materials.
2 A copy of photocopiable page 61 (also 'Microbes and illnesses' (red) available on the CD-ROM) writing materials; graph paper (or a computer and data-handling program).

PREPARATION
Fill a red balloon with as many split pins as you can, then inflate it. Make a worksheet for Group activity 1 using the table on page 53 or the diagram 'Microbe table', from the CD-ROM.

BACKGROUND
What we call 'germs' are usually viruses, bacteria, fungi or protists (one-celled organisms) and they can cause diseases. Fungi only cause a few diseases in humans, but they cause many diseases in the crops that humans grow. The destruction of potatoes, by a fungus, caused the Irish potato

famine, and a fungus known as 'brown rust' has wiped out whole crops of wheat. In this lesson, the children will learn the names, 'virus', 'bacteria' and 'fungus' and the name of a disease caused by each. (For further information, see the Main activity below.)

STARTER

Ask the children: *Hands-up if anyone here has had chicken-pox!* Next, ask whether anyone has had a sore throat; then whether anyone has had athlete's foot. Explain that these three diseases are caused by different kinds of microbes. Following on from Lesson 1, ask them to remind you what a microbe is. (A living thing too small to see with the naked eye.)

MAIN ACTIVITY

Explain that you are going to talk about three kinds of microbe: bacteria, viruses and fungi:

1 Bacteria: Explain that our bodies are covered in bacteria! We are walking bacteria hotels. Ask the children to suggest reasons why we are a good habitat for bacteria. (We are warm; our skin is sometimes moist; and best of all, when we sweat we release salts and the chemical urea – not so good for someone sitting close to us, but a feast for bacteria!) Most of the bacteria covering us are harmless; some living deep in our intestines are actually very helpful, providing vitamins that our bodies need. Some bacteria are not so useful, however. Bacteria living in the mouth produce acid as they feed on leftover sugars, and this can cause tooth decay. Explain that in the right conditions, one bacterium can divide to make two bacteria every 20 minutes (you will return to this idea later in the lesson). Bacteria cause food poisoning, sore throats, tetanus and many other infections. They can be seen under a normal microscope. Many bacteria are destroyed by antibiotics: drugs derived from moulds (and other sources) that can attack bacteria.

2 Fungi: Explain that fungi can cause terrible devastation to crops, but only cause a few diseases in humans – the most common example being athlete's foot. *Have any of you had this? How did you get rid of it? Why are conditions between the toes so good for this?* (Warm, moist, dark conditions.) Fungi can cause some types of throat infection. They can usually be seen easily – for example, mould on stale bread. Some moulds are very useful, such as yeast in bread or the veins in blue cheeses.

3 Viruses: The word 'virus' comes from the Greek word for poison. Viruses are not, strictly speaking, alive. They are little bags of trouble that inject their genes into cells, tricking them into making more copies of the virus.

Eventually they burst out of the cell. Present to the class the balloon full of split pins and pop it dramatically to show the damage that viruses do to our cells. Viruses are usually bad news – although sometimes, they can kill harmful bacteria. Antibiotics will not work against them: we have to wait for our body to learn how to fight the invasion! Viruses cause colds, 'flu, German measles, chicken-pox and polio. The HIV virus causes a loss of immunity that can lead to the syndrome known as AIDS.

To reinforce the contrasts of size and appearance, present the following models: a football as a bacterium; a ball of cotton wool as a fungus; a split pin as a virus.

GROUP ACTIVITIES

1 Give the children a worksheet with the table shown below and the following list of words and phrases, which they can use to fill in the blanks: fungus, bacteria, athlete's foot, rust on wheat, reproduces inside cells, pneumonia, sore throat.

Type of microbe	Features	Examples of diseases caused
A?	Can be treated with antibiotics	B?
Virus	C?	AIDS, chicken-pox
D?	related to the mould found on old bread	E?

The answers are: A = bacteria; B = pneumonia, sore throat; C = reproduces inside cells; D = fungus; E = athlete's foot, rust on wheat.

2 Explain that in the right conditions, one bacterium can divide to make two bacteria every 20 minutes. If one bacterium causing sore throats lands in your throat at 10pm, how many could there be at 7am the next morning?

Give the children copies of page 61 and ask them to put their calculations into the chart. If possible, ask them to put these results onto a spreadsheet and generate a graph showing the growth of the colony of bacteria.

ASSESSMENT
Have the children filled in the microbes and symptoms table accurately? Check to see how they have got on with the chart on page 53 – do they understand the principle?

PLENARY
Go through the answers to the Group activities. Relate the rate of growth of a bacterial colony to the fact that bacteria (like one-celled organisms) reproduce by dividing in half. Explain that our body has a system of specific defences or 'antibodies' that can halt most harmful intruders.

OUTCOME
● Can describe some diseases and identify their causes.

LINKS
Maths: doubling and halving.

Lesson 3 ▪ Investigation: mouldy food

Objective
● To know that mould on food is caused by micro-organisms.
● To plan and carry out a fair test.

RESOURCES 💿
Bread; small plastic self-sealing freezer bags; sticky tape; sticky labels; pens; beakers; photocopiable page 42 from Unit 6A (also 'Investigation' (red) available on the CD-ROM).

MAIN ACTIVITY
Ask the children if they have ever gone to eat a slice of bread and found that it was mouldy. *What kind of microbe is mould?* (A fungus.) Explain that eating some kinds of microbes is not dangerous: the acid in our stomachs kills most microbes before they can cause a problem. However, some kinds of microbe cause food poisoning, which can make us very sick – it can even be fatal. One type of bacteria, (botulism), can reproduce inside tinned foods and is very dangerous indeed.

Tell the children that they are going to set up an investigation to look at what conditions are best for mould to grow in. Explain that once they are set up, the bags will be sealed and not reopened. Brainstorm ideas for designing fair tests. Ideas to investigate could include the temperature the bread is left at, whether the bread has been exposed to the air before the experiment and whether the bread is wet or dry.

Let the children work in groups to design and set up their experiments. Afterwards, make sure that they dispose of all samples carefully.

ASSESSMENT
Ask the children questions about their investigation, using the guidelines on photocopiable page 42.

PLENARY
You may wish to leave the Plenary until the results have been collected, several days later. Review the children's experiments and findings. Ask them

how to prevent food spoilage. They should suggest keeping food covered up
and refrigerated.

OUTCOMES
● Can describe good practice for food hygiene.
● Can explain why food hygiene is necessary.
● Can plan and carry out a fair test.

Lesson 4 ▫ Decay

Objective
● To know that the decay
caused by micro-organisms is
useful in the environment.

Vocabulary
decomposers, decay, nutrients,
microbes, recycling,
biodegradable, non-
biodegradable

RESOURCES ◉
Group activity: One copy per child of photocopiable page 62 (also 'Decay'
(red) available on the CD-ROM), pens.
ICT link: 'Decay' interactive activity on the CD-ROM.
Plenary: Assorted rinsed litter (cans, bottles, crisp wrappers, newspaper,
half an apple) in a tray, for demonstration.

BACKGROUND
In 25–30g of soil, there are estimated to be over 4000 million tiny
organisms. These micro-organisms (or microbes) play a vital role in breaking
down organic substances and freeing nutrients that are needed by plants. In
rainforests, the soils are particularly poor because the rain quickly leaches
away the nutrients. Decomposers which break down dead plants and
animals provide the main source of important soil nutrients. Decomposers
include fungi and bacteria that can travel easily through the air and settle
on dead material. Both release enzymes: special organic chemicals that help
to break apart the remains. The rain washes the released nutrients into the
soil, while the bacteria and fungi form the start of new food chains.
Decomposers are vital in keeping the cycle of life going.

DID YOU KNOW?
● Compost heaps get very hot inside, and in the winter they sometimes
appear to be steaming. The heat is a result of the activity of billions of
decomposers.
● Decomposers work best when the compost is well ventilated – just like us,
most microbes need oxygen to stay alive.
● Water treatment works rely on microbes to break up the organic material
in sewage. The microbes are encouraged to reproduce inside warm tanks
that have oxygen bubbled through.
● Microbes are also used to clean up oil spills. In delicate coastal
environments, fertilisers are sometimes sprayed on to the rocks to
encourage bacteria to feed on the oil and break it up.

STARTER
Gather the children together. Begin by saying: *The world is not littered with
the dead bodies of pterodactyls and mammoths, dodos and sabre-toothed
tigers. Why not?* Hopefully, the suggestions offered will include the idea
that dead things rot or decay.

MAIN ACTIVITY
Explain that this lesson is about decomposers. Ask the children whether
they have a compost heap at home. *Do you know what one is? Can you
describe it?* Remind them of the work they have done on soils. *What is the
plant material found in soils called?* (Humus.) Explain that when this
material decomposes, it releases important nutrients into the soil.
Decomposers (like the mould on stale bread) play a vital role in recycling the
nutrients that are locked up in the dead bodies of animals and plants. These

Differentiation
Support children by reminding them that the decay, in a compost heap, is caused by microbes, which are living things. *What do they need to stay alive?*

To extend children, give them 'Decay' (blue), from the CD-ROM, which tests their scientific vocabulary, by asking them to complete the sentences, in Exercise A.

nutrients are released into the soil, and can be taken up through the roots of plants. Plants need nitrates, phosphates, iron compounds and potassium compounds for healthy growth. Decomposers help to provide these.

GROUP ACTIVITY
Give the children a copy each of photocopiable page 62. Ask them to label the diagram to show how decomposers return nutrients to the soil (Exercise A), then answer the questions about the action of microbes in a compost heap (Exercise B). (Exercise C will be completed in the Plenary.)

ICT LINK 💿
Children can use the 'Decay' interactive, on the CD-ROM, to sort biodegradable from non-biodegradable materials.

ASSESSMENT
Check that the children understand that microbes are living things, and that they need oxygen, moisture and warmth to be active.

PLENARY
Explain that 'biodegradable' is the term used for materials that can decay within a few years. Non-biodegradable materials are those that either do not decay or take a very long time to decay. *Which of these two types of material is a good food for microbes? Some manufacturers have made plastic bags that are biodegradable – what is the advantage of this?*

With the children contributing suggestions, sort a collection of litter into 'biodegradable' and 'non-biodegradable' materials. Ask the children to complete Exercise C on photocopiable page 62 by sorting the litter in the picture. (Non-biodegradable: soft drink can, jam jar, plastic drink bottle, burger container (compressed polystyrene), crisp packet, sweet wrapper. Biodegradable: matches, chip wrapper, apple core.) *What can we do with items of litter that are non-biodegradable, such as glass bottles or steel cans?* (Recycle them.) *What materials do your family recycle?*

OUTCOME
● Understand that the decay caused by micro-organisms allows nutrients to be recycled.

LINKS
Unit 6a, Lesson 5: Healthy plants.

Lesson 5 ▸ Finding out about yeast

Objective
● To know that yeast is a useful organism.

Vocabulary
yeast, fungus, fermentation, budding, carbon dioxide, alcohol, respire

RESOURCES 💿
Starter: A bottle of beer, a loaf of bread.
Group activity: (For each group) six test tubes; six balloons of the same size; a test tube rack; fresh or dried yeast; sugar; teaspoons; a timer; thermometers; a kettle; measuring cylinders; a copy of photocopiable page 63 (also 'Finding out about yeast' (red) available on the CD-ROM). (You may need to borrow some resources from a local secondary school, or to present the activity as a demonstration, with one set of apparatus.)

PREPARATION
Blow up the balloons and let them down again before the lesson, so that they will stretch easily. You may want to set up a microscope with some fresh yeast for the children to look at. **Safety:** Do not allow the children to handle very hot or boiling water (refer also to safety note in Chapter 6c, Lesson 4).

BACKGROUND

Yeast is the name given to a particular type of single-celled fungus. It is often associated with brewing, as it has the ability to react with sugar to produce carbon dioxide and alcohol. We call this process fermentation. The production of carbon dioxide is also useful in bread-making, as it makes the bread rise.

STARTER

Put out a bottle of beer and a loaf of bread. Ask the children to guess what these have in common (this may prompt some interesting answers). Help them by saying that the answer is a type of microbe. If necessary, reveal the answer: yeast.

MAIN ACTIVITY

Explain that yeast is a fungus, and that the children are going to find out what conditions are best for its growth and reproduction. Show them the apparatus they will need, and talk them through the experiment described on photocopiable page 63.

GROUP ACTIVITY

Explain that when yeast is growing and multiplying, it respires – that is, it uses up sugar and oxygen to make energy, and releases carbon dioxide gas. Tell the class that in this experiment, they are going to test in what conditions yeast is most active (and so makes the most carbon dioxide. Let the children set up, or demonstrate setting up, the experiment shown on page 63.

Encourage the children to record and explain their findings. These should be as follows. In tube A there is no change, because the yeast lacks water and remains inactive. In tube B there is no change, because the yeast is still inactive. In tube C a little carbon dioxide is produced, because the yeast slowly becomes active but lacks the sugar it needs to respire (make energy) and divide. In tube D carbon dioxide is rapidly produced (the balloon inflates), because the yeast has everything it needs to become active and reproduce. In tube E there is no change, because the yeast has been killed by the boiling water (if the balloon expands, it is probably because of the heated gas). In tube F a little carbon dioxide is produced, because the yeast becomes active more slowly – most living things become more active as the temperature reaches about 37°C.

ASSESSMENT

At the bottom of page 63, the children should write what conditions seem best for yeast to grow and reproduce, giving a reason for their answer. Use their answers in discussion to assess their understanding of the experiment and their ability to use their scientific knowledge.

PLENARY

Discuss the experiment and the children's answers (see Assessment). Ask the children to think why the yeast used in bread-making is left for a few hours in the bread mix before it is placed in the oven. (The yeast cells are active inside the dough mix, producing tiny pockets of carbon dioxide. Once the dough is placed in the oven, the yeast cells are killed and become part of the bread; but the bubbles expand in the heat, helping the bread to rise.

OUTCOMES

● Can identify the conditions needed for yeast to grow and reproduce.
● Know the function of yeast in bread-making.

LINKS

Unit 6d, Lessons 1, 7 and 8: irreversible changes.

Differentiation
Prompt children who need support by reminding them that yeast is a living organism. *What do all living things need to survive?* (Water, oxygen, warmth, a food source.)

Lesson 6 ▪ Micro-organisms in food production

RESOURCES
A broad bean or pea plant; wine; beer; yoghurt; butter; bread; Stilton cheese; vinegar; reference materials (such as books, CD-ROMs, the internet); old magazines with pictures of different foods; relevant food labels; scissors; adhesive; sheets of A3 paper.

MAIN ACTIVITY
Gather the class and place in front of them the resources you have collected. *What do all these things have in common?* Explain that they all depend on microbes. Bean and pea plants (legumes) have bacteria living as a partner, in their roots (in nodules). The plant provides the bacteria with sugars and the bacteria make vital nitrates for the plant (see Unit 6a, Lesson 5). Beer and wine rely on the fermentation process carried out by yeast (a fungus).

Bacteria turn ethanol (an alcohol) into vinegar. Carbon dioxide produced by yeast helps bread to rise when baked. Bacteria make milk curdle because of the acid they produce. Adding flavouring to this curdled milk produces yoghurt. If the curdled milk is allowed to ripen in the presence of a mould, it turns into cheese. Different cheeses are made using different moulds; 'blue' cheeses have veins of mould running through them. Butter is made by churning cream that has soured under the action of bacteria. Bacteria and fungi have even been used to make protein as a meat substitute for humans.

Type of food	How microbes help
Pea and bean plants	Bacteria provide vital nitrates for their growth.
Wine, beer	
Vinegar	
Yoghurt	
Cheese	
Butter	
Bread	
Protein (meat) substitute	

GROUP ACTIVITY
Ask the children to draw up a chart like the one shown above and work in pairs to fill in the blanks, using reference materials. They can then design a poster, Making Meals with Microbes, illustrating all the different ways that microbes are useful in making food. They can include food labels or pictures from magazines. Ask them to write a line under each picture explaining how microbes have helped.

ASSESSMENT
Check in the Plenary session that the children know at least four different types of food made using microbes. From previous work, they should be able to explain how yeast causes bread to rise.

PLENARY
Ask the children to feedback what they have learned about microbes and share examples of the display work produced. Now ask them to imagine that some cheese is left in the open. *What will happen to it?* Remind them that

microbes eventually cause things to decay, and that the continual recycling of materials is necessary to provide the nutrients needed for new life.

OUTCOME
● Can describe how micro-organisms are used in food production.

Lesson 7 ● Assessment

Objective
● To assess the children's understanding of micro-organisms and their functions.

RESOURCES
Copies of photocopiable page 64 (also 'Assessment' (red) on the CD-ROM) for each child; pens or pencils.

STARTER
You may want to go through the key vocabulary, covered in this unit, particularly that which relates to microbes. A word wall containing these terms would form a useful focus for the start of the lesson. You could give each group a selection of the vocabulary, and ask each of the groups to share their understanding, of each word, with the rest of the class.

ASSESSMENT ACTIVITY
Give each of the children a copy each of photocopiable page 64 and let them work through it individually.

ANSWERS
1 = e; 2 = a; 3 = b; 4 = c; 5 = d; 6 = carbon dioxide; 7= antibiotics; 8= biodegradable.

LOOKING FOR LEVELS
Most of the children should score 5+/13.
Some of the children should score 6-9/ 13
More confident learners should score 10 +/ 13

PLENARY
Having gone over the answers with the whole class, arrange the pupils into groups of five. Give each of the groups a piece of coloured card, and ask them to list five ways that the world would be different, without microbes. After five or ten minutes take one suggestion, from each group, and write each of these ideas, on the board, as a summary for the topic.

PHOTOCOPIABLE

Germs and diseases

Quarantine: the Black Death (1377) and the Great Plague (1665)

Bubonic plague caused millions of deaths worldwide. In 1377, people travelling to Ragusa in Croatia were made to stay outside the town for 40 days (anyone with the plague usually died within five days). People didn't understand how the disease spread, but quarantine (separating germ-carriers from healthy people) worked. In 1665, fleas in cloth carried the plague from London to Eyam. The village quarantined itself. Of the 350 villagers 266 died. Their bravery stopped the disease spreading.

Smallpox vaccination: Edward Jenner (1796)

Edward Jenner noticed that patients who had suffered from the mild disease cowpox (often caught by milkmaids) never caught the deadly disease smallpox. In 1796, he injected a young boy with pus from a cowpox sufferer. Six weeks later, he injected the boy with the deadly smallpox virus. The boy remained healthy. Jenner had developed the first vaccine against a disease.

Antiseptics in hospitals: Joseph Lister (1856)

Lister found that over half of the people operated on in hospitals died of gangrene. He read about Louis Pasteur's ideas on germs and started using carbolic acid to clean surgical instruments, wounds and dressings. Thanks to Lister's work, the number of people dying after operations fell to 15 out of 100.

Pasteurisation: Louis Pasteur (1860)

French wine producers had problems with their wine going sour. Louis Pasteur found that if the sugar solutions used were heated to a high temperature, it killed any bacteria present and prevented the wine from going sour. Pasteur also showed that if milk was heated to a high temperature and pressure before being bottled, it would last longer. The process called pasteurisation is still used today to treat the milk we drink. Pasteur also demonstrated that microbes (germs) cause food to go bad.

Vaccination: Louis Pasteur (1881)

Pasteur grew cultures of harmful bacteria to experiment with. One day he accidentally, let a culture of cholera bacteria die. He decided to inject the dead bacteria into some chickens. The chickens did not fall sick; they remained healthy even when they were later injected with living cholera bacteria! Pasteur realised that the dead microbes had given the chickens a chance to develop their own defences to fight cholera. On 2nd June 1881, Pasteur demonstrated his method of vaccination against anthrax. He had one pen of animals, who were grazing quietly and another pen, with similar livestock, who lay dead or dying. The animals in both pens had been injected with anthrax but the ones that survived had previously been vaccinated.

Germs: Robert Koch (1843–1910)

Koch discovered some of the deadliest germs by taking samples from sick victims, staining them so that the germs showed up better and then looking at them under a microscope. He proved that germs caused diseases by finding the killer germs, growing them on a culture plate (though he first used the liquid inside eyeballs), then injecting them into healthy animals and observing as they fell sick.

Antibiotics: Alexander Fleming (1928)

Fleming had been working on bacteria that caused influenza. He accidentally left one of his culture plates uncovered. He later found that the bacteria had all died and that there was a mould (penicillin) growing on the plate. The chemicals produced by this mould were used to make the first antibiotics.

Microbes and illnesses

■ Complete this table to show how the number of bacteria found in your throat could increase during one night.

■ Remember: the number of bacteria doubles every 20 minutes.

Time in minutes	Time of day	Number of bacteria
0	10pm	1
20		2
40		4
60	11pm	8
80		
100		
120	12 midnight	
140		
160		
180	1am	
200		
220		
240	2am	
260		
280		
300	3am	
320		
340		
360	4am	
380		
400		
420	5am	
440		
460		
480	6am	
500		
520		
540	7am	

Is it any wonder that we can feel so unwell when we wake up?

Decay

Exercise A
Write the correct letter (A–F) next to each statement.

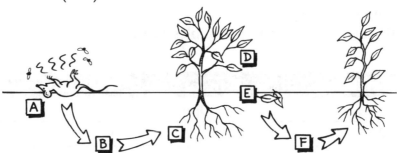

Microbes release nutrients. ☐
Animal dies and decays. ☐

Microbes decompose leaves. ☐
Soil nutrients absorbed by roots. ☐

Released nutrients absorbed by roots. ☐
Nutrients used in the growth of the plant. ☐

Exercise B
Compost bin

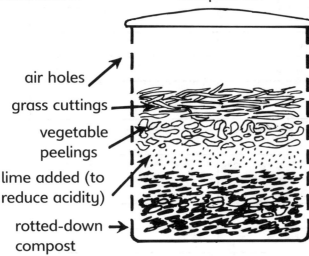

air holes
grass cuttings
vegetable peelings
lime added (to reduce acidity)
rotted-down compost

1. Why are the air holes important?

2. Why do gardeners add rotted-down compost to their soil?

3. Why do gardeners add water to the compost heap from time to time?

4. What materials could your family add to a compost bin?

_____

_____

Exercise C

 drink can   crisp wrapper   jam jar   plastic bottle   apple core   chip wrapper

Biodegradable waste

Non-biodegradable waste

1. Add the name of each piece of litter to one of the lists.
2. Write ® next to each item that could be recycled.

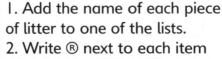

■ SCHOLASTIC

Finding out about yeast

■ Find out what conditions are best for the growth of yeast.

1. Label six test tubes A–F.
2. Put a small amount of fresh or dried yeast into each tube.
3. Set up each test tube as described below.
4. Shake each tube to mix together the contents, then place a deflated balloon over the top of each tube.

A – just the yeast (one teaspoon).
B – yeast and a pinch of sugar.
C – yeast and 10ml of tap water (record the temperature)
D – yeast, a pinch of sugar and 10ml warm water (about 35°C).
E – yeast, a pinch of sugar and 10ml boiling water. (see Safety below!)
F – yeast, a pinch of sugar and 10ml of cold water.

SAFETY: DO NOT handle boiling water – ask an adult to help you with E!

■ Record the changes that you see taking place over 30 minutes.

Test tube	Result
A	
B	
C	
D	
E	
F	

What my results show:

Assessment

Match these statements.

1. Microbes	A) Cause diseases.
2. Harmful microbes	B) Multiply inside living cells.
3. Viruses	C) Cover our skin and even make vitamins in our intestines.
4. Bacteria	D) Yeast, which helps bread to rise, is an example. Other types add flavour to cheese.
5. Fungi	E) Are living organisms. Most are very helpful.

1 =

2 =

3 =

4 =

5 =

6. To multiply, yeast needs the energy made from respiration. It uses sugar and oxygen to make this energy and the gas _____ _____. This gas causes the bread to rise.

7. Alexander Fleming discovered that a mould, called penicillin, killed bacteria. Today we use drugs that behave in the same way as penicillin to treat infections. We call these drugs _____.

8. Microbes help us to recycle waste materials and help to return nutrients to the soil. If a material can be broken down easily, by microbes, we say it is _____

CHAPTER 3   More about dissolving

Lesson	Objectives	Main activity	Group activities	Plenary	Outcomes
Lesson 1 Filtration	• To revise the concept of a mixture and ways of separating materials from mixtures. • To know that some materials dissolve in water. • To know that solids that do not dissolve in a liquid can be separated from it by filtering. • To be able to separate an insoluble solid from a liquid by filtering.	A demonstration and a 'question and answer' session to explore dissolving and filtering.	Separate soil from water using filtration. Label a diagram of a model filter bed.	A quick 'question and answer' session based on the Main and Group activities.	• Know that solids that dissolve/do not dissolve in water are soluble/ insoluble. • Know that insoluble solids can be separated from water using sieving or filtration. • Can describe how to separate a mixture such as soil and water using filtration. • Know some everyday uses of filtration. • Know that soluble solids cannot be separated from water by filtration.
Lesson 2 Evaporation	• To know that a dissolved solid can be separated from a liquid by evaporation.	A demonstration to show evaporation of water from a salt solution.	Carry out an experiment to separate salt from water using evaporation.	A 'question and answer' session based on the Group activity.	• Can describe how a dissolved solid can be separated from a liquid by evaporation.
Enrichment Lesson 3 Evaporation and condensation	• To know that when a gas is cooled it becomes a liquid, and that this process is called condensing.	A demonstration to show how to separate salt from water and then collect the water.	Label a diagram and complete a cloze text about evaporation and condensation.	Recap on the worksheet and the demonstration, using questions.	• Can describe how a liquid can be separated from a solution.
Lesson 4 The effects of temperature	• To know how the temperature of water affects the speed of dissolving. • To make a prediction based on relevant experiences. • To record results in a table	A discussion and teacher demonstration of an experiment to find out how temperature affects the speed of dissolving.	In groups carry out the same experiment as in the Main activity.	A review of the lesson's investigation.	• Can plan an investigation to find a relationship between two variables. • Know that increasing the temperature of a liquid results in quicker dissolving.
Lesson 5 Interpreting results	• To know how the temperature of water affects the rate of dissolving. • To be able to plot a line graph accurately. • To be able to interpret results.	Analyse the class results and take a close look at 'lines of best fit'.	Plot a graph of their results and draw a line of best fit. Draw a conclusion from their results.	The children plot a graph using a set of exemplary results.	• Know the relationship between the temperature of water and the rate of dissolving. • Understand why taking several measurements increases the reliability of the data. • Can decide on a line for their graph that fits the data. • Can explain why one line fits the data better than others.
Lesson 6 Checking results	• To carry out an investigation: make a prediction; decide what apparatus to use; plan a fair test; make careful observations and measurements. • To record results in an appropriate manner. • To know that repeating measurements improves the reliability of data. • To use a line graph or bar chart to present results; make comparisons and draw conclusions.	Present the information that the children will need to carry out their investigation.	Carry out an investigation to find out how the temperature of the water affects the speed at which salt dissolves in water.	Review of the lesson, highlighting the importance of fair testing and drawing 'lines of best fit' on graphs.	• Can carry out an investigation: plan a fair test to investigate a question; make a simple prediction, based on knowledge gained from a previous experiment. • Can record results in a table; present results, perhaps with some help, in the form of a bar chart or line graph; decide on a line for their graph that fits the data; explain what the results show. • Can identify the presence or absence of anomalous results.

Lesson	Objectives	Main activity	Group activities	Plenary	Outcomes
Lesson 7 The effects of particle size	• To know how particle size affects the rate of dissolving.	The children plan an investigation and carry it out, record their results and then draw a conclusion.	Review the lesson.		• Can describe how the rate of dissolving is affected by particle size.
Lesson 8 The effects of stirring	• To know how stirring affects the speed of dissolving. • To make a prediction; plan and carry out an experiment; record and interpret the results to draw a conclusion.	The children plan and carry out an investigation, record their results and then draw a conclusion.		Review the experiment and relate it to the previous lessons.	• Can describe how the rate of dissolving is affected by stirring.

Assessment	Objectives	Activity
Lesson 8	• To review learning about mixing and separating materials. • To carry out a formative or summative assessment for this unit.	Complete a worksheet on filtering and dissolving.

SC1 SCIENTIFIC ENQUIRY

How does water temperature affect the rate at which a substance dissolves?

LEARNING OBJECTIVES AND OUTCOMES
- Decide how to answer the question.
- Make predictions.
- Carry out an investigation.
- Evaluate results.
- Draw conclusions.

ACTIVITY
The children carry out an investigation into how quickly substances dissolve into water at different temperatures.

LESSON LINKS
This Sc1 activity forms an integral part of Lesson 4, The effects of the temperature.

Lesson 1 ▪ Filtration

Objective
- To revise the concept of a mixture and ways of separating materials from mixtures.
- To know that some materials dissolve in water.
- To know that solids that do not dissolve in a liquid can be separated from it by filtering.
- To be able to separate an insoluble solid from a liquid by filtering.

Vocabulary
dissolve, undissolved, soluble, insoluble, solution, filter, filtration, separate, separation, liquids, mixture

RESOURCES 💿
Starter: Mixtures of (a) flour and currants, (b) gravel and sand, (c) sand and water; a fine sieve; a coarser sieve. **Main activity:** Sand (3 tsp); water (200ml); two stirring implements (spoons or sticks); filter funnels; filter papers and beakers or jars; salt (3 tsps); a drinking straw (cut up). A microscope would be useful for examining the filter paper (your local secondary school may be able to lend you one.)
Group activities: 1 For each group (3 or 4 pupils): soil (3 tsps); water (100ml); beakers or jam jars; spoons or spatulas; glass rods or any stirring implement; filter paper; a filter funnel. **2** One copy per child of photocopiable page 86 (also 'Filtration' (red) available on the CD-ROM); a jam jar; a plant pot to fit above it (see diagram on page 68); sand; small stones; large stones; cloth; dirty water.
ICT link: 'Filtration' interactive activity, on the CD-ROM.

PREPARATION
If you wish the children to taste the water used in the teacher demonstration, you need to make sure that it, the salt and all the apparatus are very clean. Write the instructions and cloze test for Group activity 1 on the board.

It might be a good idea to organise a trip to a local water treatment plant. Most water authorities have educational services.

BACKGROUND
This lesson allows the children to revisit past work, and to learn more about solutions and filtration. They need to remind themselves what a 'mixture' is, and what is meant by the terms 'dissolving', 'insoluble' and 'soluble'. In science, a mixture is two or more materials 'mixed' together without any chemical reaction between them, and hence mixtures can be separated. There are several different kinds of mixture: solid bits and smaller solid bits;

insoluble solids in a liquid (suspension); soluble solids in a liquid (solution); and combinations of these.

The children must be steered away from the idea that when something dissolves, it disappears. When sugar or salt dissolves in water, the solid particles are broken down by the water molecules into very small pieces. These pieces are so small that they cannot be seen with the human eye. When a solid dissolves into a liquid, a solution is formed. A solution is always clear: it may be coloured, but has no bits floating around in it. For example, the solid copper sulphate takes the form of blue crystals. When these crystals are dissolved in water, a clear blue solution is formed. Other examples of water-soluble substances are sugar, salt and instant coffee.

If you put sand in water, the sand does not dissolve because the particles are not broken down by the water molecules. They remain as relatively large pieces. The children should already know that we can strain larger solid particles from a liquid with a sieve. However, the particles of sand are too small for them all to be separated from the water by a sieve.

Filter paper can be used as a very fine sieve to separate very small solid particles, that are mixed with a liquid such as water. A piece of filter paper has very tiny holes that can only be seen under a microscope. The water molecules are small enough to pass through these holes, but the sand particles are too large and so they stay behind in the filter paper. Filtration is thus a good method for separating bits of an insoluble solid (such as chalk, clay or wax) from a liquid. However, when salt or sugar dissolves in water, the solid particles are broken down into very tiny, invisible particles that can pass easily through the holes in the filter paper. Filtration is therefore not a good method for separating a soluble solid from a solution.

Filtration has many uses in our everyday life. In a coffee maker, a filter is used to separate the bits of ground bean from the dissolved coffee. Filter beds are used in the water supply to clean dirty water before it is reused. The diagram below shows how a home-made filter bed can be made.

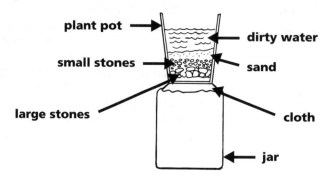

STARTER
Start by revising previous work on mixtures and ways of separating them. Offer some or all of the following examples to help the children consider their ideas. Provide mixtures of flour and currants, sand and gravel, and soil and water, as visual aids, as well as suitable equipment to separate them. Ask the children: *A chef has dropped a packet of currants accidentally into a big bowl of flour. What has he made?* (A mixture of flour and currants.) How could he separate the currants and the flour? (Using a sieve.) Demonstrate this. *What if a builder adds some gravel to a pile of sand? What has he made?* (A mixture of sand and gravel.) *If he adds too much gravel, how could he separate it from the sand?* (By using a sieve.) Demonstrate this if possible. *If you put some sand into water, what will you make?* (A mixture of sand and water.) *What is a 'mixture'?* Make sure that the children have grasped the idea that mixtures can be separated.

MAIN ACTIVITY
Ask: *How would you separate the sand from the water?* With help, the

children should suggest a sieve with very small holes. Show them a piece of filter paper. *Can anyone remember what this is?* Tell them if necessary. Explain that if you looked at the filter paper under a microscope, you would see that it is made up of lots of tiny holes. If you have access to a simple microscope, set this up for the children to take turns looking at the filter paper during the course of the day.

Ask: *Does sand dissolve in water?* (No.) Put some sand in water to demonstrate. *Is sand soluble or insoluble in water?* (Insoluble.) *How do you think we could use the filter paper to separate the mixture of sand and water?* Show the children how to fold a piece of filter paper in four so that it fits in a funnel (see illustration below) and how to set up the apparatus necessary for filtering. Demonstrate how to separate sand from water using this apparatus. Tell the children that this process is called 'filtration'. Now ask: *If you add salt to water, what do you notice?* (The salt dissolves.) Put some salt in water to demonstrate. *Is salt soluble or insoluble in water?* (Soluble.) *Can you see the salt particles when they have dissolved in water?* (No.)

Ask for a volunteer to taste the salt water, using a drop on the end of a piece of drinking straw. Make sure that all the equipment, the salt and water are clean beforehand. Ask: *Can you taste the salt in the water?* (Yes.) *So has the salt disappeared, or is it still in the water?* (Still in the water.) *When salt dissolves in water, the salt particles do not disappear even though we cannot see them. So what do you think happens to the size of the particles of salt?* (They get smaller.)

Do you think we can separate the salt from the water using filtration? Carry out filtration with the salt and water solution to demonstrate that the salt passes through the filter paper. If you want a child to taste the solution collected in the container, all the apparatus must be exceptionally clean. Again, the child should use a clean piece of cut-up drinking straw to put a drop on the tongue. *Would anyone like to see what the solution which has passed through the filter paper tastes like?* Hopefully someone will volunteer and tell the rest of the class that it tastes of salt. Then ask: Do you think the filter paper was able to catch the salt? (No.) *Why do you think the salt went through the filter paper?* (When the salt dissolves in water, the salt particles become so small that you cannot see them. They are able to pass through the tiny holes in the filter paper.) *So has filtration allowed us to separate salt from water?* (No.)

GROUP ACTIVITIES

1 The children could work in pairs or groups of three. Introduce the task: *Today we have already discussed the fact that sand is insoluble in water and that we can separate sand from water using filtration.* Direct the children to the following instructions, written on the board:
1. Add 6 teaspoonfuls (or 12 spatula measures) of soil to 200ml of water. Stir for 20 seconds.
2. Leave the soil and water mixture for about five minutes. Set up the apparatus that was used for separating sand from water.
3. After five minutes, have a close look at the soil and water mixture. What does it look like now? Draw what you see.
4. Pour the mixture of soil and water into the filter paper funnel.
5. Draw and label the

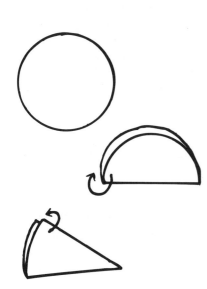

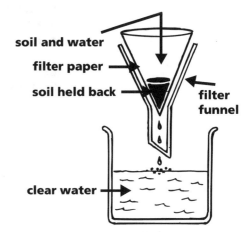

soil and water
filter paper
soil held back
filter funnel
clear water

Differentiation 💿

● Support children by setting up a 'word wall' in the classroom so that when you are asking questions, the words will act as a prompt.

Group activity 1
Some children may find it useful to have the apparatus they are to set up within their view, and a reminder sketch of how to fold the filter paper.

Children who need most support might find it useful to have a worksheet with a diagram of the apparatus and the missing words paragraph, so all they have to do is label the apparatus and fill in the words.

Extend children by asking them the following questions: *If you put some soil and chalk in water, why would filtering be no use for separating the soil from the chalk?* (They are both insoluble.) *Why do you use filter papers in a coffee percolator?* (To separate the coffee solution from the ground beans.)

Group activity 2
Support children by giving them 'Filtration' (green), from the CD-ROM, which asks them to label the diagram using words from a bank.

apparatus you have just used. (See illustration right.)
6. Copy the following, filling in the missing words:
When I looked at my mixture of soil and water, I noticed that some of the soil [sank] to the bottom and some bits of soil [floated] around in the water. Soil does not [dissolve] in water. Soil is [insoluble] in water. We can separate soil from water using [filtration]. If you look at filter paper under a microscope, you can see that it is full of [tiny holes]. The soil particles are too [large] to pass through the holes in the filter paper.

Salt [dissolves] in water. Salt is [soluble] in water. When salt is dissolved in water, it passes straight through [filter paper] because the salt particles are [smaller] than the holes in the filter paper.

2 When the children have completed the task above, tell them: *We have carried out an activity to separate soil from water using filtration. Now we are going to look at how filtration is used in everyday life.* Give each child a copy of page 86. Explain: *A filter bed is like a giant piece of filter paper. Filter beds are used to clean our water. The dirty water is passed through a filter bed at a water treatment plant before it goes back to be used again. We can make a model like this.* Demonstrate how to put the model together, inviting individuals to add parts in order and then try it out. *Let's see if it can make this dirty water clean.* Ask the children to label the diagram of the model filter bed on page 86.

ICT LINK 💿
Children can use the 'Filtration' interactive, on the CD-ROM to label the parts of a filter bed.

ASSESSMENT
Note which children can follow the instructions; understand what is meant by the terms 'soluble' and 'insoluble'; can decide when filtration is the best method of separation.

PLENARY
Finish off with a quick-fire question session based on the Main activity: *Does soil dissolve in water?* (No.) *How do you separate soil from water?* (Filtration.) *How do we fold filter paper?* (Ask a child to demonstrate.) *Name some everyday uses of filtering.* (Filter beds for water, coffee filters.) *In a filter bed, are the small stones on top of the sand or below it?* (Below it.)

OUTCOMES
● Know that solids that dissolve/do not dissolve in water are soluble/insoluble.
● Know that insoluble solids can be separated from water using sieving or filtration.
● Can describe how to separate a mixture such as soil and water using filtration.
● Know some everyday uses of filtration.
● Know that soluble solids cannot be separated from water by filtration.

LINKS
English: group discussion and interaction.

Lesson 2 ▪ Evaporation

Objective
● To know that a dissolved solid can be separated from a liquid by evaporation.

Vocabulary
evaporation, evaporate, crystals, dissolved, vapour

RESOURCES
Main activity: A watering can; bucket or cup of water; chalk; sugar or salt (2 tsp); water (100ml); a stirring implement (spoon or wooden stick); a wide dish.
Group activity: For each group: salt or sugar (about 10 tsp); water; a stirring implement; a spatula or teaspoon; a measuring cylinder or jug (to measure out water); three wide dishes (all exactly the same type).

BACKGROUND
In Lesson 1, the children saw that filtration is not a good method for separating a soluble solid from a solution (for example, salt or sugar in water). It is possible to evaporate the water from a solution by heating it with a flame, or just by putting the water and solid in a wide dish and leaving it in a warm place. The solid that was dissolved in the water is left behind as crystals. When heated, the water particles gain more energy and break free from the weak bonds between them. This results in the evaporation of water (as a gas or vapour) from the water surface. This gas is invisible, and should not be confused with the suspended water droplets that form white clouds above hot water. When liquid water is heated to its boiling point, evaporation takes place not only at the surface but all through the water, resulting in the very rapid release of water vapour.

The rate of evaporation from a water surface depends on temperature, air humidity, air movement and the surface area of the water. Places that are warm and dry and have moving air promote evaporation (for example, a sunny window sill with a warm breeze). Places that are cold, damp and still (such as a cellar) do not promote evaporation. Washing on a line dries quickest on a warm, dry, breezy day and slowest on a cold, wet, still day.

The ideas covered in this lesson are revisited from a different perspective in Lessons 3.

STARTER
Recap on Lesson 1 to focus the children on the vocabulary and concepts that were covered. Ask: *Does salt dissolve in water? So is salt soluble or insoluble in water? Can we separate salt from water by filtration? How do you think we could do it?*

MAIN ACTIVITY
At the start of the day, weather permitting, take the children into a part of the playground or school grounds that will not be disturbed. Pour water to make a puddle, and use chalk to draw around the edge of the puddle. If it is a good day for evaporation (warm, dry and breezy), you might want to send out two volunteers every hour to draw around the perimeter of the puddle.

In the afternoon, go out into the playground and observe the perimeter of the puddle again. It should have decreased, due to some of the water having evaporated. Ask: *Has the perimeter of the puddle changed in size? What will eventually happen to the puddle?* (It will disappear.) *When do puddles disappear most quickly?* (When the Sun is out.) *What do you think the Sun does to the water in the puddle that makes the water seem to disappear?* (It warms it or heats it up.) *When water is heated up, it seems to disappear. Water is a liquid (which we can see), and when a liquid is heated up it turns into a gas (which we cannot see very well). Sometimes you can see the gas turning back into tiny drops of water as it cools down. That's why there are clouds of steam above a kettle. When water turns into a gas as it is heated, we call the process 'evaporation'. The water has 'evaporated off'.*

Differentiation

Support children by giving them a diagram of the experiment (as well as the results chart) on a worksheet so that they only need to label the diagram and fill in the table. Some children may also benefit from having a list of words to choose from.

Challenge children with the following questions: *Which of the following could be separated by evaporation: a solution of yellow dye in water; salt and sugar both dissolved in water; orangeade and water?* (The first and third.) *How could you separate a mixture of gravel, sand and salt?* (Use a sieve to separate out the gravel. Add water to the sand and salt. The salt will dissolve, but the sand will not. Use filtration to separate the sand from the salt. Then use evaporation to separate the salt from the water.)

Teacher demonstration

We can use evaporation to separate salt from water. Add about two teaspoons of salt to about 100ml of water and stir. Pour the solution into a wide dish and leave it in a warm, dry place. Return to it the next day, when you should be able to show the children that all the water has evaporated, leaving behind the salt crystals.

GROUP ACTIVITY

The children could work in pairs or groups of three or four. Tell them: *You are now going to try to separate salt from water by evaporation and find out which is the best place in the classroom for evaporation.* Write on the board: 'To find the best place for evaporation'. *Which places do you think might be good for evaporation?* Draw the children's attention to the fact that when they hang washing out on the line to dry, it dries because the water evaporates from the clothes. *So on what type of day does the washing dry the quickest?* (Warm, sunny, dry, breezy days.) *How many places are you going to test? How will you make sure you are carrying out a fair test? What will you measure?* (How long it takes for the water to evaporate completely.) *How will you decide which is the best place for evaporation?* (The place where evaporation occurred most quickly.) Record the agreed plan on the board.

If the children choose three places, they will need to make up three lots of salt solution. To make the test fair, they need to make up these solutions with the same amount of water (100ml) and salt (2 tsp); the water temperature must be the same in all cases, and the containers must all present the same surface area.

The children should set up the test and then leave the dishes for a few days. Ask them to draw and describe what they have done. When all the water has evaporated, ask them to record their results in a table with the headings 'Place' and 'Time taken for all the water to evaporate (days/hours)'. They could also describe or draw what they observed in the container once all the water had evaporated. Finally, they should state which the best place for evaporation was.

NB Do not let the children taste the salt which is left behind in the dish as you don't know what may have landed in the dish, whilst it has been exposed.

ASSESSMENT

Note which children chose suitable places for their dishes, and which children were able to carry out a fair test.

PLENARY

If time does not allow children to attempt the questions from Differentiation, they could do so as a Plenary activity. The following questions could also be used to find out what the children have learned: *Does salt dissolve in water? Do you think sugar dissolves in water? How do you know?* (It dissolves in tea.) *Are sugar and salt soluble or insoluble in water? Why can we not separate salt or sugar from water by filtration? Can anyone tell me what they have done this lesson that will help them to separate salt from water?*

OUTCOME

● Can describe how a dissolved solid can be separated from a liquid by evaporation.

LINKS

English: group discussion and interaction.

ENRICHMENT
Lesson 3 ■ Evaporation and condensation

Objective
● To know that when a gas is cooled it becomes a liquid, and that this process is called condensing.

Vocabulary
evaporation, condensation, gas, liquid

RESOURCES
Main activity: A spirit burner or candle burner; a tablespoon; a cold surface (such as a ceramic tile); a salt solution (4 tsp salt dissolved in 100ml water).
Group activity: Photocopiable page 87 (also 'Evaporation and condensation' (red) available on the CD-ROM).
ICT link: 'Evaporation and condensation' interactive on the CD-ROM.

BACKGROUND
When water vapour cools, it turns into liquid water:

$$\text{Solid} \quad \overset{\text{melting} \rightarrow}{\underset{\leftarrow \text{ freezing}}{\rightleftarrows}} \quad \text{Liquid} \quad \overset{\rightarrow \text{evaporating} \rightarrow}{\underset{\leftarrow \text{condensing} \leftarrow}{\rightleftarrows}} \quad \text{Gas}$$

For example:

$$\text{Ice} \quad \overset{\rightarrow \text{melting} \rightarrow}{\underset{\leftarrow \text{freezing} \leftarrow}{\rightleftarrows}} \quad \text{Water} \quad \overset{\rightarrow \text{evaporating} \rightarrow}{\underset{\leftarrow \text{condensing} \leftarrow}{\rightleftarrows}} \quad \text{Steam}$$

If the children are unsure about melting and freezing, demonstrate these processes in the lesson. More information is available in All New 100 Science Lessons: Year 4/Primary 5.

STARTER
Tell the children: *In Year 4/Primary 5 (check with the relevant staff or school scheme of work), you looked at how a solid could be changed into a liquid and a liquid back into a solid.* Write the following on the board:

$$\text{Solid} \quad \overset{\rightarrow}{\underset{\leftarrow}{\rightleftarrows}} \quad \text{Liquid}$$

Ask the following questions and add each correct answer to the text on the board to create a flow chart diagram. *Does anyone know what we have to do to a solid to turn it into a liquid?* (Heat it up.) *What is the name of the process by which a solid turns into a liquid?* (Melting.) *Does anyone know how to turn a liquid back into a solid?* (Cool it down.) *What is the name of this process?* (Freezing.)
   By now, your diagram should look as follows:

$$\text{Solid} \quad \overset{\rightarrow \text{ 'heat (melting)} \rightarrow}{\underset{\leftarrow \text{ 'cool (freezing)'} \leftarrow}{\rightleftarrows}} \quad \text{Liquid}$$

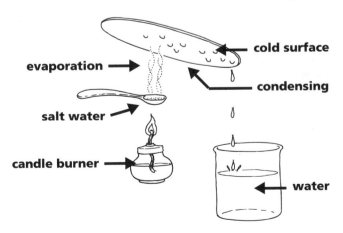

Say that in the previous lesson, we separated a soluble solid from a liquid by evaporation. By the end of today's lesson you will know a new term, 'condensation', and how to obtain the liquid from a solution.

Differentiation
Group activity
To support children, give them 'Evaporation and condensation' (green) from the CD-ROM, which provides a word list to help them fill in the blanks.

To extend children, give them 'Evaporation and condensation' (blue), which asks them to describe what is happening in the diagram in their own words.

MAIN ACTIVITY

Have the apparatus set up as shown on the bottom of page 73. As with all experiments, it is probably a good idea to practise this demonstration first. It is an established fact that more accidents occur during science lessons when the teacher is demonstrating a practical than when the children are doing the activity themselves.

Start to heat up the salt solution. Ask the following questions while you are waiting for the water to evaporate (or before you start to heat up the solution): *In the spoon, I have got some salt solution. How do you think I made the salt solution?* (Dissolved some salt in water.) *How do you think I could get the salt back on its own again?* (By evaporation.) *If I heat up this salt solution, what do you think will happen?* (We will be left with salt [crystals] in the spoon.) *What about the water – where do you think that will have gone?* Let the children offer their ideas. From Lesson 2, they may know that the water has changes into a vapour or gas.

Explain that you are going to get the salt on its own again and collect the water. Once condensation starts to form on the tile, ask the children to tell you what they can see. *Where else have you seen water collect like this?* (Perhaps condensation on a cold window or on things from the refrigerator.) Once all of the water has evaporated and you have collected some condensed water, draw the children's attention to the fact that the salt is left in the spoon. *Do you think the liquid we have collected is just water, or do you think it is a salt solution? How can we find out?*

The children may suggest tasting it – but for health and safety reasons, this is not advisable. Remind them of the previous investigation, and lead them to suggest leaving the liquid to stand in a sunny place or heating it as before. If it is a salt solution, the water can be evaporated off to leave salt behind. If it is only water, no salt will be left behind. Check this by heating up the liquid or leaving it for a few days on the windowsill. The result should demonstrate that the water collected contained no salt.

Go back to the flow chart on the board. When we heat up a liquid, it turns into a gas. This is called evaporation. Extend the flow chart:

Solid → heat (melting) → Liquid → heat (evaporating) → Gas
← cool (freezing) ← ←

If we cool the gas down, it turns back into the liquid. This is called condensation. Write 'cool (condensing)' under 'heat (evaporating)' on the flow chart. *In today's experiment, the liquid water that we evaporated turned into a gas called steam. When the gas hit the cold surface, it cooled down and turned back into a liquid. This is condensation.* Redraw the flow chart:

Ice → heat (melting) → Water → heat (evaporating) → Steam
← cool (freezing) ← ← cool (condensing) ←

GROUP ACTIVITY

Give the children a copy each of page 87. The children need to label the diagram (as on page 73) and then complete the cloze text using the key words: evaporated, salt crystals, liquid, gas, water, condensation.

ICT LINK

Children can use the 'Evaporation and condensation' interactive, on the CD-ROM, to label the diagram on the computer.

ASSESSMENT

Note which children were able to fill in the answers correctly on the sheet.

PLENARY
Review the lesson and refer back to these points on the board: *When a liquid is heated up, what does it turn into?* (A gas.) *What is this process called?* (Evaporation.) *When a gas is cooled, what does it turn into?* (A liquid.) *What is this process called?* (Condensation.) *How could I get both the water and the salt crystals from a salt solution?* (The children should be able to describe the method to you.)

OUTCOME
● Can describe how a liquid can be separated from a solution.

LINKS
English: group discussion and interaction.
Geography: weather studies.

Lesson 4 ▸ The effects of temperature

Objective
● To know how the temperature of water affects the speed of dissolving.
● To make a prediction based on relevant experiences.
● To record results in a table.

Vocabulary
temperature, dissolve, prediction, thermometer, stir, stirring

RESOURCES
Main activity: Four ordinary white sugar cubes; four beakers; four spoons; a balance (if available); four thermometers; a stopwatch; four 100ml samples of water at different temperatures (see Preparation).
Group activity: Each group needs the same set of apparatus as for the Main activity.
Safety: It is not advisable to use a kettle to heat up water, as this could lead to accidental scalding. Mercury thermometers are not suitable for use in primary schools, because the mercury released when one is broken is both toxic and difficult to clear up.

PREPARATION
Prepare 100ml samples of water, in beakers, at about 4°C (fridge temperature), 20°C (room temperature), 30°C, 40°C and 50°C. It will be useful to have an adult classroom assistant for this lesson (see Differentiation).

BACKGROUND
(This information will also be useful for lessons 5-7.) When sugar (for example) dissolves in water, the water molecules break down the sugar particles into very tiny pieces. A number of factors can affect how quickly this happens:
1 If the water is heated, the water molecules will have more energy. This means that they will move about much faster and so will collide with the sugar particles more times per second, breaking them down more quickly; so the sugar dissolves in the water more quickly.
2 Stirring the sugar into the water increases the frequency of collisions between the sugar particles and the water molecules. This means that the water molecules will break down the sugar particles more quickly. So sugar dissolves more quickly in water when it is stirred.
3 The bigger each initial sugar particle is, the longer it will take the water molecules to break it down. So it takes longer to dissolve sugar in water if it is made up of large granules as opposed to small granules (for example, brown sugar takes longer to dissolve in coffee than castor sugar, which in turn takes longer than icing sugar).
   The children do not need to know all of the above information. They only need to understand that increasing the temperature, reducing the particle size and stirring will all speed up the rate of dissolving. Offer the idea of particles and energy if it will assist their understanding.

Differentiation

Some children will need more individual help during the practical work. An adult classroom assistant could use a picture or diagram to show the experiment, or describe it on audiotape.

Some children find it very difficult to write out tables of results; it might be a good idea to have the table drawn up and photocopied for them. They could also describe their experiment orally.

STARTER

Revise the meanings of 'dissolve', 'soluble' and 'insoluble'. Discuss some examples of each process.

MAIN ACTIVITY

In this lesson, you will discuss the experiment with the children, demonstrate it and then let them carry it out for themselves. The following results might give you an idea of what to expect. The amounts of sugar and water used were constant: 1 cube and 100ml respectively.

Temperature (°C)	Time taken for sugar to dissolve (s)
4	135
20	77
30	55
40	23
50	17

The above temperatures are just a guideline. When you do the experiment, the water that has just come out of the fridge may be anywhere from 4°C to 10°C. The water from the cold tap should be about 20°C, but this can also vary. It is good practice to take the actual temperature of the water samples, and not to assume that they will have particular temperatures.

Teacher demonstration

Ask: *If I put some sugar in cold water and some in hot water, which will dissolve faster? Why?* The children might say that because sugar dissolves quicker in hot tea than in cold milk, it will dissolve quicker in hot water than in cold water. Develop a prediction based on this idea.

What experiment could we do to show that sugar dissolves faster in hot water than in cold water? With careful questioning, get the children to think about the experiment and tell you what they could do. Agree on a plan. Elicit the idea of using five temperatures of water: from the fridge, at room temperature and from the hot tap (using cold water to cool two samples a little). Emphasise the need for at least five independent variables. Decide how to make the test fair: by using the same amount of water (100ml), the same amount and type of sugar (1 cube), the same number of stirs (such as 20) and the same-sized container. The same child should do the stirring for each sample. Make sure the children understand that they must put the sugar cube in the water, then immediately start the stopwatch. As soon as all the sugar has dissolved, they should stop the stopwatch.

Discuss why you should repeat the experiment for each temperature: to obtain reliable results by taking an average. Remember to take repeats to make sure they are close. Only use close results in the average.

Once you have gone over the experiment with the children, you may wish to demonstrate it and show the children how to record their results. Then ask the children to carry out the experiment for themselves. When they have completed the Group activity and recorded their results, collect in the tables and keep them for the next lesson.

GROUP ACTIVITY

Divide the children into groups of three or four to carry out the experiment. Encourage them to use a thermometer to measure the temperature of the water for themselves. Write the investigation title and the class prediction on the board or flipchart. The children can copy this and then describe the experiment in writing and drawings.

ASSESSMENT

Note which children were able to plan and carry out a fair test, use a thermometer accurately and record their results in the form of a table.

PLENARY
Review the lesson: *Can anyone describe our experiment to find out how temperature affects the rate at which sugar dissolves in water?*

OUTCOMES
● Can plan an investigation to find a relationship between two variables.
● Know that increasing the temperature of a liquid results in quicker dissolving.

LINKS
Maths: understanding measures.

Lesson 5 ◘ Interpreting results

Objective
● To know how the temperature of water affects the rate of dissolving.
● To be able to plot a line graph accurately.
● To be able to interpret results.

Vocabulary
dissolve, undissolved, soluble, insoluble, solution, filter, filtration, separate, separation, liquids, mixture

RESOURCES 💿
Main activity: The children's group results tables from Lesson 4; copies of a table of the class results (see Preparation); an OHP and two OHTs with graph axes already drawn on them (see Graphs 1 and 2 opposite), OHP pens.
Group activities: Graph paper (or a computer and data-handling software), paper, pens and pencils or use the graphing tool from the CD-ROM.

PREPARATION
On an OHT or on the board, have ready a blank 'class results' table. Below is an example, with some typical results. Prepare a sheet of the completed table (using the group results from the previous lesson, but without the averages) and make a copy of this for each child.

Group	Temperature (°C)	Time for sugar to dissolve (s)	Average time taken (s)
1	4	134	
2	4	140	144.6 (including 180)
3	4	180 *	135.8 (excluding 180)
4	4	138	
5	4	131	
1	20	55	
2	20	84	77.2
3	20	60	
4	20	99	
5	20	88	
1	30	54	
2	30	59	55.4
3	30	52	
4	30	57	
5	30	55	
1	40	24	
2	40	26	23
3	40	20	
4	40	24	
5	40	21	

The result marked * can be judged an error or anomalous result.

BACKGROUND
See Background for Lesson 4.

STARTER

Remind the children of their experiment in Lesson 4. *Can anyone tell me how they did the experiment? How did you record your results?* This lesson, we are going to look at your results and find out what they tell us.

MAIN ACTIVITY

Give the children their results tables back. Ask them: *Look at your results table. How long did it take the sugar to dissolve at 4°C?* Take a result from each group. Record the results in the table on the board. Repeat the same procedure for all the temperatures. Now plot each group's result on a graph, using prepared axes on an OHT (see Graph 1).

Identify a temperature where the results are spread out (for example, 20°C in Graph 1). *At __°C, you can see that one group found it took __ seconds for the sugar to dissolve in the water, but another group found that it took __ seconds. So it is difficult to say which is the most accurate result. Would you be able to trust that set of results?* (No.) *At __°C, the results are quite close together. Do you think you could trust these results?* (Yes.) Consider a result such as the one marked * (if appropriate). Explain that this is an anomalous result: one that does not fit the trend or pattern. This result is probably due to experimental error. On the graph, where the other results are bunched together, this one is separate.

Explain that you now have to join up the points on the graph. *We call this 'drawing a line of best fit'.* Attempt to draw a line through the highest points (see line 1 on Graph 1). *If I draw the line through these points, do you think that would be the line of best fit?* (No.) *Can anyone suggest where I could draw a better line?* (Working out the line of best fit for a scatter of results is very subjective. However, in general, a good rule when drawing a line of best fit is to ensure that there are a similar number of points above and below the line.) Agree on a line of best fit with the children (see line 2 on Graph 1).

Hand out copies of the completed results table (this should be the same as the results table on the OHT). *For each temperature, work out the average time it takes for the sugar to dissolve. Then write your answer on the results table I have just given you.*

At this point, have the second OHT ready with the graph axes drawn on it. Ask, for example: *Sarah, can you tell me what the average time was for 4°C? Does everyone else agree with Sarah's answer? Does anyone disagree with it?* When you have been given the correct answer and you are sure the children know how to work out an average, plot the answer onto the graph on the OHT. Repeat the same procedure for all temperatures. *Draw a line of*

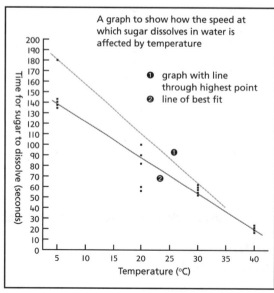

A graph to show how the speed at which sugar dissolves in water is affected by temperature

❶ graph with line through highest point
❷ line of best fit

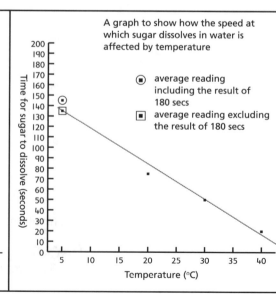

A graph to show how the speed at which sugar dissolves in water is affected by temperature

⊙ average reading including the result of 180 secs
⊡ average reading excluding the result of 180 secs

best fit through the points you have just plotted (see Graph 2).
    Once the two graphs are complete, overlay Graph 2 on top of Graph 1. Point out how the line of best fit on the first graph is in a similar position to the line of best fit for the average values - but the latter was much easier to draw. Emphasise to the class that finding average values, in this way, improves the reliability of their results.

GROUP ACTIVITY
The children should plot a line graph and draw a line of best fit for the average results. This is a very good opportunity to use a computer with data-handling software. Use questions to help the children to reach and write up a conclusion: *Which temperature made the sugar dissolve the quickest? Which temperature made the sugar dissolve the slowest? Do your results match your prediction? Use your graph to find out how long it would take for one sugar cube to dissolve in 100ml of water at 35°C. What could you have done to make sure that your results were reliable? What else dissolves in water? Do you think salt will dissolve faster or slower in hot water?*

ICT LINKS
The children could plot their graphs using a computer and data-handling software, or the children may wish to use the graphing tool from the CD-ROM, to plot their line graphs.

ASSESSMENT
Note which children are able to work out average results; plot their results accurately (on a line graph or bar chart); draw a line of best fit (on a line graph); and draw a conclusion from their graph.

PLENARY
Give the children the set of results, which were used as an example in Lesson 4. Ask the children to plot a graph of the results and draw a line of best fit.

OUTCOMES
● Know the relationship between the temperature of water and the rate of dissolving.
● Understand why taking several measurements increases the reliability of data.
● Can decide on a line for their graph that fits the data.
● Can explain why one line fits the data better than others.

LINKS
Maths: processing, representing and understanding data.

Lesson 6 ▪ Checking results

Objective
● To carry out an investigation; make a prediction; decide what apparatus to use; plan a fair test; make careful observations and measurements.
● To record results in an appropriate manner.
● To know that repeating measurements improves the reliability of data.
● To use a line graph or bar chart to present results; make comparisons and draw conclusions.

RESOURCES
Group activity: For each group: four lots of 1 tsp of salt; beakers, spoons, thermometers; a stopwatch; three 100ml samples of water at about 4°C (fridge temperature), about 20°C (room temperature), and about 30–40°C (from the hot tap, but not so hot that it would scald a child). See the safety note on kettles and mercury thermometers in Lesson 4.

BACKGROUND
In Lesson 5, the children reached the conclusion that salt is soluble in water and so can be expected to dissolve faster in hot water than in cold water. This lesson gives the children an opportunity to test that idea. The lesson also allows you to assess the children on all three skill areas of 'Experimental and Investigative Science'. The children will need to make a prediction, plan a fair test, carry out the experiment (repeating the test twice for each temperature), draw a table of results, plot a line graph, draw a line of best fit and make a concluding statement.

STARTER
What did you find out from your last experiment? (That sugar dissolves faster in hot water than it does in cold water.) *How could you have made the results more reliable?* (By repeating the test at each temperature.) This lesson, you are going to plan and carry out your own experiment.

MAIN ACTIVITY
Write the following on the board:
To find out if salt dissolves faster in hot water or cold water
Plan
Think about the last experiment. and reread what you wrote.
What apparatus will you use?
How much salt and water will you use?
What will you measure?
What will you keep the same?
What temperatures will you use?
How can you make your results more reliable?
Prediction
At which temperature do you expect the salt to dissolve fastest?
At which temperature do you expect the salt to dissolve slowest?
Why?
Results
Draw a table of results. Use the results table from the last experiment to help you. Don't forget to add an extra column for the average time.

GROUP ACTIVITY
The children should work in groups of three or four to carry out the experiment and record their results. Before they do so, talk it through with them. The procedure is the same as that in Lesson 4, but using salt instead of sugar. The children should repeat the test for each temperature twice, then find the average time for the salt to dissolve in the water at each temperature. They should draw a line graph of their average results (perhaps using a computer), deciding on a line for their graph that fits the data. Finally, they should make some kind of concluding statement about their results. To help them do this, write the following questions on the board:
At which temperature did salt dissolve fastest?
At which temperature did salt dissolve slowest?
Are these results what you expected?

Differentiation

For some children, a worksheet with the prediction and plan written out, would be useful. You could also provide a blank results table.

Some children may also need help with practical tasks such as, using a stopwatch. Other children may have difficulty working out averages, and might prefer taking one reading for each temperature. They may also prefer to draw a bar chart instead of a line graph.

To extend children, you could discuss their results, focusing on any that do not fit the general trend. Explain that such results are called 'anomalous'. You might ask: *Do you think that result is right?* (No.) *Why not?* (Because the salt took longer to dissolve in the water at 40°C than it did at 20°C. I thought that it would dissolve faster at 40°C.) *So what could you do?* (Do that test again.) If time permits, the child could repeat a test that gave an anomalous result. Encourage them to reocord the results in their results table and comment on them in their conclusions.

If there are no anomalous results, you could encourage children to comment on this fact in their conclusion. *Do you think all of your results are right?* (Yes.) *Why?* (Because the salt dissolved faster in water at 40°C than at 20°C, and it dissolved faster in water at 20°C than at 4°C.)

- *Why did you expect/not expect to get these results?*
- *How could you make your results even more reliable?*
- *How long would it take for salt to dissolve in water that was at 35°C?*

A typical conclusion that might be expected from the children is as follows:

> My results showed that salt dissolved faster in water at 40°C than it did in water at 4°C. These results match my prediction, where I said that salt would dissolve faster in hot water than it would in cold water. I thought this because, in another experiment, I saw that sugar dissolved faster in water at 40°C than it did in water at 4°C.
>
> In the last experiment, I did not repeat my results. To make my results more reliable this time, I have done the experiment twice at each temperature. If I had the time to repeat the experiment three or four times at each temperature, that would make my results even more reliable.
>
> From my graph, I can see that 1 teaspoon of salt would dissolve in 100ml of water at 35°C in ___ seconds.

ICT LINKS

Graphs can be plotted on a computer, using data handling software or you may wish to use the graphing tool from the CD-ROM.

ASSESSMENT

This activity gives you an opportunity to assess all three areas of Sc1: Experimental and Investigative Science using the Statements of Attainment. The three areas to be assessed are 'Planning experimental work', 'Obtaining evidence' and 'Considering evidence'.

PLENARY

Review the lesson. Highlight the fact that the higher the temperature of water, the higher the rate at which salt will dissolve in it. Also highlight aspects of the experimental procedure such as fair testing and drawing the line of best fit. (Children who have drawn a bar graph should be encouraged to identify the trend in their results without drawing a line.)

OUTCOMES

- Can carry out an investigation: plan a fair test to investigate a question; make a simple prediction, based on knowledge gained from a previous experiment.
- Can record results in a table; present results, perhaps with some help, in the form of a bar chart or line graph; decide on a line for their graph that fits the data; explain what the results show.
- Can identify the presence or absence of anomalous results.

Lesson 7 ▪ The effects of particle size

RESOURCES
Group activity: For each group: 2g or 1tsp samples of icing sugar; caster sugar and brown sugar; a stirring implement; 3 × 100ml water in beakers; a stopwatch; a thermometer.

PREPARATION
Have amounts of each type of sugar and the water already measured out. Write the following questions on the board, to help the children plan their experiment and consider their results:

Plan
What are the three types of sugar that you are going to use?
What apparatus will you need?
What will you do?
What things will you keep the same? What will you measure?

Explain that only three independent variables will be used because it is difficult to obtain five different types of sugar. Remind the children that it important to do repeats and take an average to obtain reliable results.

Prediction
What do you think will happen? Why?

Results
Which type of sugar dissolved the fastest?
Which type of sugar dissolved the slowest?
Why do you think one type of sugar dissolved faster than another?
Which type of sugar did you say would dissolve the fastest?
Does this prediction match with your results?

BACKGROUND
This activity addresses the following skills for Scientific Enquiry: 'Planning experimental work', 'Obtaining evidence' and 'Considering evidence'. Expect the children's prediction, plan and recording to contain the following:

Prediction
I think icing sugar will dissolve in water faster than caster or brown sugar. This is because icing sugar is made of very small pieces. The pieces in caster sugar are larger than in icing sugar and the pieces in brown sugar are larger than those in caster sugar. When sugar dissolves in water, the water breaks down the sugar pieces and they become too small to be seen. So if the pieces of sugar are big, as in brown sugar, it will take longer to break them down. Pieces of icing sugar are tiny to begin with, so it will not take as long for the water to break them down.

Plan
I will put 2g/1 tsp of icing sugar in 100ml of water. I will stir until it has all dissolved. I will time how long it takes. I will repeat the test using caster sugar and brown sugar.

Fair test
Same amount of water (100ml) for each experiment.
Same amount of sugar (2g/1tsp).
Same temperature of water.
Same person stirring (to keep rate of stirring the same).

Results

Type of sugar	Time to dissolve (s)
Icing	
Caster	
Brown	

Differentiation

Children who need support could use pictures or diagrams to describe the experiment and/or describe it orally onto audio tape. Provide a blank results table and a cloze text for the conclusion, such as: *The results showed that the [icing] sugar dissolved the fastest and the [brown] sugar dissolved the slowest. This shows that the [smaller] the particle size, the [faster] it dissolves.*

Extend children by asking them to write up the experiment, in their own words, evaluate their results and write their own conclusions.

STARTER

Remind the children what happens to salt when it is put in water: it dissolves. *Can anyone remember what happens when salt dissolves in water?* (The water breaks down the salt into pieces that are too small to be seen.)

Present the three types of sugar for today's experiment. *Which type of sugar is made of the smallest pieces?* (Icing sugar.) *Which is made of the largest pieces?* (Brown sugar.) *Which do you think will take the longest to dissolve in water?* (Brown sugar.) *Why?* (Brown sugar is made up of big pieces of sugar. It will take the water longer to break down these big bits into pieces that are too small to see, compared to the smaller bits of caster or icing sugar.)

Tell the children that they are going to plan and carry out an experiment. Write the title on the board: *To find out if particle size affects the speed at which sugar dissolves.*

MAIN ACTIVITY AND GROUP ACTIVITY

Let the children devise and carry out an experiment, using the questions, written on the board, to help them. They should draw a bar chart of their results (perhaps using a computer). Finally, they should use the second set of questions on the board to help them decide what their results show and write a conclusion.

ICT LINKS

Bar charts can be plotted on a computer, using data handling software or the children may wish to use the graphing tool from the CD-ROM.

ASSESSMENT

This activity gives you an opportunity to assess all three areas of Sc1: Experimental and Investigative Science using the Statements of Attainment. The three areas to be assessed are 'Planning experimental work', 'Obtaining evidence' and 'Considering evidence'.

PLENARY

Review the lesson. Highlight the conclusion that larger particles take longer to dissolve. Discuss why this is: smaller particles present a greater surface area to the liquid.

OUTCOME

● Can describe how the rate of dissolving is affected by particle size.

Lesson 8 ▸ The effects of stirring

RESOURCES
Two white sugar cubes; a stirring implement; two 100ml samples of water in beakers (both at room temperature); a stopwatch.

MAIN ACTIVITY
Ask some questions about the work covered in Lessons 4-7. Tell the children that today, they are going to look at how stirring affects the rate at which sugar dissolves in water. Write the title of the investigation on the board: *Do you think stirring will make sugar dissolve in water faster or slower? Why?* Discuss the children's answers and their reasons (for example, the experience of stirring a cup of tea). Ask them to write down their own prediction. Discuss and plan the investigation as a class or in groups, depending on their ability. The children will need to add sugar to water, stir and time how long it takes for the sugar to dissolve; then repeat the test, but without stirring. Discuss how the test can be made fair.
   The children should work in groups of three or four to carry out the experiment and record their results. Individually or as a class, they should analyse the results and decide whether the results match their prediction, then write a conclusion.

ASSESSMENT
As for Lesson 7.

PLENARY
Review the experiment and relate it to the two previous lessons: *Did the sugar dissolve faster when stirred or not stirred? What other things affect the rate at which sugar dissolves in water?*

OUTCOME
● Can describe how the rate of dissolving is affected by stirring.

Lesson 9 ▸ Assessment

RESOURCES ◉
Photocopiable page 88 (also 'Assessment' (red) available on the CD-ROM); pens.

STARTER
You may wish to begin the Assessment activity straight away, or you may like to begin by helping the children prepare for the test. Devise and ten questions from the work you have covered in this unit and question the class in quck succession. You may want to let the children pose questions to each other and evaluate the answers with your help. This could be done as a quiz where the class is split up into teams, or children can just answer their questions individually.

ASSESSMENT ACTIVITY
Give out copies of photocopiable page 88 for the children to complete individually. You may wish to mark the sheets yourself, or exchange them around the class and let the children mark each other's sheets to encourage discussion.

ANSWERS
1. Soluble: salt, instant coffee, artificial sweetener, Insoluble: sand, soil,

chalk (3 marks for all 6 correct, 2 marks for 4 or 5 correct, 1 mark for 2 or 3 correct). 2a. Filtration (1 mark); 2b. Evaporation (1 mark). 3. Below the sand (1 mark). 4. To clean water by filtering; 5. Catch it on a cold surface (1 mark).

The water vapour condenses back to a liquid (1 mark). 6. Increase the temperature of the water (1 mark), stir the water (1 mark), make the size of the particles smaller (1 mark). 7. Use the same amount of water; use the same amount and type of sugar; stir the mixture equal amounts (1 mark only for any of these).

LOOKING FOR LEVELS

All the children should be able to identify common substances which are soluble and those which are insoluble. Most children should be able to describe how to separate certain mixtures; understand how a filter bed works to clean water; and be able to identify the conditions that help to speed up dissolving. Some children will also be able to explain how David can make his experiment fair.

PLENARY

You may wish to go through the answers to the test, with the children, after you have collected in their work for marking.

There may be a question that many of the children get wrong (for example, question 2b). If this is the case, it is advisable that you go over the concepts that relate to this question, with the children, and then pose the same question again, in a different way for example: *How would you separate sugar from water?*.

PHOTOCOPIABLE

Filtration

◼ Filter beds are used to clean water. The dirty water is passed through a filter bed before it goes back to the river.

Home-made filter bed:

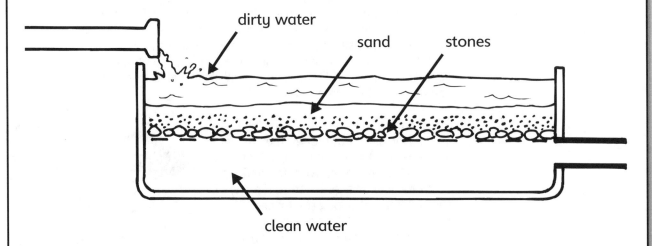

◼ Label the following diagram:

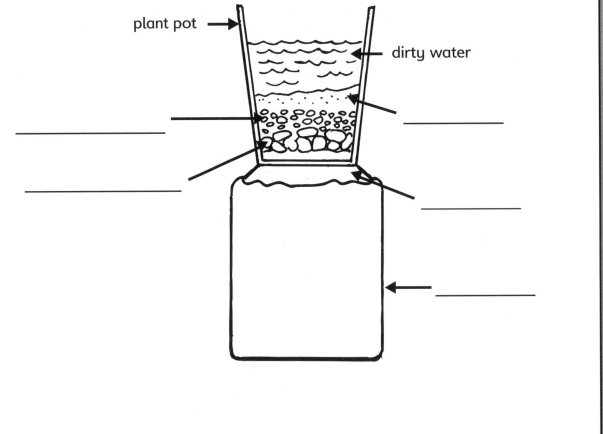

◾SCHOLASTIC

Illustrations © Tony O'Donnell © Sarah Wimperis

Evaporation and condensation

◧ Label the diagram below.

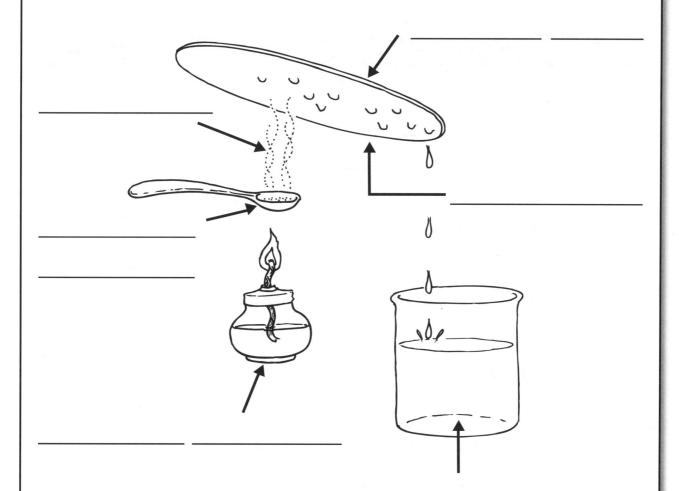

◧ Complete the paragraph below.

When the salt solution was heated up the water _____, leaving

_____ behind in the spoon. Water is a _____, and so

when it is heated it turns into steam, which is a _____. When the

steam hit the cold surface it cooled down and turned back into _____,

which is a liquid. When a gas turns back into a liquid, this is called

_____.

Illustrations © Tony O'Donnell © Sarah Wimperis

PHOTOCOPIABLE

Assessment

1. Put the following substances into the correct list in the table:
sand, salt, soil, chalk, instant coffee, artificial sweeteners.

Soluble	Insoluble

2. (a) To separate sand from water, I would use _____

(b) To separate salt from water, I would use _____

3. In a filter bed, are the small stones on top of the sand or below the sand?

_____

4. What is a filter bed used for?

_____

5. When water evaporates into the air, how can you catch the water and

turn it back into liquid? _____

6. What three things can you do to increase the speed at which sugar dissolves in

water? _____

_____

_____

7. David has decided to test how the temperature of water affects how quickly
something dissolves. He is going to put sugar in water that is cold, warm and hot. He
will time how long the sugar takes to dissolve in each one. What can David do to
make sure the test is fair?

_____

_____

CHAPTER 4 Reversible and irreversible changes

Lesson	Objectives	Main activity	Group activities	Plenary	Outcomes
Lesson 1 Irreversible changes	• To understand that changes sometimes happen when materials are mixed together, and that these changes cannot be reversed easily. • To observe an irreversible change.	Discuss the instructions for the Group activities. Demonstration of an irreversible change that happens when materials are mixed.	Carry out experiments that show irreversible changes happening when materials are mixed.	Review the Group activities.	• Recognise that mixing materials can cause them to change. • Can describe some ways in which mixing materials causes a gas to be produced. • Know that some changes are not reversible.
Lesson 2 Reversible changes	• To know that mixing materials can cause them to change. • To know that some changes can be reversed easily, and so are called 'reversible' changes. • To carry out an experiment to reverse the change that occurs when sand, salt and water are mixed together.	Discuss ways of separating the components of a mixture. A demonstration of how to separate components of a mixture.	The children carry out an experiment to separate a mixture of salt, sand and water.	Review the observed changes and how they could be reversed.	• Can use previous knowledge to solve a problem. • Can explain what happens in the process of filtering and evaporating. Understand what is meant by 'reversible' and 'irreversible' changes.
Lesson 3 Heating and cooling	• To know that heating and cooling can cause changes. • To observe how heating can cause irreversible changes. • To observe how heating can cause a reversible change. • To observe how cooling can cause a reversible change.	Demonstrations to show how heating and cooling can cause reversible changes and how heating can cause an irreversible change.	The children record their observations in words and/or diagrams.	Review the examples from the lesson.	• Know that some changes, that take place when materials are heated, cannot be reversed. • Know that changes made by cooling materials can be reversed.
Lesson 4 Burning	• To know that burning brings about changes that are irreversible. • To confirm this knowledge through observation.	Discussion in the course of the Group activities to help the children interpret what they have seen.	A circus of observation and recording activities related to burning (the activities do not require the children to burn anything).	The children feedback their observations to the class.	• Can describe observations of what happens when different materials burn. • Know that when burning occurs, new materials are made such as ash and gases. • Know that burning is an irreversible change.
Lesson 5 The hazards of burning	• To know that burning materials can be dangerous. • To know what to do to reduce the hazards of burning. • To know what to do if a problem arises when something is burning.	A group discussion of how to make burning materials safe.	Some children design a poster about the hazards of burning materials. Other children use role-play to highlight the safety procedures needed when burning things.	Review the children's work and draw up a class list of safety precautions.	• Can recognise hazards associated with burning materials.
Enrichment Lesson 6 Safety signs	• To know which household products are hazardous. • To know the warning symbols used on such products.	Explanation of the most common safety/warning symbols.	Record the safety symbols that appear on various products. Identify the correct safety signs for various situations.	A quick quiz about safety signs and their meaning.	• Can describe some materials that are flammable, some that are poisonous and some that are corrosive. • Know some common safety signs and their meanings.
Enrichment Lesson 7 Rusting	• To carry out an experiment to show what causes rusting. • To carry out an experiment to show that only iron and steel rust.	Discuss the experiment with the children.	The children carry out an experiment to find out which metals rust and what causes rusting.	A 'question and answer' session to test the children's understanding.	• Know that only iron and steel rust. • Know that oxygen and water are needed for rusting. • Know that rusting is an irreversible reaction.

Lesson	Objectives	Main activity	Group activities	Plenary	Outcomes
Enrichment Lesson 8 Rust prevention	• To carry out an experiment. • To know how to prevent iron and steel from rusting.	Review Lesson 7. Plan an experiment to find out how to prevent iron and steel from rusting.	The children carry out the experiment.	Review the children's work.	• Can describe ways to prevent rusting.
Lesson 9 Making paper	• To know that some materials that we use in everyday life (such as paper) are made by changes that are irreversible.	Watch a video about how paper is made. Demonstrate how to make paper.	A written activity related to making paper.	Build up a concept map about reversible and irreversible changes.	• Know that many manufacturing processes involve permanent changes.
Enrichment Lesson 10 Things that need energy	• To know that there are many energy sources in the home. • To know what these energy sources are used for.	Discuss what energy is and what it is used for.	Identify uses and sources of energy in the home.	Discuss uses and sources of energy in the school.	• Can recognise items in the home that need energy to work. • Can recognise sources of energy in the home.
Enrichment Lesson 11 Power generation	• To know how electricity is made from non-renewable fuels.	Discussion and explanation of how electricity is made.	Match pictures to captions on how electricity is made. Use a CD-ROM to research Michael Faraday.	Consolidate the children's learning through a 'question and answer' session.	• Can describe how a non-renewable source of energy is used in power stations.
Enrichment Lesson 12 Non-renewable energy	• To know that there are non-renewable sources of energy.	Discuss the nature and uses of fossil fuels.	The children make posters to show the chain of events from fossil fuels being formed to electricity being used.	Question and answer session on fossil fuels.	• Can describe how non-renewable sources of energy are used in power stations.
Enrichment Lesson 13 Saving fossil fuels	• To understand why we need to be economical in our use of fuels. • To interpret a graph.	Explain why we need to be economical with the use of fossil fuels.	The children answer questions about energy consumption.	Build up a concept map on fuels and other energy sources.	• Can explain why there is a need for fuel economy.

Lesson	Objectives	Activity
Lesson 14	• To review the topic of reversible and irreversible change. • To carry out a formative or summative assessment for this unit.	Children answer questions on reversible and irreversible changes and non-renewable energy.

SC1 SCIENTIFIC ENQUIRY

How can we stop things from rusting?

LEARNING OBJECTIVES AND OUTCOMES
- Decide how to answer the question.
- Plan and carry out an investigation.
- Draw conclusions.

ACTIVITY
The children carry out an investigation to test different methods of preventing iron nails from rusting.

LESSON LINKS
This Sc1 activity is an integral part of Lesson 8 , Rust prevention.

Lesson 1 ▪ Irreversible changes

Objective
- To understand that changes sometimes happen when materials are mixed together, and that these changes cannot be reversed easily.
- To observe an irreversible change.

Vocabulary
Plaster of Paris, carbon dioxide, irreversible, reversible

RESOURCES
Main activity: Baking powder, vinegar, a beaker, a spoon.
Group activities: 1 Plaster of Paris; water; spoons; beakers; modelling moulds. **2** Andrew's Liver Salts; water; spoons; beakers.

PREPARATION
Obtain the necessary materials. DAP (Bandex) plaster of Paris should be mixed with two parts plaster to one part cold water, until smooth. It sets in 20-30 minutes.

BACKGROUND
When different materials are mixed together, they may change by reacting with each other. Sometimes these changes can be reversed. For example, if you dissolve salt in water, you can get the salt back by evaporating, and get the pure water back by condensing. Dissolving salt in water is an example of a reversible change.

Lesson 2 looks at the use of reversible changes to separate sand and salt: the salt can be dissolved in water; the sand can be removed from the salt solution by filtration; and the salt can be separated from the water by evaporation.

However, when some materials are mixed together, a change occurs that cannot be reversed. This lesson looks at two examples of irreversible changes:
Adding water to plaster of Paris: Plaster of Paris is a white powder; but when water is added to it, it dries into a hard solid mass. It is used to make plaster casts to protect injured limbs. We cannot get back to plaster of Paris and water. Adding water to cement (powder) has a similar effect.
Adding Andrew's liver salts to water: You will see bubbles of carbon dioxide gas being given off. The gas escapes and once it is gone, it cannot be put back. You cannot get back to the original powder and water. Adding baking soda to vinegar has a similar effect.

STARTER
Briefly review the children's work on mixtures and separating mixtures. Explain that when you mix certain materials together, they change - for example, salt dissolves in water. Because you can get the salt back by evaporation, this change, or 'reaction', is called a 'reversible reaction'. Make

Differentiation
Group activities
For some children, provide a worksheet with titles and diagrams of the activities so they can label the diagrams and write their observations underneath. Let them copy the following text and fill in the missing words: *When plaster of Paris is added to water and left to dry, it cannot be changed back into [plaster of Paris] and water. The change is said to be [irreversible]. When Andrew's Liver Salts are added to water, the result is [fizzing or bubbles]. This shows that a [gas] is being given off. This gas is called [carbon dioxide]. Once the gas has escaped, it cannot be put back, so we cannot get back the Liver Salts and water. This is another [irreversible] change. When vinegar is added to baking powder, [carbon dioxide] gas is given off. Once the gas has escaped, it cannot be put back. We cannot get back the vinegar and baking powder. This is another example of an [irreversible] change.*

Some children will be able to write their own account, but may find a word bank useful.

sure the children understand the term 'reversible': relate it to their experience of vehicles reversing (going backwards). Continue: *However, certain materials when mixed together cannot be separated again. A change takes place in the materials that cannot be reversed. Reactions of this kind are called 'irreversible' reactions. Today, we are going to look at some irreversible reactions. You may remember some of these reactions from Year 5/Primary 6.*

MAIN ACTIVITY – PART 1
You may wish to write a set of instructions on the board for the children to follow. Go through these instructions before the children start the Group activities.

GROUP ACTIVITIES
1 The children should work in groups of three or four. Ask them to mix some plaster of Paris with water (see Preparation), pour the mixture into a mould and leave until set. The moulded shapes can then be painted in art lessons, or used to create a science display that represents irreversible changes. Ask the children to describe what they did and what they observed.
2 Ask the children to add a teaspoon of Andrew's Liver Salts to 100ml water, then observe and record what happens.

MAIN ACTIVITY – PART 2
Demonstrate the effect of adding baking powder to vinegar. Ask the children: *What did you notice? What did you notice when you added Andrew's Liver Salts to water? The bubbles you can see mean that a gas is being produced. The gas is called carbon dioxide. The carbon dioxide escapes, and once it has gone it cannot be put back. That is why these two changes are said to be irreversible. When the plaster of Paris dries, you cannot get back the original powder and water. So this is another example of an irreversible change.*

ASSESSMENT
Note which children are able complete the worksheet or write their own account.

PLENARY
Review what has been discovered. *Why do we say these changes are irreversible?* For homework, the children can complete the worksheet or finish writing their own account.

OUTCOMES
● Recognise that mixing materials can cause them to change.
● Can describe some ways in which mixing materials can cause a gas to be produced.
● Know that some changes are not reversible.

Lesson 2 ◘ Reversible changes

Objective
● To know that mixing materials can cause them to change.
● To know that some changes can be reversed easily, and so are called 'reversible'.
● To carry out an experiment to reverse the change that occurs when sand, salt and water are mixed together.

Differentiation
Some children may prefer to describe the experiment orally into a cassette recorder. You could provide a cloze text as a worksheet, describing the experiment and drawing conclusions, for these children to complete.
The children who tackled the extension questions in Unit 6c, Lesson 2, Evaporation will be more familiar with this experiment. It might be useful to put them into mixed ability groups where they can assist each other.

RESOURCES
Sand; salt; water; filter papers; filter funnels; beakers; wide dishes; paper; pens.

MAIN ACTIVITY
Review the previous lesson, emphasising how and why the mixtures were different from the original starting materials. Introduce the term 'reversible changes', reminding the children how salt and water could be separated. Explain that because we can get salt and water back from the solution, we say that the dissolving of salt in water is reversible. Discuss the methods used to separate salt from water in detail.

Ask the children, working in groups of three or four, to work out how they could separate a mixture of salt, sand and water. Provide each group with a large sheet of paper and a felt-tipped pen to jot down their ideas. Give them 10–15 minutes to do this, then ask each group to feed back their ideas to the class.

You could demonstrate the experiment according to an agreed method or, if time and resources permit, the children could carry out the experiment themselves. You may prefer to separate the sand and the salt by dissolving and filtration, then discuss how the salt and the water could be separated (by evaporation). Encourage the children to write up the experiment using diagrams and their own words. You may wish to display their written work as a summary of this topic.

ASSESSMENT
Note which children come up with an idea for separating the components of the mixture. Note which of the less able children complete the worksheet.

PLENARY
Review how the materials changed when they were mixed together, and how they could be changed back. Why do we call this a reversible change?

OUTCOMES
● Can use previous knowledge to solve a problem.
● Can explain what happens in the process of filtering and evaporating.
● Understand what is meant by 'reversible' and 'irreversible' changes.

Lesson 3 ◘ Heating and cooling

Objective
● To know that heating and cooling can cause changes.
● To observe how heating can cause irreversible changes.
● To observe how heating can cause a reversible change.
● To observe how cooling can cause a reversible change.

Vocabulary
heating, cooling, reversible, irreversible

RESOURCES
Starter: An egg box with one raw egg and one, two or three hard-boiled eggs in it; a glass bowl or jug, a raw potato, a baked potato (cut in half), a plate.
Main activity: The ingredients and equipment necessary to make bread, pancakes, Christmas cake or Simnel cake; ice cubes; a glass; a second prepare cake or pancake if required (See Main activity).

BACKGROUND
This lesson looks at how, when some mixtures are heated, changes take place that cannot be reversed. If a mixture of flour, eggs, sugar and butter is heated, the cake made is very different from the raw mixture. This change cannot be reversed: it is impossible to get the ingredients back. When an egg is boiled, it is changed irreversibly. To make bread, you mix together flour and yeast to make a dough, then put the dough in a tin and bake it.

The baked bread is very different from the dough; it is impossible to get the flour back.

The above are all examples of irreversible changes. These tend to be 'chemical' changes. In chemical reactions, the materials break down completely into their constituent atoms. The atoms rearrange themselves and recombine, forming a new substance. It can often be seen that the original materials have undergone a change. This change is permanent: it cannot be reversed. Irreversible changes often produce new materials. Those chemical changes that are irreversible are often triggered by heat.

During this lesson, the children will also observe some changes that can be reversed. Reversible changes can be brought about by cooling and heating. For example, ice cubes (solid) melt when warmed above 0°C to form liquid water. This water can then be cooled below 0°C to in order to re-form the ice cubes. Chocolate behaves in a similar way. Reversible changes tend to be 'physical' changes or changes of state: the materials do not break down, but change in appearance and form. No new materials are made.

STARTER

Gather the class around you. Crack an egg into a glass bowl or jug. Ask the children to make observations. *What does the egg look like?* Now take a hard-boiled egg out of the egg box (do not say that it is hard-boiled). Drop the egg accidentally on purpose. *Why did it not smash?* (Because it has been hard-boiled.)

Give a child a raw potato and ask: *Would you eat this?* Show him or her a baked potato, cut in half and say: *Would you eat this?* When the child says 'Yes', ask: *If you would eat this, why would you not eat the first potato?* (Because this one is cooked and the first one is not.)

Ask the class: *When you boil or cook something, what do you need?* (Heat.) *Could you turn the boiled egg back into the raw egg?* (No.) *Could you turn the baked potato back into a raw potato?* (No.) *Do you think that by heating the egg and the potato, you have caused them to change forever?* (Yes.) *So would you say that when you cook an egg or a potato, the change is reversible or irreversible?* (Irreversible.)

Introduce a cooking activity suitable for Shrove Tuesday, Harvest Festival and as appropriate.

MAIN ACTIVITY

Show the children some ice cubes in a glass. Leave these to melt while you carry out the following demonstration. Show the children the ingredients for bread, pancakes or a cake. Mix the ingredients together (or ask a couple of children to help). Ask: *Would you eat this now?* Most of the children will say 'No'. Be prepared for those who like eating cake mixture and so say 'Yes'. In that case, you might say: *Is this the best way to eat cake?* Do not allow the children to eat the cake mixture, as there is a risk of catching salmonella from the uncooked eggs.

What do we have to do to turn this mixture into bread/cake/pancake? (Adapt the wording according to item you are cooking.) Pour (the cake) mixture into a tin and place in an oven. If an oven is not available, you might have to have a pre-cooked example already 'waiting in the wings': If you are using pancakes they will have to be pre-cooked.

Ask: *Does (the cake) look anything like the original materials?* (No.) *What do you think has caused the change?* (Heating or cooking.) *Could I get back to the original ingredients?* (No.) *Do you think the heating has made something new?* (Yes.) *Do you think the heating has caused a reversible change or an irreversible change?* (Irreversible.)

Look at the ice cubes now. *Did the ice cubes that we started with look the same as the water we have got now? What did we do to the ice cubes to turn them into water?* (Melted them or warmed them up.) *To melt*

something, what do we need? (Heat or warmth.) *Can we turn the water
back into ice?* (Yes.) *What do we have to do to turn the water back into ice?*
(Freeze it or make it cold.) *If you can turn ice into water and then back into
ice, do you think these changes are reversible or irreversible?* (Reversible.)
    Discuss how heating can cause both reversible and irreversible changes
by comparing how ice melts with how food is cooked. Say that changes
caused by cooling can generally be reversed.

GROUP ACTIVITY
Encourage the children to write up or draw one or more of the irreversible
changes that have been discussed and then the reversible change of ice
melting and water freezing. They can work individually or in groups. For
example:

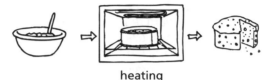

heating

Heating some materials causes irreversible changes. It is not possible to get
the flour, eggs, sugar and butter back after the cake has been baked.

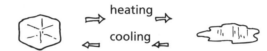

Heating some materials causes a reversible reaction. The liquid water made
when ice melts can be frozen again by cooling. No new materials are made.

ASSESSMENT
Note which children are able to complete the Group activity with confidence.

ICT LINK
The children could present their work on changes as a short multimedia
presentation, or they could design a poster on the computer.

PLENARY
Review the examples from the lesson to make sure the children understand
which changes were reversible and irreversible. For homework, ask the
children to do (or finish off) the tasks outlined in Differentiation.

OUTCOMES
● Know that some changes that take place when materials are heated
cannot be reversed.
● Know that changes made by cooling materials can be reversed.

LINKS
English: group discussion and interpretation.

Lesson 4 ▪ Burning

Objective
● To know that burning brings
about changes that are
irreversible.
● To confirm this knowledge
by observation.

RESOURCES
Starter: A wooden splint, matches, a heat-resistant mat.
Main activity: A prepared worksheet (see Preparation); candles in secure
holders; matches; tongs; materials for burning (see Background); heat-
resistant mats.

Vocabulary
irreversible, burning, materials, smoke, ash, hazards, fire blanket, heat-resistant, fuel

Group activities: A TV and video player, a video showing a short clip of something burning; a candle in a secure holder; pictures of objects burning.

PREPARATION
Prepare a worksheet with the following table for the children to record their observations:

What material is burning?	What do you notice when it burns?	Are any new materials made?	Is the reaction reversible or irreversible?

BACKGROUND
Burning is an irreversible change. It is often called 'combustion'. Materials that burn react with oxygen in the air to produce a new material, usually called an oxide. Carbon-based fuels such as wood, coal and oil produce the gas carbon dioxide when they burn. Because oil and wood are hydrocarbons (they contain hydrogen), burning them also produces water.

A fuel is a material that has energy 'locked up' in it. Most fuels are carbon-based 'fossil fuels' such as coal, crude oil and natural gas, formed from long-dead vegetable matter. By refining crude oil, we obtain purer fuels such as petrol, diesel and propane. During combustion, the energy in a fuel is 'unlocked'. The energy (heat and light) released can be used for heating, cooking, transport and industry.

The oxygen required for burning is usually obtained from the air (oxygen makes up about 20% of air). Where carbon dioxide and water are formed, they are released into the atmosphere. These products of fuel combustion cannot be converted back into fuel and oxygen, so we can say that combustion is an irreversible chemical reaction. During combustion, a flame appears and smoke and ash (carbon) are also produced. Whereas carbon dioxide and water vapour cannot be seen, flame and smoke can – so they provide an indication that combustion is occurring.

Heating and burning are not the same thing, though some heat is needed to start something burning. We burn fuels to generate heat energy, which can then be used to heat things. Burning is an irreversible reaction, whereas heating can cause both reversible and irreversible reactions.

IMPORTANT: Only set up experiments and demonstrations for which you feel confident to take responsibility. When demonstrating burning materials, it is essential to consider the risks and necessary health and safety precautions. Never leave children unattended with matches and candles. When a candle is used, keep a heat-resistant mat under it (if possible) so as not to risk burning the table. You and the children should tie back long hair, tuck ties into shirts (or take them off) and fasten any loose clothing in place.

The burning material could cause other things to catch fire. Have a fire blanket and a bucket of sand close by in case clothing or other materials catch fire. Be aware of the immediate first aid measures for the treatment of burns (for example, see CLEAPS' Model Safety Policy). Make sure the children know that if they suffer a burn, they must tell you or another adult immediately. Make it clear to them that if the end product of burning is touched, it could cause serious burns: just because it's not red, that doesn't mean it's not hot. Even if you are outside, make sure the children are not too close to the demonstration in case the breeze catches a spark.

STARTER
Discuss the previous lesson, drawing out the children's understanding that cooking is an irreversible chemical

Differentiation

Children who need support could draw a picture or poster to warn people of the dangers of burning things. Extend children by asking them to answer the following questions: 1. *When something burns, what do you see and feel?* (Flames, smoke, heat.) 2. *What do we call a material that burns?* (A fuel.) 3. *Does burning create new materials?* (Yes.) 4. *Is burning a reversible or an irreversible reaction?* (Irreversible.) 5. *When something burns, do you think an invisible gas might be formed?* (Yes.) 6. *How could you show that an invisible gas is formed?* (Find the mass of the starting material and the mass of the new material. If the mass of the new material is less than the mass of the starting material, some mass has been lost during burning. This could have been because some gas escaped into the atmosphere.)

change whereas the melting of ice is a reversible physical change. *How do you know if something is a chemical reaction?* (New products are made and the reaction cannot be reversed.) *How do you know if something is a physical reaction?* (New materials are not made and the reaction can be reversed.)

Take a splint and burn it in front of the class. Ask the children: *What did you see when the wooden splint burned?* (Flames, smoke.) *Has there been a change?* (Yes.) *What is the change?* (The stick has turned into burnt wood. You may have to explain that the burnt wood is called ash.) *Have any new materials been made?* (Yes, ash. Some children may also say 'smoke' and 'flame'. If necessary, explain that flame is just heat and light.) *Could I turn the ash and smoke back into the wooden splint?* (No.) *So do you think burning is an irreversible or reversible reaction?* (Irreversible.) *Why?* (Because something new has been made that cannot be turned back into the wooden splint.)

MAIN ACTIVITY

The children should work in groups to look at examples of burning (see Group activities). They should do different tasks and swap around every five minutes. Distribute copies of the worksheet (see Preparation) to help the children record their observations. When the children have completed the activity, tell them that a material that burns in a useful way is called a 'fuel'. Ask them for examples of fuels and situations where they are used, such as natural gas in cookers, wood in bonfires, lighter fuel in barbecues and petrol in vehicles.

Discuss the children's observations. *What did you notice when the materials burned? Were any new materials made?* They will have noticed flames, smoke and heat when burning was taking place. They will have also noticed ash as a new material. Discuss whether you could get the original material back. *Was the burning of this material reversible or irreversible?*

Discuss whether the children think a gas was made. The more observant children may comment that you appear to end up with a lot less of the new material than there was of the original material. You could prove this by finding the mass of a wooden splint before burning, then finding out the mass of the ash. *How much mass has been lost?* Explain that the lost mass could have been released as an invisible gas, though some of it could have been released as smoke.

GROUP ACTIVITIES

1 Ask the children to look at pictures of burning objects and record what they see (answering the same questions as before).
2 Show a brief video clip of something burning (perhaps only a couple of minutes). Ask the children to record what they see.
3 Let the children watch a candle burning and ask them to record their observations. Do not leave them unattended while they are carrying out this activity.
4 Ask the children to record their observations of the teacher demonstration of burning a wooden splint.

ASSESSMENT

Note which children are using the scientific vocabulary correctly in the Plenary session.

PLENARY

Ask some children to feedback their observations to the rest of the class.

Differentiation
Some children may need help with spelling and general organisation when making their posters. They may find the role-play more suitable.

OUTCOMES
● Can describe what they observed when different materials were burned.
● Know that when burning occurs, new materials are made such as ash and gases.
● Know that burning is an irreversible change.

Lesson 5 ▪ The hazards of burning

Objective
● To know that burning materials can be dangerous.
● To know what to do to reduce the hazards of burning.
● To know what to do if a problem arises when something is burning.

RESOURCES
A bucket of sand; a fire blanket; colouring pencils; A3 paper; pencils.

MAIN ACTIVITY
Why is burning things dangerous? Discuss the dangers of intense heat, smoke and spreading fire. Consider the risks of barbecues, camping stoves and Bonfire Night. Note that some children may have had traumatic experiences with fire.

Ask: *What things could you do to make burning materials safe?* Write down suggestions on the board or flipchart. Show the children the bucket of sand and the fire blanket. Ask the children (working individually or in groups) to research and then make a poster about the hazards of burning materials. Some children could design a poster to show how to make the burning of materials more safe. They should include the following: long hair tied back; ties tucked out of the way; safety glasses; standing up, so you can move out of the way if a heat source falls over; keeping desks clear of books and paper.

Alternatively, the children could practise and perform a role-play to highlight the safety precautions that should be followed when burning something or present what they would do if they were burning something and it went wrong. The children should not actually burn anything during the role-play.

ICT LINK
The children could research the dangers of burning using the internet and the design a poster on the computer. The website www.fireservice.co.uk/safety/index.php provides some useful information on fire safety.

ASSESSMENT
Note which children are able to convey the necessary fire precautions.

PLENARY
Make a class list of fire precautions to use when burning materials.

OUTCOME
● Can recognise the hazards associated with burning materials.

ENRICHMENT
Lesson 6 ▪ Safety signs

Objective
● To know which household products are hazardous.
● To know the meaning of warning symbols.

RESOURCES 💿
Main activity: A4-sized photocopies of some of the signs on photocopiable page 110 (also 'Safety signs' (red) available on the CD-ROM); one copy per child of photocopiable page 110.
Group activities: 1 Examples of a few containers for household chemicals with warning signs (see Background); a worksheet of safety signs (see Preparation). **2** Five A4 cards with scenarios (see Preparation); A4 photocopies of the safety signs for 'corrosive', 'highly flammable' and

Vocabulary
corrosive, flammable,
radioactive, explosive, toxic,
harmful, irritant, electric shock

'harmful/irritant', without a square or triangle; yellow crayons, black crayons, rulers.
ICT link: 'Safety signs' interactive activity, on the CD-ROM.

PREPARATION
Prepare copies of page 110 and enlarged copies of the safety signs, as listed above. Prepare a worksheet (not the same as page 110) featuring only the signs that appear on the products you are showing the children Ensure that if for example, there are four products with the 'corrosive' sign, there are four 'corrosive' signs on the worksheet.
Prepare a set of five A4 cards with scenarios, as follows:

---

1. A tanker is carrying a substance that is extremely or highly flammable.
Colour in the safety sign and decide what shape should go around it.
2. Paintbrush cleaner is harmful and also an irritant. It is normally kept in a bottle.
Colour in the safety sign and decide what shape should go around it.
3. Oven cleaner is corrosive. It is normally kept in a spray can.
Colour in the safety sign and decide what shape should go around it.
4. You find a bottle of clear liquid in the garden shed. You don't know what the liquid is (it might just be an empty bottle that someone has found and filled up with water), but on the bottle there is a safety sign that means 'toxic'.
Would you taste it to find out whether it was water?
Colour in the safety sign and decide what shape should go around it.
5. On a cupboard door, you see the sign for danger. Would you open the door?
Colour in the safety sign and decide what shape should go around it.

BACKGROUND
We all come across potentially dangerous substances in our everyday lives – but because we use them in the home, we tend to forget about the hazards they can present. To help us identify potentially hazardous substances, safety signs are used as warning symbols. These signs are essential for our health and safety. They are used to give information: they tell us whether a substance is corrosive, flammable and so on. Photocopiable page 110 shows all of the safety signs you will come across on containers.

Safety signs should be black on a yellow background. The signs are usually shown in a triangle if displayed on a wall, in a square if on bottles, and in a diamond if on vehicles. Some examples of familiar hazardous substances are: dishwasher tablets (irritant/harmful), antifreeze (irritant/harmful), cleaning spray for suede shoes (extremely or highly flammable), fly spray (extremely or highly flammable), oven cleaner (extremely or highly flammable, corrosive), descaler (irritant/harmful), room spray (extremely or highly flammable), paintbrush cleaner (irritant/harmful), spray adhesive (irritant/harmful), hair mousse (extremely or highly flammable).

For further information about safety signs, consult the latest edition of the CLEAPSS publications, 'Hazcards®' or 'Laboratory Handbook'.
IMPORTANT: For health and safety reasons, it is not recommended that the children handle the containers of dangerous substances. In the home, these products are normally kept out of the reach of children so when you display these items, make sure that the lids are on tightly and that the containers are well-sealed. When the items are not being used, make sure they are stored in a safe place.

STARTER
Refer to the safety factors considered when you burned materials in Lesson 5. Explain that you are going to carry on thinking about safety. *We all come*

Differentiation 💿
To support children, give them 'Safety signs' (green) from the CD-ROM, which includes only the most common symbols. To extend children, give them 'Safety signs' (blue), which asks them to match the symbols to their meanings.

across dangerous and poisonous substances everyday but they are not always obvious. To help us identify them, we use safety signs and symbols.

MAIN ACTIVITY

Give out copies of page 110 and briefly explain the most common symbols. For example, hold up an A4-sized version of the safety sign for 'corrosive', and ask the children to find it on their sheet. *If you see this symbol on a bottle, it means that the substance inside is corrosive. Does anyone know what we mean by this word?* (Like an acid, it can cause burns and damage the eyes.) Repeat the same questions for 'toxic', 'irritant' and 'extremely or highly flammable'. Explain that safety signs are usually black and on a yellow background; the signs displayed on walls are often in a triangle; on bottles, the picture will be in a square; on vehicles it will be in a diamond.

GROUP ACTIVITIES

1 Show a small group of children several household products with safety signs. Hold up each household product and ask the children identify these warning signs. Fill in the following table together, on the board or flipchart: Give out copies of the worksheet (see Preparation). Ask the children to copy the chart into their own books, then cut out the signs from the worksheet and stick each one, next to the appropriate item, in the right-hand column.
2 Give each of the other small groups a set of enlarged safety signs and an A4 card with a scenario written on it (see Resources and Preparation). Leave them to work independently, following the instruction(s) on the card.

Item	Safety signs

ICT LINK 💿

Children can use the 'Safety signs' interactive on the CD-ROM.

ASSESSMENT

Note which children can answer the questions in the Plenary session.

PLENARY

Quiz the class: *What is the warning sign for something that is corrosive? Can you name a corrosive household substance? If you had to put a warning sign on a tanker, what shape would it be? If you were going to put a warning sign on a bottle, what shape would it be? If you were going to put a warning sign on a wall, what shape would it be?*

OUTCOMES

● Can describe some materials that are flammable, some that are poisonous, and some that are corrosive.
● Know some common safety signs and their meanings.

LINKS

PSHE: dangerous substances in the home.

ENRICHMENT
Lesson 7 ▸ Rusting

Objective
● To carry out an experiment to show what causes rusting.
● To carry out an experiment to show that only iron and steel rust.

RESOURCES

Group activity: Iron nails; steel panel pins; pieces of aluminium foil; pieces of copper; pieces of plastic; jam jars with lids (or test tubes with bungs borrowed from your local secondary school); tap water; salt water; cooled boiled water; packets of silica gel; paraffin.

PREPARATION

Write the title of the investigation, 'Finding out what causes things to rust', and draw the diagram shown below on the board or flipchart.

Vocabulary
prevent, rust, rusting,
conditions, grease, oxygen

BACKGROUND

Rusting is the corrosion of iron (or steel, which is mostly iron) to iron oxide. Water and oxygen are both needed for rusting to occur. Iron in dry air, or in water that is free of dissolved oxygen, will not rust. Metal salts, such as sodium chloride (table salt), help to speed up the process.

Rusting can be prevented by keeping the iron object near to a substance that absorbs water from the air, such as silica gel. Iron can be coated with paint, grease or oil to stop air and water getting to it. Plating iron involves putting a thin coat of a metal that does not rust over the iron. Chromium and zinc plating are commonly used for this process. When iron is coated in zinc, it is said to be 'galvanised'. The zinc will protect the iron even if it is scratched. Stainless steel is made by mixing iron with other metals such as chromium and nickel; it does not rust at all.

This lesson will look at what causes rusting and which types of materials are prone to rust. It will also highlight the fact that rusting is an irreversible reaction. Following the experiment in this lesson, the recording of results will need a little time, every day, for a week. Use a lesson in the following week to review the overall outcome.

STARTER

Does anyone here have a bike? Does it tend to rust in bad weather? Can you give me an example of something else that rusts? List suggestions (such as cars and railings) on the board. *What are these objects made from?* You might get answers such as 'metal', 'chrome', 'iron', 'steel'. Iron and steel are the correct answers. *Can anyone describe to me what rust looks like? Where else have you seen rust?*

Rusting causes millions of pounds worth of damage every year. Many companies spend lots of money trying to stop things rusting. To know how to stop rusting, we have to know what causes it. *What do you think causes things to rust?* 'Rain' and 'water' will be the two most popular answers. Today, you are going to find out what causes rusting.

MAIN ACTIVITY

Draw the children's attention to the title and diagram on the board. Discuss the experiment so that they know what to do with each jam jar. Explain to the children that by boiling water, you get rid of any oxygen that might be contained in the water, and that oxygen gets into water from the air. Discuss why they need to put paraffin on top of the boiled water. Also explain that silica gel takes any moisture out of the air in the jar. Discuss how the test can be made fair – for example, using the same amounts of water and salt for each metal. Tell the children that they will need to check their experiments every day and record their observations.

GROUP ACTIVITY

The children can work in groups of three or four. One group should set up four jars, as shown in the diagram, on the board. Other groups should carry out the same experiment with pieces of steel, copper, aluminium and plastic.

By observing over a period of time, they should establish how many days it takes for each sample to become rusty (if it happens at all). The class results can then be shared.

After a week of observations, you should come to the following

Differentiation
Some children may need support to record their observations and conclusions.
   Other children could attempt to answer the following questions: *Will your car or bike rust more quickly if you live by the sea? Why do you think this is?*

conclusions together:
1. Iron and steel both rust, but other metals and plastic do not.
2. Both water and air are needed to make iron or steel rust.
3. Salt speeds up rusting.
Explain that scientists call rust 'iron oxide'. It is formed by iron reacting with oxygen in the presence of water. Salt speeds up the reaction because it dissolves in the water and helps to 'break down' the iron. The children can copy out and complete the following conclusion:
[Water] and [oxygen] are needed for iron to rust. [Salt] speeds up the rusting of iron. Boiling water removes any [oxygen] that might be in it. Silica gel is a chemical that takes the [water] out of air. Metals such as [copper] and [zinc] do not rust. [Plastic] does not rust. Scientists call rust [iron oxide].

ASSESSMENT
Note which children can answer the questions in the Plenary session.

PLENARY
Test the children's understanding of the lesson with a quick 'question and answer' session. *Does iron rust? Does steel rust? Does copper rust? Does zinc rust? What is needed for rusting? What speeds up rusting? Rust is called 'iron oxide'. You have seen what iron oxide looks like. Do you think it is a new material compared to the iron, water and oxygen? Do you think it would be possible to turn the iron oxide back into iron, oxygen and water? So do you think rusting is a reversible or an irreversible reaction?*

OUTCOMES
● Know that only iron and steel rust.
● Know that oxygen and water are needed for rusting.
● Know that rusting is an irreversible reaction.

LINKS
English: group discussion and interaction.

ENRICHMENT
Lesson 8 ▶ Rust prevention

Objective
● To carry out an experiment.
● To know how to prevent iron and steel from rusting.

RESOURCES
Iron nails; petroleum jelly; painted iron nails; water; jam jars.

MAIN ACTIVITY
Review what causes iron and steel to rust. Emphasise that rusting is an irreversible reaction. *How can we stop things rusting?* Discuss why painting an iron bridge might slow down rusting. *How could we investigate this using a fair test?* Plan an experiment to coat iron nails in petroleum jelly or paint and see how quickly they rust in tap water or in air. The children should check the nails every day and record what they see. They should find that only the uncoated nails rust. Lead them to conclude that to stop things rusting, we have to keep air and water from touching them.

ASSESSMENT

Note which children are able to: plan and carry out a fair test; make observations and record them in an appropriate way; say what their results show them.

PLENARY

Review the children's work. Ask: *How do we stop iron from rusting?*

OUTCOME

● Can describe ways of preventing rusting.

Lesson 9 ▪ Making paper

RESOURCES

Main activity: The video *Materials We Need* (Channel 4, 254255); a TV and video; a wooden picture frame (the size of the paper you wish to make); a bowl (large enough to hold the picture frame); straw; fabric; a kitchen blender; newspaper; two kitchen cloths; a rolling pin; a staple gun. (If the children carry out the activity, more sets of these things will be needed.)
Group activities: 1 Photocopiable page 111 (also 'Making paper' (red) available on the CD-ROM); writing materials. **2** Paper; writing materials.

BACKGROUND

Paper and plastic are materials that we use every day. They are manufactured materials that have been made from natural raw materials.

Paper is made from wood and other fibrous materials such as straw, fabric or leaves. The choice of raw materials depends on what the paper will be used for (for example, banknotes are made from cotton, which is more durable than wood pulp). When wood is changed into paper, the change is irreversible. The wood fibres have been broken down and cannot re-form.

When plastic is made from crude oil, the change is also irreversible: the oil molecules have been chemically transformed and cannot be restored.

STARTER

Review previous work on reversible and irreversible changes. Hold up a piece of paper and ask the children what it is. *What do we use paper for? Does anyone know how we make paper? This lesson, we are going to look at how paper is made.*

MAIN ACTIVITY

Show the children the video about paper. Reinforce the idea that paper is made from wood, which comes from trees. Explain that you are going to make paper, using straw instead of wood.

The following activity could be done as a teacher demonstration. Alternatively, if you wish the children to make their own sheet of paper, they could carry out Step 1 during a design and technology lesson. Steps 2 to 4 could then be done as a demonstration. Each child could carry out Steps 5 to 10 (to save time, you might want to have a few bowls of pulp already made).

1. Make a paper-making frame by stretching some fabric across an old picture frame and stapling it in place so it is taut. The frame needs to be small enough to fit inside a bowl during Step 5.
2. Take four generous handfuls of straw and cut it into lengths of about 3cm. Boil the straw in a pan of water for about one hour (keep the water topped up so the straw is always covered).
3. Place the boiled straw and water in a blender. Make sure the straw is covered with water – top up if necessary. You might not get all the straw in

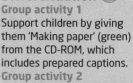
the blender at once. Blend until the straw pulp is well mashed-up. Only the teacher should use the blender.
4. Pour the pulp into the bowl. There should be enough pulp to half-fill it.
5. Put the frame into the bowl and swish it around to get a layer of pulp in the frame. You may need to do this a few times to ensure that the pulp is evenly spread across the frame.
6. Cover the work surface with newspaper and lay a kitchen cloth over it.
7. Take the frame out of the pulp. Tip the layer of pulp out of the frame and on to the kitchen cloth. You may need to give the frame a knock to get the pulp out. Place another kitchen cloth over the top of the pulp and press down firmly.
8. Use a rolling-pin to press down evenly and firmly on the cloth, removing any excess water.
9. Leave the sheet of paper to dry.
10. It will take practice to get the amount of pulp right and to learn how to spread the pulp evenly across the frame.

GROUP ACTIVITIES

1 Give the children photocopiable page 111 and ask them to cut out and rearrange the pictures into the correct order. They should then write a caption for each picture.
2 Ask the children to copy and complete the following from the board:
In factories, paper is made from [wood]. Today we made paper from [straw]. To help turn the straw into paper, we had to [heat] it up. We started with straw and made a new material, [paper]. We could not turn the paper back into straw. Paper-making is an [irreversible reaction], because a new material is made that cannot be turned back into straw.

ASSESSMENT

A concept map (see Plenary) shows the connections between different ideas in a particular topic, and is a useful source of information about children's understanding. Use the Plenary session to assess which children understand what is meant by the terms 'reversible change' and 'irreversible change', and can give examples.

PLENARY

Use questions to build up a concept map on the board. What material did we use today to make paper? (Straw.) *In today's activity, did we make a new material from straw?* (Yes, paper.) *What did we do to the straw that you think might have turned it into a new material?* (Boiled/heated it.) *So the starting material was straw and the new material is paper. Do you think we could turn the paper back into straw?* (No.) *When we make paper from straw or wood, do you think this is a reversible or an irreversible reaction?* (Irreversible.) *Why?* (Because a new material has been made that cannot be turned back into straw or wood.)

OUTCOME

● Know that many manufacturing processes involve permanent changes.

LINKS

Design and technology: working with tools, equipment, materials and components to make quality products.

ENRICHMENT
Lesson 10 ▢ Things that need energy

Objective
● To know that there are many energy sources in the home.
● To know what these energy sources are used for.

Vocabulary
energy, chemical, kinetic, light, heat, electrical

RESOURCES ◉
Main activity: A lamp; a battery-operated toy with batteries.
Group activities: 1 Photocopiable pages 112 and 113 (also 'Things that need energy - 1' (red) and 'Things that need energy – 2' (red) available on the CD-ROM); paper; writing materials. **2** Catalogues containing household items; scissors; adhesive; A3 paper.
ICT link: 'Things that need energy' interactive activity, on the CD-ROM.

BACKGROUND
To make things move, change or do work, you need energy. You cannot see energy (apart from some kinds of light energy), but it takes many different forms. Chemical energy is stored in batteries. Food is also a source of chemical energy. Other types of energy are heat energy, sound energy, light energy, kinetic (movement) energy and electrical energy.

Fuels are a source of heat energy. The energy stored in them is released during combustion, which generates heat and light energy (see Lesson 4). Carbon-based 'fossil fuels', such as coal, oil and natural gas, are a major natural source of energy. They are burned in power stations to release heat energy, which is used to boil water into steam. The steam builds up, and its pressure drives turbines that generate electricity. The electricity is itself used as a source of energy.

STARTER
Tell the children that they are going to look at energy, what it does and where it comes from.

MAIN ACTIVITY
Display a lamp which is not plugged in. Switch it on and exclaim: *Oh, it's not working!* Hopefully one of the children will spot that it is not plugged in. *Why do I need to plug it in?* (Because the lamp needs electricity to make it work.) Plug the lamp in and switch it on.

Try working a toy, that needs batteries, without the batteries. Say to the class, *I wonder why it's not working?* The children might tell you that the batteries have run out. Some might ask you whether you have put the batteries in. Check the toy and notice that the batteries are missing. Put the batteries in and show the children that the toy is now working.

Then say: *Do you know, on my way to school this morning, my car just stopped. I have no idea what is wrong with it. Perhaps I should phone up the garage and ask them to help.* Hopefully someone will say that it has probably run out of petrol.

Does anyone know what we mean by the word 'energy'? Explain that energy is needed to get jobs done, or to make things work. So the lamp needs energy to work. The energy comes from electricity. The toy also needs energy to work. *Where do you think the energy comes from?* (Batteries.) *What does a car need to work?* (Energy.) *Where does the energy come from?* (Petrol.) Lots of things that are in our homes need energy to work. Now we are going to look at where these things get their energy from.

GROUP ACTIVITIES
1 Give each child a copy of pages 112 and 113. For each room in the house, the children have to list the items that need energy to work and then say where the energy is coming from. For example:

Room	Which things need energy?	Where does the energy come from?
Bedroom	Lamp	Electricity
Bedroom	Alarm clock	Batteries
Garage	Car	Petrol
Lounge	Fire	Coal/wood
Kitchen	People	Food
Kitchen	Cooker	Gas/electricity
Garden	Barbeque	Lighter fuel, briquettes

2 Ask the children to look through some old catalogues and find items that need energy, cut them out and stick them onto a large sheet of paper to make a collage. The collages could then be used for a classroom display.

ICT LINK 💿
Children can use the 'Things that need energy' interactive, from the CD-ROM to highlight things in the house that need energy.

ASSESSMENT
Note which children are able to identify items which require energy in order to work, and which children can name different types of energy that we use in the home.

PLENARY
Can anyone give me an example of something we have in school that needs energy? Can anyone tell me the source of energy this item needs in order to work? Elicit several suggestions and discuss what energy sources they use.

OUTCOMES
● Can recognise items in the home that need energy to work.
● Can recognise sources of energy in the home.

LINKS
PSHE and citizenship: preparing to play an active role as citizens.

ENRICHMENT
Lesson 11 💿 Power generation

Objective
● To know how electricity is made from non-renewable fuels.

Vocabulary
electricity, generate, generator, turbines, steam, fossil fuels, renewable, non-renewable, power station, biomass

RESOURCES 💿
Main activity: A video about electricity generation, such as *Cat's Eyes: Electricity Light and Sound* (BBC, 37604X); a TV and video.
Group activities: 1 Photocopiable page 114 (also 'Power generation' (red) available on the CD-ROM); scissors; glue. **2** CD-ROMs such as Encarta®.

BACKGROUND
We say that electricity is 'generated' rather than 'made', because it is a form of energy and not a material. Electricity is generated in power stations, which can be identified by their distinctive cooling towers. Fossil fuels (coal, oil and natural gas) are burned in power stations, releasing heat energy which boils water; the steam drives turbines which generate electricity.

Fossil fuels are 'non-renewable' forms of energy. It has taken millions of years to form them. Once they have all been used up, they will not be replaced, within a human timescale. Uranium is also used in nuclear power stations to generate electricity; but as well as producing dangerous waste, nuclear power uses up the non-renewable supplies of uranium. It is important to be economical in the use of fossil fuels because one day these resources will run out. The burning of fossil fuels also releases carbon dioxide into the atmosphere, which causes global warming and it also

Differentiation 💿
Group activity 1
To extend children, give them 'Power generation' (blue) which shows a diagram of a power station and asks them to explain what is happening in the picture.

releases sulphur dioxide into the atmosphere, which causes acid rain.

Some energy sources are said to be 'renewable', because they are naturally replaced as quickly as they are used up and so will not run out. Examples are solar energy, tidal energy, geothermal energy (heat from naturally hot springs) and energy from wind, rivers and biomass. Biomass is living material such as wood; the energy stored in it is released when the wood is burned. Biomass is renewable through the replanting of forests.

Some of these renewable forms of energy are sources of heat energy (solar or geothermal) that can be used to heat up water, making steam that can be used to generate electricity. Other renewable forms of energy are sources of kinetic (movement) energy that can be used directly to turn the turbines that generate electricity. When renewable forms of energy are used to generate heat energy there is no burning involved (with the exception of biomass). These forms of energy are therefore better for the environment, in terms of avoiding pollution.

STARTER
Say: *Last lesson, we saw that many items in our homes need energy to work. Can anyone give me an example? Where does the energy come from?* (Electricity provides many things with the energy that they need in order to work.) *This lesson, we are going to find out more about electricity.*

MAIN ACTIVITY
Does anyone have any idea where electricity comes from or how it is made? Collect the children's ideas and write them on the board or flipchart. Explain how electricity is made, using careful questioning and drawing a flow chart on the board. *When you burn something like coal, what is produced?* (Heat, light, smoke.) *The heat produced when coal burns is used to heat up water. When you heat up water and it starts to boil, what is produced?* (Steam.) *The steam pushes against some turbines. Turbines are like big fans that turn. As they turn, they make electricity.*

Coal burned → Heats up water → Steam → Turns turbines → Electricity.

This would be a good point to show the children a video about how electricity is made.

GROUP ACTIVITIES
1 Give each child a copy of page 114. Ask them to cut out the pictures, stick them into their exercise book in the correct sequence, then stick the correct caption beside each picture.
2 Ask some children to use the CD-ROM encyclopedia to find the answers to the following questions: *Who discovered electricity? When was electricity discovered? How did Michael Faraday become interested in science? What two new materials did Michael Faraday discover?*

ASSESSMENT
Note which children are able to describe how electricity is made from coal.

PLENARY
Review how electricity is made. As homework, they could continue their research (using textbooks) and write a project on Michael Faraday.

OUTCOME
● Can describe how a non-renewable source of energy is used in power stations.

LINKS
ICT: using ICT to find information.

ENRICHMENT
Lesson 12 ▫ Non-renewable energy

Objective
● To know that there are non-renewable sources of energy.

RESOURCES
A video on fossil fuels (such as Channel 4's *Pl@net.com*, 254278); a TV and video; A3 paper; collage materials; adhesive; colouring pencils.

MAIN ACTIVITY
Recap on Lessons 10 and 11. Explain why coal, oil and gas are called 'fossil fuels', and why they are non-renewable sources of energy. Show a video that explains how fossil fuels were formed. Ask the children to draw a poster to illustrate the sequence of events from: the formation of fossil fuels, to electricity being generated in power stations through to how electricity is used in the home.

ASSESSMENT
Note which children can answer the questions asked in the Plenary session.

PLENARY
Ask the children which fossil fuels are used in the home and where; how fossil fuels were formed; why fossil fuels are called non-renewable sources of energy.

OUTCOME
● Can describe how non-renewable sources of energy are used in power stations.

Differentiation
Some children might find the poster difficult to produce, and may prefer to explain the sequence orally. They might also find using the computer to find out how fossil fuels were made a more rewarding alternative.
   To extend children, ask them to find out about the use of another non-renewable source of energy: uranium.

ENRICHMENT
Lesson 13 ▫ Saving fossil fuels

Objective
● To understand why we need to be economical in our use of fuels.
● To interpret a graph.

RESOURCES
Writing and poster-making materials (as for Lesson 4).

MAIN ACTIVITY
Recap on fossil fuels: how they are used and why they are non-renewable. Explain that there is a need for everyone to be economical with the use of fossil fuels, because we are using them up and cannot remake them, so they will eventually run out. Ask the children what they think would happen if fossil fuels were to run out.

Explain that another reason why we need to reduce the burning of fossil fuels is because burning them releases massive amounts of carbon dioxide (which causes global warming) and sulphur dioxide (which is thought to cause the formation of acid rain) into the atmosphere.

Ask the children to design a poster to show why people should save fossil fuels and how this could be done. This activity could be done as an individual task, in pairs, or in groups.

ASSESSMENT
The concept map activity (see Plenary) will be a useful source of information about the children's understanding of the topic. If they have not previously made a concept map, they will need to be taught how to do so.

PLENARY
Can you name a fuel that we use to make electricity? Is this a renewable or a non-renewable source? Repeat for several examples. *Why do we have to be economical in our use of fossil fuels?* Use this discussion to build up a concept map on the board.

Differentiation
Extend children by asking them to design a poster to say why we need to be more economical with fossil fuels and how we could achieve this.

OUTCOME
● Can explain why there is a need for fuel economy.

ENRICHMENT
Lesson 14 ▪ Assessment

Objective
● To review the topic of reversible and irreversible change.
● To carry out a formative or summative assessment for this unit.

Vocabulary
Plaster of Paris, carbon dioxide, irreversible, reversible

RESOURCES
One copy per pupils of photocopiable page 115 (also 'Assessment' (red) available on the CD-ROM); pens.

STARTER
You may wish to begin the Assessment activities straight away, or you may like to begin by helping the children prepare for the test. Create a mind map for everything the children remember from the topic, for example: *Which changes are reversible? Which are irreversible? Can you remember any ways of correcting reversible changes?*

ASSESSMENT ACTIVITY
Give out copies of photocopiable page 115 for the children to complete individually. You may wish to mark the sheets yourself or let the children mark each other's sheets, to encourage discussion of the questions and answers.

ANSWERS
1a. Carbon dioxide (1 mark). 1b. Irreversible (1 mark). 1c. We cannot get Andrew's Liver Salts and water back (1 mark); a new material has been made (1 mark). 2. Reversible change (1 mark). 3. See table below (2 marks for 4 correct, 1 mark for 2 or 3 correct). 4. Water and oxygen (1 mark - accept 'air' instead of 'oxygen'). 5. Non-renewable sources of energy (1 mark). 6a–c. Answers will vary.
(1 mark each); 6d Gas and oil will run out (1 mark). 6e. We will only have coal for energy; there will not be enough fossil fuels (1 mark for any reasonable answer).

Safety Sign	Meaning
☠	Toxic
🔥	Flammable
✕	Harmful
🜂	Corrosive

LOOKING FOR LEVELS
Most children should know the conditions needed for rusting; and will be able to identify the common safety symbols. Some children will be able to identify reversible and irreversible changes, and understand what is meant by a renewable or non-renewable form of energy. These children will also be able to answer the rest of question 6.

PLENARY
You may wish to go through the answers to the tests with the children after you have collected in the work for marking.

There may be a question that many of the children got wrong (for example, question 6e). If this is the case, it is advisable that you go over the concepts that relate to this question or re-phrase the question (for example: *what would happen if we ran out of gas and oil?*)

On the other hand, there may be a question that the majority of children got right. In this case, it would be a good idea to give them an extension question or task that covers the same concepts. For example, if most children get question 4 right, you could ask them to describe how they would prevent their bike from rusting and why these methods would work.

PHOTOCOPIABLE

Safety signs

Explosive		Corrosive	
Oxidising		Irritant	
Extremely or highly flammable		Biohazard	
Radioactive		Risk of electric shock	
Laser radiation		You MUST wear eye protection	
Harmful to the environment		You MUST wear protective gloves	
Danger		You MUST NOT have naked flames	
Toxic		You MUST NOT drink this water	
Harmful		You MUST NOT use water to put out fires	

Notes: Symbols inside squares are used only on bottles and other containers. Safety signs that are circular are required by law: you MUST or MUST NOT.

Illustrations © Tony O'Donnell © Sarah Wimperis

Making paper

- The pictures below show you how to make paper.
- Cut each one out.
- Put the pictures in the correct order.

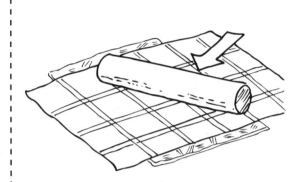

Remove excess water by rolling

Boil up straw with water

Blend into pulp

Place another kitchen cloth over the top of the pulp and press down

Scoop up pulp and spread evenly on surface of fabric inside frame

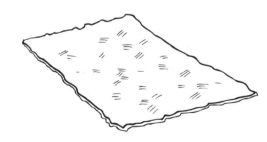

Leave the sheet of paper to dry

Old picture frame

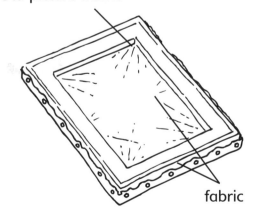

fabric

Illustrations © Tony O'Donnell © Sarah Winperis

PHOTOCOPIABLE

Things that need energy – 1

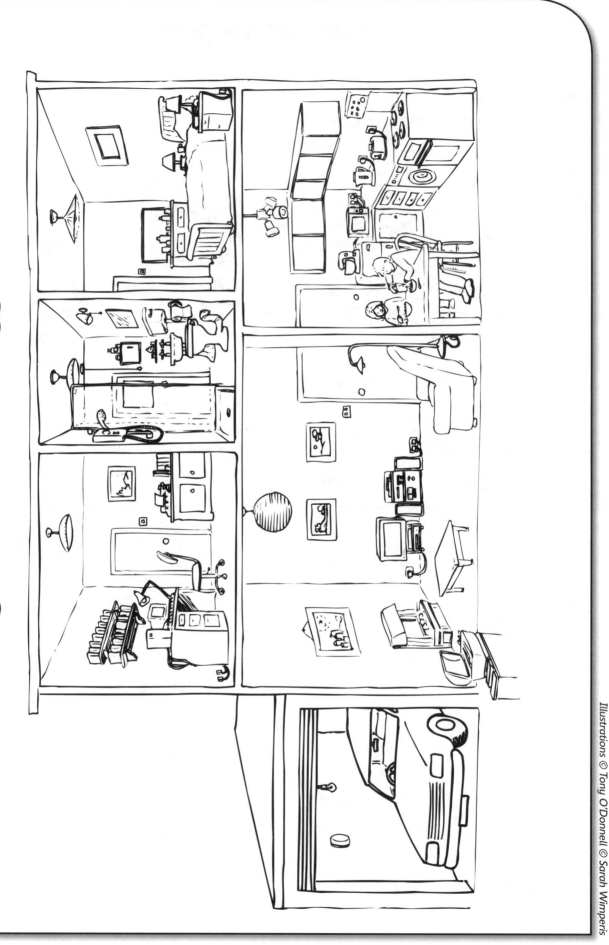

Illustrations © Tony O'Donnell © Sarah Wimperis

■SCHOLASTIC

Things that need energy – 2

■ Look at the picture of a house. Use the following words to help you fill in the chart. Words can be used more than once and you can add words of your own.

bedroom   petrol   gas   garage   car   fire   electricity
batteries   alarm clock   lounge   people   cooker   lamp   barbeque
coal   wood   kitchen   garden   food   lighter fuel   briquettes

Room	Which things need energy?	Where does the energy come from?
Bedroom		
Lounge		
Kitchen		
Bathroom		
Garage		

PHOTOCOPIABLE

Power generation

◼ Cut out and match together the pictures and captions. Arrange them in the correct order.

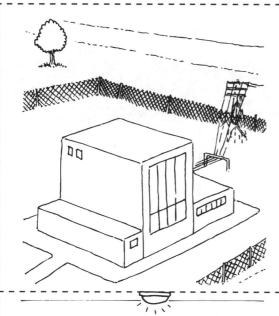

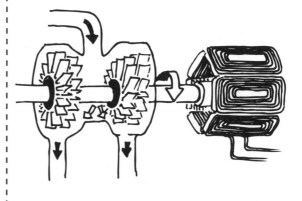

Electricity is generated in power stations. Coal is burned to boil water and turn it into steam.

The steam is forced through large fans called turbines. As these turn they generate electricity.

When coal is burned, heat and light are produced.

Electricity is used in the home for many things, such as heating up water in a kettle and making the lights work.

Illustrations © Tony O'Donnell © Sarah Wimperis

Assessment

1. When you add liver salts to water, you see fizzing and bubbles.

a) What is the name of the gas that is given off?_____

b) Is this a reversible or irreversible change?_____

c) Give reasons for your answer to 1b. _____

_____

2. When an ice cube melts and forms liquid water, is this a reversible or irreversible

change? _____

3. On the back of this sheet, draw the safety signs that mean: toxic, flammable, harmful, corrosive.

4. What conditions are needed for rusting of iron to take place?

_____

5. Fossil fuels are non-renewable sources of energy. Once we have used them up, they are gone for ever. Use the time chart to answer the questions below.

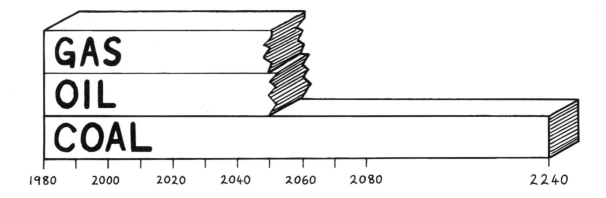

a) When were you born? Mark the year on the time chart and write it here: _____

b) What year is it now? Mark it on the time chart and write it here: _____

c) When you are 30, what year will it be? Mark it on the chart and write it here: ____

d) When you are 60, what year will it be? Mark it on the chart and write it here: ____

e) From the chart, what do you notice about the fuels? _____

f) What can you predict about your life when you are 60? _____

Illustrations © Tony O'Donnell © Sarah Wimperis

CHAPTER 5 Forces in action

Lesson	Objectives	Main activity	Group activities	Plenary	Outcomes
Lesson 1 Magnetic force	• To know that forces can be measured. • To know that a force exists between two magnets, and between magnets and magnetic materials.	Demonstrate that a magnet can be used to pick up a steel paper clip. Demonstrate that a force meter can be used to measure a force.	Measure the force between a magnet and a paper clip when different thicknesses of card are placed between them. Use secondary sources to find out about the uses of magnets and electromagnets.	Discuss how the strength of a magnetic field is reduced as the distance from the magnet increases.	• Understand that a force has a value that can be measured. • Can measure a force with a force meter. • Can describe the forces existing between two magnets, and a magnet and magnetic materials.
Lesson 2 Gravity and weight	• To know that the force of gravity is responsible for the weight of an object.	Use a force meter to measure the weight of an object. Compare this with its mass found by placing it on a balance	Find out the weight and mass of various objects. Use secondary sources to find out what their own weight would be on other planets.	Find the value of the strength of gravity and use this to calculate corresponding weights. Think about differences in the gravitational strength of Earth and other planets.	• Can find the mass of an object. • Know that 'mass' and 'weight' are not the same. • Understand that the weight of an object will differ on other planets of our solar system.
Enrichment Lesson 3 Magnetic and non-magnetic materials	• To know that only a limited number of metals are magnetic. • To know that the magnetic property of some metals allows them to be separated from other metals.	The children test various metals with a magnet to see whether they are attracted to it.		Discuss the fact that few metals are magnetic, and how this knowledge is used, in the recycling industry, to separate metals.	• Know that only a limited number of metals are magnetic. • Can use a magnet to separate metals.
Lesson 4 Streamlining	• To look at how objects that move through fluids are streamlined.	The children use secondary sources to put together a display of streamlined objects and explain their uses.		Review streamlined shapes and the importance of streamlining in sports.	• Can identify streamlined shapes in the natural and manufactured world.
Lesson 5 Force diagrams	• To be able to explain how objects stay at rest or move by considering the forces acting on them.	Demonstrate the forces acting on a hanging object, a held object, and a moving toy car.	Exert forces in various ways on different objects and draw force diagrams. Label force diagrams provided.	Discuss how forces affect the movement or shape of an object.	• Can explain how forces make things stay at rest or move.
Lesson 6 Weight in water	• To know that water exerts an upward force on a solid object which is suspended in it.	Compare the weight of objects when hanging in the air, with their weight when suspended in water.	Use this experiment to introduce the concept of upthrust.		• Recognise the change in the weight of an object when suspended in water due to upthrust. • Can explain the forces acting on an object in water. • Can make and record observations.
Enrichment Lesson 7 Floating objects	• To know that when an object floats, the upthrust acting on it is equal to the force of gravity, acting in the opposite direction.	The children repeat the above experiment using objects that float and ones that sink in water.		Discuss the forces of gravity and upthrust when an object is floating.	• Can explain why an object floats.
Lesson 8 Load and extension	• To know that when a stretch force on an elastic band is increased, its length increases in proportion. • To record observations, draw a graph, analyse results and draw conclusions.	Demonstrate the relationship between load and extension using a spring.	Carry out the test, from Lesson 6 to determine the relationship between load and extension for a hanging elastic band. Answer questions about elastic bands' breaking points.	Observe the spring mechanism in a force meter.	• Know that the extent to which an elastic material stretches is proportional to the force applied. • Can make and record observations and select results from a table to draw a conclusion.
Lesson 9 Sinking slowly	• To know that air resistance can slow down a moving object. • To conduct an investigation.	Demonstrate how varying the size of a parachute affects the speed at which it falls.	Test the rate at which different-sized parachutes fall. Answer questions about drag in liquids.	Discuss drag and streamlining.	• Can describe how air resistance affects a falling object. • Can carry out an investigation.

Lesson	Objectives	Main activity	Group activities	Plenary	Outcomes
Lesson 10 Spinner test	• To investigate factors that affect how fast a 'spinner' falls to the ground.	The children investigate how rotor size affects the speed at which 'spinners' fall.		Draw a scatter or bar chart graph of the results. Discuss the findings and review the experimental method.	• Can investigate how the size of a spinner affects the amount of time it takes to fall. • Can explain this result in terms of the effects of drag.

Assessment	Objectives	Activity 1	Activity 2
Lesson 11	• To assess the children's knowledge and understanding of forces: their nature, relative sizes and direction. • To assess the children's ability to plan an investigation and predict the results.	Answer questions about forces, including magnets, gravity, springs and balanced forces.	Look at some data from an experiment and analyse it to draw a conclusion

SC1 SCIENTIFIC ENQUIRY

Does an elastic band stretch evenly?

LEARNING OBJECTIVES AND OUTCOMES
● Read a force meter accurately.
● Measure length with care.
● Collect results and plot on a graph.
● Interpret results to answer original question.

ACTIVITY
Children stretch an elastic band with a force meter attached to one end. They record the amount of stretch when different forces are applied. Children input data into a table or Excel® spreadsheet to plot a graph and interpret graph.

LESSON LINKS
This Sc1 activity forms an integral part of Lesson 8 , Load and extension.

Lesson 1 ▶ Magnetic force

Objective
● To know that forces can be measured.
● To know that a force which exist between two magnets, and between magnets and magnetic materials.

Vocabulary
magnetic field, magnetism, poles, newton, attract, repel

RESOURCES 💿
Main teaching activity: A magnet, a paper clip, a copy of *Dead Famous: Isaac Newton and his Apple* by Kjartan Poskitt (Scholastic, 1999) (optional).
Group activities: 1A copy of photocopiable page 132 (also 'Magnetic force' (red) available on the CD-ROM); a magnet; a paper clip; a force meter, capable of reading 0 –1N; string and card (for each group). **2** Secondary sources such as library books and CD-ROMs.

BACKGROUND
The children will already have experienced the pushing and pulling effects of the poles of a magnet, and will know that magnets can pick up certain metallic objects. Magnets are magnetic due to the alignment of the particles (atoms) inside the material. This alignment causes one end of the material to be attracted to the Earth's magnetic north pole, while the other is attracted to the magnetic south pole. (These do not exactly coincide with the geographical North and South Poles.) The North and South poles of the magnet will both attract a magnetic material such as steel, and will attract each other. However, if two north poles or two south poles are put close together, their magnetic properties will cause them to repel each other.

The children may have previously used force meters to measure force. A force meter (see illustration) is a simple device, containing a spring which extends when a force is used to stretch it (by pulling with it or hanging something from it); the amount of stretch is measured on a calibrated scale, to show the value of the force being applied.

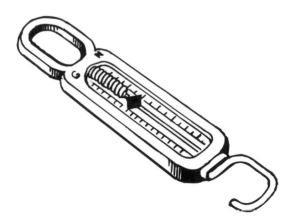

Differentiation
Group activity 1
Children who need support could concentrate on repeating their measurement for two sheets of card to improve the reliability of their experimental readings.

To extend children, ask them to look at the effect of other materials, as well as card.
Group activity 2
All the children should be able to participate in this activity, which revises work from Year 5.

STARTER
Gather the children around you. Tell them that they are going to explore the force of a magnet. Ask them what a magnet can do. *Does it matter which part of the magnet is used to attract an object? Will all materials be picked up by a magnet?* Emphasise that when magnets pull/attract or push/repel, they are exerting a force.

Show the children a force meter. *What is this called? What does it do? How does it do that?* If necessary, demonstrate how to use the meter and read the scale. Tell the children that the unit of force is the newton (symbol N), which is named after the scientist Sir Isaac Newton. You may wish to refer page 150 of 'Dead Famous: Isaac Newton and his Apple' by Kjartan Poskitt, as a source of further information on the newton.

MAIN ACTIVITY
Use a magnet to pick up a paper clip. Show the children that the paper clip will actually move towards (be attracted to) the magnet it without initially being in contact with it. Say that this shows that the force or pull of a magnet exists beyond the magnet: there is a 'magnetic field' around the magnet that is strongest at each pole. Demonstrate how to use a force meter to measure the force needed to pull the paper clip away from the end of the magnet. Discuss with the children how they could use this equipment to measure how strong the force of the magnet is at different distances .

Encourage them to think of a way of keeping the magnet and the paper clip a set distance apart; remind them that magnetic forces can travel through card and paper.

GROUP ACTIVITIES
1 Using photocopiable page 132 as a guide and record sheet, let the children carry out an experiment to measure the force between a magnet and a paper clip when pieces of card, of varying thickness, are placed between them.
2 Ask the children to use secondary sources to find out about uses of magnets and electromagnets.

ASSESSMENT
Assess whether the children make accurate measurements of the strength of the magnetic force, acting on an object, at different distances from the magnet? Did they conclude that a magnetic field becomes weaker as you move away from the magnet?

PLENARY
Discuss the results of the experiment to establish the idea that a magnetic field becomes weaker as distance from the magnet increases. Ask the children how they think the extent of the magnetic field is affected by the strength of the magnet. Show the children a compass and remind them that it always points north. *Do you know why that is? If you were using a compass to find your way around, do you think it would matter if there were lots of magnets close by? What about magnetic materials such as iron and steel?* Show the children that the compass is affected by iron and steel objects around it by passing it over a steel box. *Why is the compass needle deflected, but the box does not move?* (The attraction between them is relatively weak, and the needle can move because it is lighter than the box.)

Time could also spent discussing how easy or difficult the force meters are to read and finding average measurements, by comparing the results from different groups. Explain why average measurements should be more accurate than individual measurements. The closer the children's results are, the more reliable they are likely to be.

OUTCOMES
- Understand that a force has a value that can be measured.
- Can measure a force with a force meter.
- Can describe the force of attraction between magnets and magnetic materials.
- Can describe the forces existing between two magnets and a magnetic and magnetic materials.

Lesson 2 ▫ Gravity and weight

Objective
- To know that the force of gravity is responsible for the weight of an object.

Vocabulary
gravity, mass, weight, gravitational field

RESOURCES
Main teaching activity: A force meter; Plasticine®.
Group activities: 1 A force meter; weighing scales; small objects for weighing; a bag for hanging objects from the force meter; graph paper (or a computer and spreadsheet/graphing software). **2** A secondary source of information about the planets; calculators; bathroom scales (measuring in kilograms).
ICT link: The 'Graphing tool', on the CD-ROM.

BACKGROUND
Every day, we pick things up and put them down without much thought. Only when an object is particularly heavy do we make a comment. So what makes things 'heavy'? All objects on or near the Earth are attracted to the centre of the Earth. Even the Moon is attracted to the Earth by a force that keeps it in orbit (like a ball on a string). This force is known as 'gravity'. A gravitational attraction exists between all objects due to their mass (the amount of material from which they are made) but it is only when objects are extremely massive, that this force becomes noticeable. The Earth is massive, and so attracts objects to it. When you 'fall down', you are actually being attracted, to the Earth, by gravity.

An object's weight is a measure of the force of gravity acting on it. The weight of an object is its mass (in kilograms) multiplied by the strength of gravity (in newtons per kilogram). The strength of the Earth's gravitational field is approximately 10 newtons for every kilogram of mass. The Moon is smaller than the Earth and consists of a different material, so it has a different strength of gravity: about one-sixth that of the Earth. So a 1kg bag of sugar has a weight of 10N on Earth, but only 1.6N on the Moon. Other planets in the solar system also have their own gravitational forces. We can measure the force of gravity acting on an object in the classroom by hanging it from a force meter.

STARTER
Gather the children in a group and ask a volunteer to stand, in a space, on one foot. Ask the child how he or she is feeling (besides tired). After a while, the child may start to topple. Ask the child: *Why do you keep falling over? What is making you fall?* (The invisible force of gravity.)

Throw a ball into the air. Ask the children to describe its path. (It goes up, then stops for a brief moment and then falls.) *What made it stop and then fall?* (The force of gravity.) The children should already know that forces change the speed and direction of moving objects. Tell them that they are going to measure the force of gravity in the classroom.

MAIN ACTIVITY
Show the children the force meter and hang a lump of Plasticine® from it. Say that the force meter measures the weight of the object. Compare this with the value for its mass found by placing the Plasticine® on a balance. Tell the children that they will repeat this with several objects to see

whether there is a link between the weight in newtons and the mass in grams.

GROUP ACTIVITIES

1 Ask groups to use a force meter to measure the weight of an object, then find the object's mass by placing it on a balance. They should repeat this for at least six objects, record the results in a table, then plot a line graph of weight against mass on graph paper (or using a computer). This work can be used to assess children's understanding of weight as a force.
2 Ask the children to use secondary sources to find out what the strength of gravity is on the Moon and on different planets in the solar system. Using a set of bathroom scales, they can measure their own mass and then work out what their weight would be on different planets (by multiplying their mass by the strength of gravity on each planet). Use this work to assess their understanding.

ICT LINK
The children could use the graphing tool, from the CD-ROM, to plot their line graphs.

PLENARY
Discuss Group activity 1, and try to encourage the children to look for a 'magic number' that links the mass and the weight. The number is 10, which is an approximate value for the gravitational field strength on Earth (actually 9.81N/kg). Once this number has been established, random values for greater masses and weights can be chosen for the children to calculate the corresponding weight or mass by multiplying or dividing as appropriate. Explain that the Earth has a gravitational field that affects objects around it, and that like the magnetic field around a magnet, this field gets weaker further away from the Earth.

Discuss Group activity 2. Encourage the children to think about how the differences in gravity between the Earth and the other planets would affect astronauts. *Are people heavier or lighter on Mars than on Earth? How would this affect how fast they could run/high they could jump?*

OUTCOMES
● Can find the mass of an object.
● Know that 'mass' and 'weight' are not the same.
● Understand that the weight of an object will differ on the other planets of our solar system.

LINKS
Enrichment unit, Lessons 4 and 5: the composition of the solar system.
Maths: developing mental strategies for multiplying and dividing by 10.

Differentiation
Group activity 1
Support children by giving them labelled masses and asking them to concentrate solely on measuring the weight.
Extend children by asking them to discuss how the graph produced would allow them to find the mass of an object given its weight, and vice versa.
Group activity 2
Some children may need help with finding the gravitational field strength data for each planet. It may be appropriate to provide a simplified table for use in their calculations.
To extend children, ask them: *Would these scales still be accurate on the Moon? Why/why not?*

ENRICHMENT
Lesson 3 ▪ Magnetic and non-magnetic materials

Objective
● To know that only a limited number of metals are magnetic.
● To know that the magnetic property of some metals allows them to be separated from other metals.

RESOURCES
Labelled samples of magnetic metals (iron, steel, cobalt, nickel) and of some other metals; magnets; paper; writing materials. Metal samples are available from commercial sources.

MAIN ACTIVITY
Ask the children to test a selection of metal samples with a magnet to see whether they are attracted to it. To do this, they should place the magnet on

the sample and record whether it is possible to lift the sample off the desk with the magnet.

ASSESSMENT
Can the children correctly separate the magnetic and non-magnetic materials?

PLENARY
Discuss the fact that only a few metals are magnetic, and how this fact is used in the recycling industry to separate steel and iron (e.g. steel cans) from other metals.

OUTCOMES
- Know that only a limited number of metals are magnetic.
- Can use a magnet to separate metals.

Lesson 4 ▪ Streamlining

Objective
- To look at how objects that move through fluids are streamlined.

RESOURCES
A selection of secondary sources and pictures showing streamlined shapes, both natural (e.g. fish) and manufactured (e.g. racing cars).

MAIN ACTIVITY
Ask the children to use the secondary sources to put together a display of streamlined objects and add appropriate comments to explain why streamlining is necessary.

ASSESSMENT
Can the children identify streamlined shapes?

PLENARY
Review the kinds of shapes that are streamlined. *Does the direction of movement affect whether a shape is streamlined?* Discuss the importance of streamlining in sports such as cycling and skiing, and how the athletes change their body shapes to become streamlined.

OUTCOME
- Can identify streamlined shapes, both in the natural and manufactured world.

Lesson 5 ▪ Force diagrams

Objective
- To be able to explain how objects stay at rest or move by considering the forces acting on them.

Vocabulary
balanced forces, opposite forces

RESOURCES
Main teaching activity: A simple plumb-bob; a tennis ball; a model car; a stiff board.
Group activities: 1 A 'stress ball' or a ball of Plasticine®; a marble; an elastic band; a large mass (such as a brick or a box of books); a lollipop stick; sandpaper; thick card; scissors; paper; writing materials. **2** Photocopiable page 133 (also 'Force diagrams' (red) available on the CD-ROM).
ICT Link: 'Force diagrams' interactive from the CD-ROM.

BACKGROUND
No force ever acts on its own. As Newton's third law states, 'for every action there is an equal and opposite reaction.' For example, when you sit on a

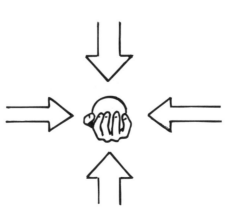

Differentiation 💿

Group activity 1
Support children by providing them with diagrams of the activities on a sheet, leaving them to draw the force arrows; this will prevent them from getting slowed down and distracted by the task of drawing the objects.
    To extend children, ask them to arrows of different sizes to give an indication of the relative size of the forces, as well as showing the direction of the forces.

Group activity 2
To support children, give them 'Force diagrams' (green), which includes fewer diagrams than the core sheet.
    To extend children, give them 'Force diagrams' (blue), which asks them to add the names of the different forces to the diagrams.

soft-cushioned chair, it gives to start with, but then supports your weight. The force of gravity acting downwards on you has a reaction from the chair providing support: the springs and cushioning pushing up. These two forces are therefore in opposition. There are always a couple of forces, and sometimes more, acting on any given object, at the same time. The direction and magnitude of the forces determines what happens to the object.

Consider a ball resting on a table. There are two forces acting on the ball: its weight and the upwards push from the table. These forces are equal and opposite, and so cancel each other out. They are known as 'balanced' forces. The ball will remain stationary. However, if we apply a sideways force, the ball moves in the direction of that force. The bigger the push, the greater the effect on the motion of the ball. However, this very motion immediately introduces a force that tends to reduce the speed of the motion: 'friction'. Unless the propelling force is continued, the force of friction will eventually stop the ball. In this situation, friction is the larger force and it will slow the moving object down. These forces are not cancelling each other out (they are not balanced), and so they are changing the motion of the ball.

In summary, if the forces acting on it are balanced, the object will either stay at rest or continue to move at the same speed in the same direction. If the forces are unbalanced, then a change in speed or direction (or in the shape of the object) will occur. The terminology of balanced and unbalanced forces is not required for children at primary level, but you may find these ideas valuable in helping the children to understand how forces act.

STARTER

Ask the children to name a force that is acting on them at this moment. Their answers should include 'weight' or 'gravity'. Ask them which direction this force is acting in. (Downwards.) *So what is stopping them falling to the centre of the Earth?* (The upthrust from the ground.) Remind them that every force has a direction, and that the forces they have mentioned are acting in opposite directions. (It may also be worth discussing the idea, with more able children, that the forces are of equal magnitude and hence balanced.) Explain that they are going to look at the forces acting on an object to see why it moves or stays still.

MAIN ACTIVITY

Ask a volunteer to hold a small mass (such as a plumb-bob) hanging on a string. Ask the children to identify the forces acting on this mass. It should be easy for the class to spot the force of gravity giving the mass its weight. Say: *But If gravity were the only force acting on it, the object would fall. Where is the other force?* (The tension in the string provides an upward force.) This situation can be represented on a diagram, using arrows to show the directions of the forces. Draw a diagram (see below) on the board or flipchart, with equal-sized arrows to represent the tension in the string (pulling upwards) and the weight (pulling downwards).

Hold a tennis ball (or similar) between your thumb and finger. Ask the children to describe the forces acting on the ball. Weight is present as always, in a downwards direction, but the opposing force is provided by the finger and thumb grip and the strength of your arm. Ask a volunteer to draw the forces on a diagram on the board.

As a final demonstration, place a small toy car (or similar) on a stiff board. Explain that the car is not moving, because there are equal forces acting downwards (the car's weight) and upwards (upwards push from the board).

Push the car in one direction, so that it moves and then stops. Ask the children to describe the forces acting on the car. As the car is pushed, there is a force from one side. The car slows down because of a friction force in the opposite direction. Diagrams could be drawn to show this. *How are the forces different if the board is on a slope?* (If the board is tilted slightly, initially the car will not move, because, although the board provides less upthrust when it is at an angle, friction holds the car in place. Eventually the slope is great enough for gravity to overcome the friction and upthrust, so the car moves down the slope.)

GROUP ACTIVITIES

1 Ask the children to carry out the following simple activities, in a circus. Each time they must draw the object and the forces acting on it, naming the forces and describing (in writing) how they affect the object: squashing a stress ball or ball of Plasticine®; flicking a marble; pulling an elastic band; lifting a large mass; sliding a lollipop stick along a desk and over sandpaper; cutting thick card with scissors.
2 Give the children a copy each of page 133. Ask them to label the drawings with arrows to show the forces acting in each situation.

ASSESSMENT

From their written work, assess whether the children have an idea of the direction of a given force and the relative strength of the forces acting on an object; are able to comment on whether an object will move faster, slow down, stay the same or change shape as a result of the forces acting on it.

PLENARY

Go through the activities in the experiment circus, giving the children opportunities to explain what they have found out. Ask them to confirm the findings or otherwise. Emphasise the names of the forces, the directions in which they act, and whether they are balanced.

OUTCOME

● Can explain how forces make things stay at rest or move.

Lesson 6 ▪ Weight in water

Objective
● To know that water exerts an upward force on a solid object which is suspended in it.

RESOURCES

A water trough or large beaker; a force meter; some objects that sink in water.

MAIN ACTIVITY

Ask the children to assist you in a demonstration. Use a force meter to measure the weight of an object hanging in air. Repeat the measurement of the weight with the object immersed in water (not floating). Record the following information, in a table, on the board: the object, its weight in air (N), its weight in water (N), the difference in weight (N). Repeat for a number of different objects that sink in water. After weighing about six objects, ask the children to look for a pattern in the results.

ASSESSMENT

Can the children make the measurements required accurately? Do they notice the difference in the measured force? Can they give a reason for the difference?

PLENARY
Discuss the difference between the results for an object hanging in air and in water. *What is the force pulling down on the object?* (Gravity or weight.) Explain that the difference between the results is due to another force from the water. *Which direction is this force acting in?* (Upwards.) Say that this force is given the name 'upthrust'.

OUTCOMES
● Recognise the apparent change in the weight of an object when suspended in water due to upthrust.
● Can explain the forces acting on an object suspended in water.
● Can make and record observations.

ENRICHMENT
Lesson 7 ◾ Floating objects

Objective
● To know that when an object floats, the upthrust acting on it is equal to the force of gravity acting in the opposite direction.

RESOURCES
A water trough or large beaker; a force meter; some objects that float in water, (enough for each group)

MAIN ACTIVITY
Ask the children to carry out an experiment similar to the one in the previous Lesson, but this time using a mixture of objects that float and ones that do not. An additional column, 'Floats or sinks?', can be added to those used previously. After the children have collected the results, ask them to calculate the upthrust for each object and to look for a link between the upthrust on floating objects and their weight in air.

Differentiation
Support children by providing a worksheet with the table already drawn. With these children, it may be more helpful just to look at the fact that the weight of a floating object in water is zero, without using calculations, then use the Plenary to deduce the link with upthrust.

ASSESSMENT
Can the children take measurements in a suitable way to allow a conclusion to be drawn from them?

PLENARY
Discuss the children's results and calculations of upthrust. Ask them to suggest why things float, using the terms 'upthrust' and 'weight'. Develop the idea that these forces are balanced for floating objects.

OUTCOME
● Can explain why an object floats.

Lesson 8 ◾ Load and extension

Objectives
● To know that when a stretch force on an elastic band is increased, its length increases in proportion.
● To record observations, draw a graph, analyse results and draw conclusions.

RESOURCES 💿
Main teaching activity: A light spring; a strong hook or laboratory stand; hanging masses; a strong elastic band; a ruler.
Group activities: 1 Strong elastic bands; force meters; rulers; calculators; paper; writing materials. **2** Photocopiable page 134 (also 'Load and extension' (red) available on the CD-ROM); writing materials.

BACKGROUND
Consider the effect of lifting a bag of shopping: the handles stretch a little. The greater the weight of the shopping in the bag, the greater the stretch on the handles. Sometimes the stretch is too great for the material that the

Vocabulary
elastic, extension, deform, stretch, proportional

bag is made from, and the handles snap. The same rules apply to all elastic materials. An elastic material, in scientific terms, is one that can be stretched but will then return to its original shape (provided the force applied is not too great). Sometimes the force is great enough to cause permanent deformation and the material will either remain in a 'stretched' shape or will break apart. The extent to which a material stretches, up to the point of permanent deformation (its extension), is directly proportional to the amount of force applied. This law is known as Hooke's Law, after Robert Hooke (1635-1703). We can use this relationship to measure forces: a force meter is a spring in a plastic case. Conversely, the force required to stretch an object by a certain amount increases as the extension increases.

STARTER
Gather the children around you and show them a spring. Demonstrate that it can be pushed (compressed) or pulled (extended), but it returns to its original shape. Ask the children what they think will happen if the spring is pulled with a small force. (It will stretch.) *What would happen if the force were greater?* (The spring would get even longer.) *Will the spring go back to the same shape? What if a very strong force were used?* (The spring would straighten out and not go back to its coiled shape.) Say that they are going to look at the effects of forces on stretchy materials.

MAIN ACTIVITY
Hang a light spring on a strong hook or laboratory stand. Select a couple of volunteers to carry out the demonstration. One child should measure the length of the spring while the other adds hanging masses to it and then records each length (as reported by the first child) on the board or flipchart. Tell them to measure the unloaded spring first and write this result down.

To work out the extension produced by the hanging masses that will be added, this first value must be subtracted from the new length value each time. Ask the volunteers to hang a mass on the spring, record the mass and length and calculate the extension. Repeat for four or five results. *Can the children see a relationship between the mass and the extension? If the mass is doubled or tripled, what happens to the extension?*

GROUP ACTIVITIES
1 Ask the children to carry out an experiment (similar to the demonstration) to see whether the effect is the same for an elastic band. They must record the length of an unstretched band, then measure the length of the band as the amount of force is increased. By pulling the band with a force meter, the force applied can easily be observed and recorded. The children must then make calculations to find out whether the extension is proportional to the force applied. It is possible that the results will not show a proportional relationship for rubber bands in certain regions of its extension.
2 Give each child or group a copy of photocopiable page 134. The data on the sheet shows how different types of plastic bag perform when stretched to breaking point. The children can use this information to infer the answers to the questions on the sheet: 1. Savamarket; 2. Shopsafe; 3. Pricemate, Shopsafe, Worthmore; 4. Shopsafe - it is the strongest (can take the most weight); 5. Savamarket - since it is the weakest, it will stretch the most when the weight is not enough to break it.

ASSESSMENT
In Group activity 1, note whether the children make the appropriate measurements to a good degree of accuracy. Can they select appropriate information from the chart in order to draw a conclusion? In Group activity 2, note if the children can interpret the information from the chart, to complete the worksheet correctly.

Differentiation
Group activity 1
Some children may find it easier to mark out the extension if the experiment is placed on a sheet of paper and the taut but unstretched length of the elastic band is drawn on the paper.

Measurements of extension can be made from that point without the need to subtract the original length from the stretched length.
Group activity 2
To support children, give them 'Load and extension' (green) from the CD-ROM, which includes fewer questions than the core sheet.

To extend children, give them 'Load and extension' (blue), which presents the information in tabular form and asks children to draw their own bar chart.

PLENARY

As Group activity 1 is discussed, hand around a force meter (of the type where the spring is exposed) in order to reinforce the idea that springs are used to measure pulling forces because the relationship between force and extension is so consistent. Group activity 2 provides an opportunity to for the children to attempt interpretation type questions.

OUTCOMES

● Know that the extent to which an elastic material stretches is proportional to the force applied.
● Can make observations, record them and select results from a table to draw a conclusion.

Lesson 9 ▪ Sinking slowly

Objective
● To know that air resistance can slow down a moving object.
● To conduct an investigation.

Vocabulary
friction, lubrication, drag, air resistance, streamlined

RESOURCES

Main teaching activity: Three small home-made parachutes of different sizes; three identical small hanging weights; a stopwatch; a metre ruler.
Group activities: 1 Parachutes made by the children, using paper, plastic bags or light fabric; paper clips, stopwatches; paper; writing materials; graph paper (or a computer and data-handling software) or the graphing tool from the CD-ROM **2** One copy per child of photocopiable page 135 (also 'Sinking slowly' (red on the CD-ROM).

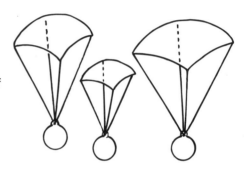

PREPARATION

Prepare three small parachutes of different sizes, using thin cloth and string. Attach identical small hanging weights to the three parachutes (see diagram).

BACKGROUND

The children will previously have studied the effect of friction, and will understand it as the force acting between two surfaces. They may have looked briefly at ways of making objects move easily, reducing friction through use of lubrication. This activity deals with the friction that occurs between a solid object and a fluid. In order to move through a fluid (that is, a gas or a liquid), a solid object has to part the fluid material so that the fluid can move around it. Some shapes move through fluids more easily than others. For example, the bow of a boat is pointed but the stern is flatter, so a boat moves forward more easily than backward.

This activity also focuses on objects moving through air, and looks at the shapes that move through air more easily and less easily. The force that restricts the ease of movement through a fluid or gas is called 'drag'. We experience drag when we go out on a windy day. In this situation, not only are we trying to move through the wind, but the wind is being obstructed in its path by our bodies. When 'drag' occurs in the air, we call this 'air resistance'.

STARTER

Gather the children around you. Ask them to imagine a park with people walking, children playing ball games and frisbee, with trees all around. Say that at fisrt the air is still but then a strong wind starts to build up. *What happens in the park?* (The trees sway and the balls and frisbees start to go

Differentiation
Group activities
Support children by giving
them blanks of the two tables.
   Children who complete the
tasks quickly could calculate
the average height of the
children in the class (this is
easy if the results are in a
spreadsheet). These children
could also use reference books
to find out the names of the
different blood groups. *What
kind of variation is this?* Ask
them to find out their own
blood group. This data can be
added to the chart for the
next lesson.

where the wind blows.) Ask a volunteer to show how the people might have
to walk. Ask the children to explain why these things are happening. (The
force of the wind is causing these effects.) The effects can be observed, but
how they are applied cannot be seen: wind exerts an invisible force, like
gravity and magnetism. But unlike these, it is not operating at a distance
from the material producing the force: the material producing wind force is
the air.
   Explain that the reason it is difficult to move through a strong wind is a
force called 'drag' that opposes movement in that direction. Drag is a friction
type of force. It happens when objects try to move through a liquid or a gas,
or when a liquid or gas passes a stationary object. If the gas is air, we also
call it 'air resistance'.

MAIN ACTIVITY

Tell the children that they are going to look at the effect of drag on different
parachutes. Show the children the three parachutes and explain that they
are of different sizes, but each is carrying the same mass. *Why is this
important?* (It is necessary for a fair test to take place.) *What other factors
must be kept the same to make a fair test?* (Same height, same shape of
parachute, same length of strings, same material for parachutes.) Drop each
of the parachutes in turn, asking a child to time the fall carefully. *What do
the children notice about how the larger, middle-sized and smaller
parachutes compare?* (The largest parachute takes longest to fall, the
smallest takes the least time.) Ask them to explain these results, using their
knowledge of forces.
   Discuss their explanations: gravity pulls all the different parachutes down
with equal force (because they have virtually the same mass), but larger
parachutes have a greater drag and therefore experience less overall
downward force. NB Some anomalous results may be due to the fact that
drag is speed-dependent. Different-sized parachutes will take different
times to reach their terminal velocity (the maximum speed of the parachute,
when the gravitational and drag forces are balanced).

GROUP ACTIVITIES

1 Ask the children to carry out a fair test to examine the experiment in more
detail. They should make parachutes and load each one with a couple of
paper clips, then measure the time taken for it to fall to the ground from a
constant height (about 1.5m). The results can then be put into a scatter
graph or bar chart. This is a good opportunity to use data-handling software
to transfer data from a spreadsheet to a graph. The children should then
write a conclusion about what they have found out from the experiment,
and what patterns they have observed in their results. They should try to
give a scientific explanation of these results, using their knowledge of
forces. Finally, they can evaluate the experiment, look for possible problems
and errors in it, and suggest how they might improve it (perhaps giving tips
to a future group). Use this work to assess children's understanding of air
resistance and their ability to carry out an investigation.
2 Ask the children to work individually through page 135, analysing data on
different-shaped pieces of Plasticine® falling through different liquids to
decide whether there is high or low drag in each case. Use this sheet to
assess their understanding of drag. The answers are: 2. Dome in paste. (The
dome is the least streamlined shape (encounters most resistance) and the
paste is more resistant to movement through it.) 3. Cone in water. (The cone
is the most streamlined shape (encounters least resistance) and the water is
less resistant to movement through it.) 4. Paste. 5. Cone.

ICT LINK
The children could use the graphing tool from the CD-ROM to create their graphs.

PLENARY
Use both Group activities to stimulate discussion of how objects that are designed to move through fluids are shaped. The children may remember work from Year 4/Primary 5 on streamlining and how a streamlined shape has low drag. Group activity 1 should be discussed with an emphasis on how the investigation went and how improvements could be made.

OUTCOMES
● Can describe how air resistance affects the speed of a falling object.
● Can carry out an investigation.

Lesson 10 ◗ Spinner test

Objective
● To investigate factors that affect how fast a 'spinner' falls to the ground.

RESOURCES
Card; scissors; paper clips; stopwatches; paper; writing materials; graph paper (or a computer and data-handling software).

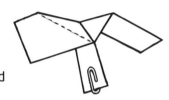

MAIN ACTIVITY
'Spinners' are a popular way of investigating air resistance at Key Stage 2/ Primary 4–7. Explain to the children that they are going to look at how spinners with different-sized rotors fall, by carrying out a fair test. They need to find out whether the rule that worked for the parachutes is also applicable to a two-armed spinner (the bigger the area, the slower the spinner will fall due to the increase in air resistance). They should make the spinners and load them with a couple of paper clips (this adds stability and holds the spinner together). They should record the size of the rotor blades on each spinner and the time taken for it to fall to the ground. Ask each group to use a different-sized spinner, with several repeats.

ASSESSMENT
Have the children carried out a fair test in order to gather their results? Have they recorded the results in an appropriate manner?

PLENARY
Collate the class results and use them to draw a scatter graph or bar chart. Discuss the results obtained and how the experiment could be improved to make the results more reliable. *Why is it useful to repeat the test two or three times with each size of spinner?* (To check and improve the overall reliability of the investigation, and to show more clearly any pattern in the results.)

Differentiation
Extend children by asking them to look at how spinner size affects how far the spinner travels horizontally after being dropped, and relate this to seed dispersal.

OUTCOMES
● Can investigate how the size of a spinner affects the time it takes to fall to the ground.
● Can explain their results in terms of the effects of drag.

Lesson 11 ▶ Assessment

RESOURCES ◉
Photocopiable pages 136 and 137 (also 'Assessment – 1' (red) and 'Assessment – 2' (red) available on the CD-ROM; pencils; pens.

STARTER
You may wish to start with the written tasks, or to give the children a short oral test as revision. You may also wish to review the key vocabulary from the topic.

ASSESSMENT ACTIVITY 1
Give the children a copy each of photocopiable page 136 and let them complete it individually. When they have finished, you may prefer either to mark the answers yourself or to collect the papers and redistribute them for the children to mark, creating an opportunity to discuss the questions and the relative merits of different answers.

ANSWERS
1. gravity; 2. friction; 3. 4cm; 4. The second and third pairs will attract, the other pairs will repel; 5a. upthrust; 5b. 2 newtons; 6. zero; 7. Answers might include the friction between the tyres and the ground, the push of feet on the pedals, the weight of the rider on the saddle, the upthrust of the saddle on the rider, the weight of the bicycle and rider on the ground, the upthrust of the ground on the wheels, the friction (air resistance) between the air and the rider, the push (in a constant direction) from the wind, and so on.

LOOKING FOR LEVELS

Most children will correctly answer questions 1, 2, 3 and 4, and give a short description of how they may feel on a windy day, without the qualification using scientific terminology for example, referring to 'air resistance'. Some children may answer questions 1, 2 and 4 correctly, but will find the application of scientific theory difficult in the other questions. Other children will complete the test giving scientific explanations for their observations in question 7.

ASSESSMENT ACTIVITY 2
This task focuses on selecting information in order to draw a conclusion from an experiment. Give each child a copy of photocopiable page 137 and ask them to complete the questions.

ANSWERS
Look for a line graph with correctly labelled axes. The explanation should point to a consistent relationship between the weight applied and the degree of stretching up to the point where the bag breaks.

ICT LINK ◉
The children could use the graphing tool, from the CD-ROM, in order to create their line graphs.

LOOKING FOR LEVELS
Most children should be able to draw an appropriate graph of the data. Some children may space out the markings on the graph incorrectly and not label the axes. Other children may correctly space out and label the axes. When

Differentiation 💿

Group activity 1
Extend children by asking them to examine how other factors, such as the load, affect the time of fall.

Group activity 2
Support children by asking them to complete the activity in 'Sinking slowly' (green) from the CD-ROM, in which only one liquid is investigated. This means that children can concentrate on the effect of shape on drag.

analysing the results, most children will note that as the force (or weight) is increased, the handles on the bag become longer. Some children may state briefly that the handles are longer when there is more in the bag. Other children may comment that doubling the weight in the bag makes the handles twice as long.

PLENARY

Following Assessment activity 1, it is important to discuss with the children the need to use the precise scientific vocabulary when answering questions. Following Assessment activity 2, use 'anonymous' quotes from the children's graphs and conclusions to reinforce the ideas that graphs should be completed with labelled axes; when describing patterns in results and writing a conclusions, scientific language should be used correctly.

PHOTOCOPIABLE

Magnetic force

Number of pieces of card	Force needed to pull paper clip off magnet (N)

Illustrations © Tony O'Donnell © Sarah Wimperis

■ SCHOLASTIC

Force diagrams

■ Draw arrows to show the forces on each diagram.

Illustrations © Tony O'Donnell © Sarah Wimperis

PHOTOCOPIABLE

Load and extension

■ The graph below shows the force needed to break the handles of carrier bags from different grocery stores. Use this information to answer the questions below.

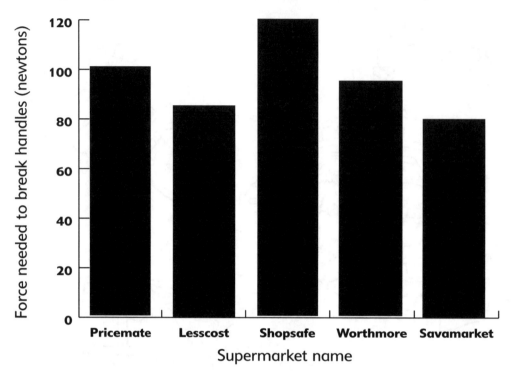

1. Which shop has the weakest bag?_____

2. Which shop has the strongest bag?_____

3. A bottle of cola has a weight of 22 newtons. Which bag or bags could carry four bottles without breaking?

_____

4. Which bag is likely to have been made from the thickest plastic? Explain your answer.

_____

_____

5. If a weight of 50 newtons is placed in each carrier bag, which one is likely to have its handles stretched the most? Explain the reason for your prediction.

_____

_____

■SCHOLASTIC

Sinking slowly

Shape	Time taken to fall through paste (seconds)	Time taken to fall through water (seconds)
ball	2.5	1.0
sausage	3.0	2.0
cone	2.0	0.5
cylinder	3.5	1.5
cube	5.0	2.0
dome	6.0	2.5

◼ This table shows the results for an experiment using several objects, water and wallpaper paste.

1. Plot two bar charts to show the two sets of results.

2. Which shape takes the longest to fall, and in which liquid? _____ through _____

Explain why this is. _____

_____

_____

3. Which shape falls through the fastest, and in which liquid? _____ through _____

Explain why this is. _____

_____

_____

4. Which liquid has more drag? _____

_____

5. Which shape falls faster through paste than the dome falls through water?

_____ Explain why this is _____

_____

PHOTOCOPIABLE

Assessment – 1

1. The force that makes an object fall when you let go is called:

_____

2. The force that helps you to grip is called:

_____

3. A force of 10N pulls on a spring that stretches 2cm. If a force of 20N were used, how far would you expect the spring to stretch?

_____

4. Look at the following pictures of pairs of magnets.

a)
   N   S   S   N

b)
   S   N   S   N

c)
   N   S   N   S

d)
   S   N   N   S

Which will attract each other?

_____

Which will repel each other?

_____

5. A snooker ball has a weight of 7 newtons when in air. In water, the weight of the same ball is 5 newtons.

(a) What force causes the difference?

_____

(b) What is the size of this force?

_____

6. A tennis ball floats on water. In air, it has a weight of 2 newtons. What will its weight be in water?

_____

7. Describe how forces affect you when cycling on a windy day.

_____

_____

_____

_____

_____

_____

_____

_____

■ S C H O L A S T I C

Assessment – 2

◧ Use the following information to draw a graph, then explain any patterns that you see in your results.

Rose and Malik carry out an experiment to find out how much a piece of plastic from a carrier bag would stretch when they hung different masses from it. Here are their results:

Mass used (grams)	Amount of stretch (mm)
50	2
100	4
150	6
200	8
250	10
300	Plastic snapped

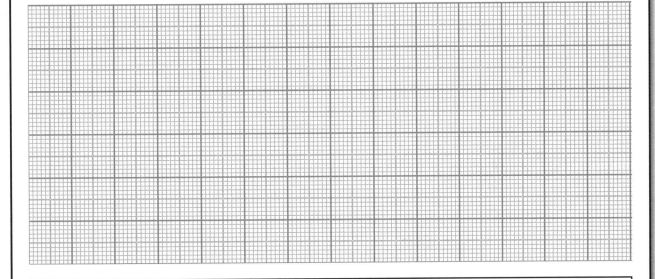

Explanation:

CHAPTER 6 The solar system

Lesson	Objectives	Main activity	Group activities	Plenary	Outcomes
Lesson 1 Sun, Earth and Moon	• To know that the Earth spins as it goes around the Sun and that the Moon travels with the Earth, in orbit around it. • To reinforce the relative sizes of the Sun, Moon and Earth.	Watch a video about the Earth, Sun and Moon. Discuss the relative sizes of the Sun, Moon and Earth, and how these could be modelled.	Make a scale to represent the distances between the Earth, Sun and Moon.	A quick-fire 'question and answer' session.	• Know that the Earth moves around the Sun. • Know that the Sun is larger than the Earth and that the Earth is larger than the Moon. • Appreciate the scale of the distances between the Earth, Sun and Moon.
Lesson 2 Eclipse of the Sun	• To know how a solar eclipse occurs.	Use a model to demonstrate what happens during a solar eclipse, pointing out the Moon's umbra and penumbra.	Label a diagram and complete a cloze text. Use a search engine to find out about the solar eclipse which took place, in Cornwall, in 1999.	A quick-fire 'question and answer' session about the solar eclipse. Reinforce the ideas with the eclipse model.	• Can explain how an eclipse of the Sun occurs.
Lesson 3 Moon craters	• To be able to describe the surface of the Moon. • To know how the craters on the Moon were formed.	Use a photograph to discuss what the surface of the Moon looks like. Use a model to demonstrate how the craters on the Moon's surface were formed.	In groups, repeat the crater formation activity to find out how the height from which an object is dropped and the mass affects the size of the craters formed.	Some of the children read out their work and then others offer constructive feedback. Finished work could be used in a wall display.	• Can explain how some of the craters on the Moon were formed.
Lesson 4 Facts about our solar system	• To know what makes up our solar system. • To know the order of the planets in our solar system. • To know what a comet, an asteroid, a meteor and a meteorite are. • To know which planets have moons.	Show a video on our solar system. Introduce the children to a variety of sources of information, including CD-ROMs and the internet.	Find answers to questions about our solar system. Find out information about each planet. Make pictures or models of the planets. Find out about comets or meteorites.	The children make up a nonsense poem to help them remember the order of the planets.	• Can name the nine planets of the solar system. • Know which of the planets have moons.
Lesson 5 Modelling the solar system	• To know what makes up our solar system. • To know the order of the planets in our solar system.	Play music excerpts from *The Planets*, by Holst. Discuss how the mood of the music describes the planets. Review information from lesson 4 about the size and order of the planets.	The children make scale models of the solar system or paint pictures of the planet gods.	Children explain their scale models of the solar system, or display and describe their paintings.	• Can name the nine planets of the solar system.
Lesson 6 Space travel	• To know about space exploration in the past. • To know about space exploration in the future.	Explain that the children will use a variety of sources of information to help them carry out research about telescopes, rockets, satellites, space probes, humans in space and space stations.	Groups research into different aspects of space travel in order to answer the questions provided.	Groups present their findings to the class. Make a list of ways in which space can be explored.	• Know about the different methods that are used to explore space.
Lesson 7 Science fiction	• To think about space exploration in the future.	Read excerpts from the novel *The War of the Worlds*, as a stimulus for discussion.	The children write their own science fiction story and record it as a 'broadcast'.	Play some of the broadcasts to the class. The cassettes can be added to the class bookshelf or school library.	• Can use scientific knowledge to create a science fiction story.
Lesson 8 Space exploration	• To recognise how quickly space exploration has progressed.	Research space exploration using the internet and the prompt questions.	The children prepare posters or a timeline, based on the findings of their research.	Discuss the children's findings and predict the future of space travel.	• Know the main milestones of space exploration.

Assessment	Objectives	Activity 1	Activity 2
Lesson 9	• To review learning about the Earth, Moon and Sun. • To assess the children's knowledge about the Earth, Moon and Sun.	Individually or in teams, use a range of resources (including ICT) to devise questions for a class quiz based on the content of this unit.	Complete a written test on the content of this unit.

SC1 SCIENTIFIC ENQUIRY

What caused the craters on the Moon?

LEARNING OBJECTIVES AND OUTCOMES
- Carry out an investigation.
- Measure width and depth with care.
- Draw conclusions.

ACTIVITY
The children drop balls into the sand to investigate how height and weight affect the size of the craters that form.

LESSON LINKS
This Sc1 activity forms an integral part of Lesson 3, Moon craters.

Lesson 1 ▸ Sun, Earth and Moon

Objectives
- To know that the Earth spins as it goes around the Sun, and that the Moon travels with the Earth and in orbit around it.
- To reinforce the relative sizes of the Sun, Moon and Earth

Vocabulary
Earth, orbit, spherical, gravity, gravitational, rotate, axis

RESOURCES 💿
Starter: Posters or pictures of the Earth (viewed from space); pictures of the Moon and the Sun; a version of the Icarus myth – for example, from the *Illustrated Dictionary of Mythology* (Dorling Kindersley).
Main activity: A TV and video, the *Our Earth* video (Channel 4 Learning; 217785); photocopiable page 155 (also 'Sun, Earth and Moon - 1' (red) available on the CD-ROM); a tray of spherical objects of different sizes including poppy seeds, dried peas and a beach ball; calculators.
Group activity: Spherical objects, (as above); the school field or an alternative large, open space.
Plenary: Photocopiable page 156 (also 'Sun, Earth and Moon - 2' (red) available on the CD-ROM).

BACKGROUND
The Earth is approximately spherical, and it rotates (spins) on its own axis. The axis is an imaginary line drawn through the centre of the Earth from the North Pole to the South Pole. One complete rotation of the Earth takes 24 hours (one day). The Earth's axis is tilted at a constant angle of 23.5° to the plane of its rotation. The side of the Earth facing the Sun is lit up, and we say it is 'daytime' on this side. The side of the Earth facing away from the Sun is in darkness, and so it is 'night-time' on that side. The Sun does not move (relative to the solar system) – the Earth moves around the Sun. It takes the Earth one year (365¼ days) to orbit the Sun. To take account of the extra quarter-day, the calendar has an extra day every four years (leap year).

The Earth is held in orbit around the Sun by the Sun's gravitational pull. The Earth's tilt relative to the plane of the orbit causes the seasons. For half of its orbit, the tilt leans the northern hemisphere towards the Sun. Six months later, when the Earth is on the other side of the Sun, the southern hemisphere leans towards the Sun. In the hemisphere leaning towards the Sun, the Sun appears to rise

Differentiation
To support children, give them 'Sun, Earth and Moon' (red) from the CD-ROM, a simplified version of the core sheet.

Extend children by asking the following questions: *Light travels at 300,000 kilometres per second. How long does it take reflected light to reach us from the Moon? How long does it take light to reach us directly from the Sun?*

high in the sky; the number of daylight hours is greater, and the air is warmer. This is summer. In the hemisphere leaning away from the Sun, the Sun appears to rise lower in the sky; the number of daylight hours is smaller and the air is colder. This is winter.

The Sun is a star. All stars give out a large amount of heat, light and other forms of energy. The surface of the Sun is a seething mass of hydrogen, which acts as a fuel. The heat of the Sun is produced from nuclear fusion reactions in the middle, or core, of the Sun, where the temperature reaches millions of degrees. At the surface, the temperature is only about 600°C.

Compared with other stars, the Sun is of average size and brightness. There are many stars which are in fact larger than the Sun. Betelgeuse is over 100 times larger and Rigel an even brighter star ,is 50,000 times brighter.

The Moon is a ball of rock that orbits the Earth and travels with it around the Sun. The Moon is held in its orbit by the Earth's gravitational pull. The Moon does not spin on its axis, so we always see the same side of it. All the planets in the Solar system, except Mercury and Venus, have moons. The Earth's moon is one of the largest. It is roughly one-quarter the size of the Earth. It takes 28 days for the Moon to orbit the Earth.

This lesson reinforces work that the children will have done in Years 4–5/ Primary 6–7. It is important to revise these concepts as the children like adults can often find them confusing. Further details can be found in *All New 100 Science Lessons: Year 5/Primary 6, Chapter 6, Unit 5e 'Earth, Sun and Moon'.*

STARTER

Read the story of *Icarus* to the children. This will capture their imagination and help them to develop a mental picture of the heat and power of the Sun. Show them some pictures or posters of the Sun, the Moon and the Earth. Use these pictures to help them focus their minds on the ideas which they have covered, over the previous two years. Try a brainstorming session, recording key words on the board, to revisit important concepts such as: *What are the Earth, Sun and Moon? What is meant by the terms 'day', 'year' and 'seasons'?*

MAIN ACTIVITY

Show the children the video *Our Earth*. Give out copies of photocopiable page 154 and look at the data together. Explain that it is hard to visualise what these numbers tell us but we can use a models to help. Show the children the tray of spherical objects and decide together which three objects would make good models of the Earth, Sun and Moon. The proportion of Earth to Moon is about 4:1; that of Sun to Earth is about 109: 1; that of Sun to Moon is about 400:1. A beach ball, pea and poppy seed would be good choices for the models.

Draw the children's attention to the fact that the Sun's diameter is 400 times greater than the Moon's and that the Sun is 400 times further away from the Earth than the Moon. This is why the Sun and the Moon appear to be about the same size in the sky. Invite a child to use one of the balls to 'cover' a large object, such as a parked car, that is visible from afar, through the classroom window. Discuss the size of an aeroplane which is parked at the airport compared to the size it appears when it is in the sky.

GROUP ACTIVITY

Divide the class into groups of three or four to work on the second part of photocopiable page 154, making up a scale to represent the distances between the Earth, Sun and Moon. The Sun is about 390 times further from the Earth than the Moon. For example, if a group adopts a scale of 1mm: 10,000km, the Moon (poppy seed) will be about 4cm and the Sun (beach ball) about 15m from the Earth (pea). At a scale of 1mm:1000km, the Moon will be about 38cm and the Sun 150m from the Earth. The groups will need a large open space to work in. At the end of this session, ask one group to model the scaled-down distances for the rest of the class, using suitable objects.

ASSESSMENT
Note which children are able to calculate the relative diameters correctly, and which make a plausible choice of spheres to represent the Sun, Moon and Earth.

PLENARY
Finish with a quick-fire 'question and answer' session. What shape is the Earth? Which is the largest: the Earth, the Sun or the Moon? Which is greater, the distance between the Sun and the Earth or the distance between the Earth and the Moon? What do we call the imaginary line through the centre of the Earth? On which side of the Earth is it daytime? How long does it take the Earth to make one complete rotation on its axis? How long does it take the Earth to orbit the Sun? How long does it take the Moon to orbit the Earth? Why does the Sun appear to move across the sky during the day?

Give out copies of photocopiable page 155 as homework. Ask the children to record their observations of the Moon, for the next month, using the sheet to help them.

OUTCOMES
- Know that the Earth moves around the Sun.
- Know that the Sun is larger than the Earth and the Earth is larger than the Moon.
- Appreciate the scale of the distances between the Earth, Sun and Moon.

LINKS
Geography: time zones.

Lesson 2 ▪ Eclipse of the Sun

Objectives
- To know how a solar eclipse occurs.

Vocabulary
eclipse, solar, umbra, penumbra

RESOURCES ◉
Starter: A collection of spherical objects of different sizes (as for Lesson 1).
Main activity: A TV and video player; a video showing a solar eclipse; a globe; a torch or OHP; a tennis or table-tennis ball.
Group activities: 1 Photocopiable page 157 (also 'Eclipse of the Sun' (red) available on the CD-ROM); writing materials. **2** Access to the internet; highlighter pens.

PREPARATION
The teacher demonstration will need some practice (See Main activity).

BACKGROUND
A solar eclipse (eclipse of the Sun) happens when the Earth, Moon and Sun line up in such a way that the Moon blocks the Sun's light from the Earth –It occurs when the Moon lies directly between the Earth and the Sun. The Moon's shadow (or 'umbra') covers a small area of the Earth's surface so anyone who is standing in the umbra (or 'zone of totality') will see the Sun totally eclipsed by the Moon. People standing within the wider surrounding area may see the Moon covering part of the Sun. This is called a partial eclipse. The region of partial shadow is known as the 'penumbra'.

During a total eclipse, the Moon blots out all of the Sun's light, making day suddenly turn into night. This only occurs within a small area of the

Differentiation 💿
Group activity 1
Support children by giving them a list of words they can use to fill in the blanks on page 157. They (and/or other children who have completed the sheet) could also work on a poster or collage showing the Sun, the Earth and the Moon lined up to cause a solar eclipse.
Extend children by giving them 'Eclipse of the Sun' (blue) which does not include the words children need to label the diagram.
Group activity 2
Some children will need help with typing in the search words, skimming and selecting information.

Earth's surface at a time and for only a few minutes because the Moon is so far away, that it casts a relatively small shadow on the Earth. As the Moon moves across the Sun, its shadow races across the Earth's surface along what is called the 'path of totality'. Just before the Sun disappears in a total eclipse, a 'diamond ring effect' occurs: the Sun's normally invisible corona (outer atmosphere) flashes into view. If the Moon were further away from the Earth it would not cause a total eclipse when it moved between the Earth and the Sun. If the Moon were nearer to the Earth, the 'zone of totality would be greater'.

STARTER

Ask questions to recap on the work from the previous lesson. *Which is the largest: the Sun, Moon or Earth?* Illustrate this with a beach ball, a pea and a poppy seed. *Which is further away from us: the Sun or the Moon?* Show the relative distances using the same objects. (See Lesson 1.) *Does the Sun move within the Solar system, or does it stay in the same position? Does the Earth move or stay in the same position? How long does it take the Earth to orbit the Sun? What about the Moon: does that move or stay in the same position? What does the Moon move around? How long does it take the Moon to move around the Earth? Does anyone know what a solar eclipse is?* Some children may remember the solar eclipse from the summer of 1999. *Did any of them go to Cornwall or abroad to see the eclipse?* A member of staff may be able to visit your class to give his or her recollections.

MAIN ACTIVITY

Tell the children that you are going to show them what happens during a solar eclipse. Using a model set up as shown below, line up the Sun, Moon and Earth. Point to the shadow that is produced on the Earth. If you were in this spot, then you would be in darkness. Say that this area is called the umbra. Then point to the penumbra and explain that if you were in this area, you would see part of the Sun. If you are using an OHP, it might be useful to show what would happen to the shadow if the Moon were further away from the Earth. Reinforce these ideas by showing a relevant video.

GROUP ACTIVITIES

1 Give out copies of page 157 and ask the children to complete it individually by labelling the diagram and filling in the missing words.
2 Demonstrate using an internet search engine to look for the word 'Moon'. Ask the children to count how many hits were found. Now ask the children to use the search engine to look for the word 'Cornwall' and write down the number of hits found. Then should then use another search engine for the

word 'Eclipse' and write down the number of hits found. Finally, they should search for 'Eclipse and Cornwall'. They should print what they have found in this final search, and mark any key facts with a highlighter pen.

All the groups should be given the opportunity to carry out this ICT activity. When they have all completed the activity, they could share their findings. For example, if groups carried out the activity on different days, they could compare the number of hits in each search. *Did the number of hits vary? If they did, why was this? Did they find the search helpful?*

ASSESSMENT
Note which children are able to use a search engine correctly, print out information, highlight key facts and explain what happens during a solar eclipse.

PLENARY
Ask the class: *Is the Moon the same size as the Sun? Why do the Sun and the Moon appear to be the same size? What does the Moon do to cause a solar eclipse? What would happen if the Moon were further from the Earth?* Once again, show the children the model of a solar eclipse.

OUTCOME
- Can explain how an eclipse of the Sun occurs.

LINKS
ICT: using the internet to search for information.
Geography: visibility of a solar eclipse in different parts of the world.

Lesson 3 ▪ Moon craters

Objectives
- To be able to describe the surface of the Moon.
- To know how the craters on the Moon were formed.

Vocabulary
Moon rock, Moon crater, mountain, asteroid

RESOURCES ●
Starter: A source of Moon myths and legends, such as *Golden Myths and Legends of the World* by Geraldine McCaughrean (Orion).
Main activity: A photograph of the Moon showing its craters (available from the NASA website – www.nasa.gov.uk); a tray of damp sand to a depth of 3–4cm; objects to drop such as, a ping-pong ball, a ball-bearing wrapped in Plasticine®; stones of various sizes wrapped in Plasticine®.
Group activities: Photocopiable page 158 (also 'Moon craters (red) available on the CD-ROM) **1** Trays (the type that children use to put their equipment in, i.e. a drawer tray) with damp sand to a depth of 3–4cm; a ball made of Plasticine®; a metre ruler; a 30cm ruler. **2** Trays of sand (as above); objects to drop such as, a ping-pong ball, a ball bearing wrapped in Plasticine®, stones of various sizes wrapped in Plasticine® (try to keep the size of the balls dropped the same – just change the mass); weighing scales, a metre ruler, a 30cm ruler.

BACKGROUND
Once the telescope had been invented, people drew detailed maps of the side of the Moon, facing the Earth. The Italian astronomer Galileo Galilei (1564–1642) built the most powerful telescope of his time. It could magnify things to about 30 times their real size. This meant that he could see the planet Jupiter and its four moons. In 1609, Galileo became the first person to make a study of the skies with a telescope. When he

Differentiation
Group activities 1 and 2
Arrange children in mixed-ability groups so that they can support each other. Some children may need help to find the mass of the objects in Group activity 2. Children may or may not get as far as drawing a bar chart. If they do not manage to draw a bar chart of their own results, then the teacher could draw it for them and ask them to interpret it through questioning. For example: *Which mass gave the deepest crater? Do heavier objects produce deeper craters?*

Extend children by asking them to work out the average of their results and then draw a line graph.

observed the Moon he saw craters and mountains that were not invisible to the naked eye.

The Moon is a ball of rock that orbits the Earth and travels with it, around the Sun. The Moon is held in its orbit by the Earth's gravitational pull. The Moon does not spin on its axis, so we always see the same side of it. All the planets in the solar system, except Mercury and Venus, have moons. The Earth's moon is one of the largest. It is about one-quarter of the diameter of the Earth. It takes 28 days for the Moon to orbit the Earth. It is very quiet on the Moon as it has no atmosphere (air), so sound cannot travel. People would also not be able to breathe on the Moon unaided. If you look at the Moon through binoculars, you can see the craters on its surface. These can be hundreds of kilometres in width. The dark patches that can be seen, are flat areas of land called 'maria' or 'seas'. The lighter areas are mountains.

The craters are thought to have been formed around 4000 million years ago, when asteroids (different-sized lumps of rock) collided with the Moon. Asteroids were once thought to be the remains of other planets. These planets were formed thousands of millions of years ago, when chunks of ice-covered of rock joined together. Some rocks were left over and became asteroids. A large collection of these asteroids ended up circling the Sun, in a broad band, between the orbits of Mars and Jupiter and this phenomenon became known as the 'asteroid belt'.

STARTER
Capture the children's imaginations by reading one of the many myths and legends that relate to the Moon. Brainstorm words that describe the Moon on the board or flipchart. Accept both scientific and descriptive language.

MAIN ACTIVITY
Pass around the photograph showing the surface of the Moon. Ask the children to describe what they see. Compare their observations with the word list. *Does the Moon look as you imagined?* Discuss how the image of the Moon and explain what the light and dark patches are. Say that the larger craters are actually hundreds of kilometres wide. *Does anyone have any idea how these craters were formed?* Explain that they were formed by rocks hitting the Moon's surface.

To demonstrate crater formation by placing a tray of damp sand on the floor and asking a child to drop different-sized pebbles and marbles into it. This should create a similar effect to that on the Moon's surface.

GROUP ACTIVITIES
1 Explain to the children that they are going to investigate how the height from which an object is dropped affects the size of the crater formed. Before the children begin their experiment, they may wish to carry out a few trial runs to find out if the amount of sand they are using is adequate. Pupils can work in groups of two, three or four. The independent variable is the height from which the ball is dropped and the dependent variables are the depth and diameter of the crater. In order to ensure a fair test, the balls should have the same mass and the same depth and the same type of sand should be used each time. (The children can make the balls out of Plasticine, or you can have them already prepared.)

One child should hold the metre ruler or tape it to the wall, so that 0cm is lined up with the top of the sand, in the tray. Another child should drop the ball from a height of 20cm. Another child should measure the depth and diameter of the crater using the 30cm ruler. To ensure reliable results, the procedure should be repeated twice, from 20cm.

The next step is to repeat the drop from the heights of 40cm, 60cm, 80cm and 100cm. (Remind the children that they need to use at least 5 independent variables to ensure reliable results). You will need to add more water to the sand if it begins to get dry (damp sand makes better craters).

2 Tell the children that this time they will investigate how the mass of the object dropped affects the size of the crater formed. The independent variable is the mass of the ball dropped and the dependent variables are the depth and diameter of the crater. In order to ensure a fair test, the children should use the same sized balls - dropped from the same height and use the same depth and type of sand each time.

Ask the children to find the mass of a ping-pong ball and then to repeat the procedure from Group activity 1, dropping the ping-pong ball from a specific height e.g. 40cm. They should then repeat the drop for at least three other balls of different masses, which are, as near as possible, the same size. **Safety:** Be aware that some children might be tempted to throw objects, especially ball-bearings, which can cause harm.

For both activities, the children will need to make a prediction about what they think their results will show and they should record results in a table (photocopiable page 158, could be used for this). Emphasise the need to record measurements, using standard units.

ASSESSMENT

Can they measure accurately using standard units? Can they write up their investigations and results accurately?

PLENARY

Ask: *What do your results show? Do the results match what you predicted? Did the experiment work well? Were there any results that did not fit the pattern? Were there any problems with the investigation? How do you think you could improve upon the investigation?*

OUTCOME

● Can explain how some of the craters on the Moon were formed.

Lesson 4 ▪ Facts about our solar system

Objectives
● To know what makes up our solar system.
● To know the order of the planets in our solar system.
● To know what a comet, an asteroid, a meteor and a meteorite are.
● To know which planets have moons.

Vocabulary
solar system, comet, asteroid, meteor, meteorite, Mercury, Venus, Earth, Mars, Jupiter, Saturn, Uranus, Neptune, Pluto

RESOURCES

Starter: A poster showing the planets in our solar system (from Channel 4 Learning).
Main activity: A video about the solar system, such as *Our Solar System and Beyond* (Channel 4 Learning); books; magazines and comics about space and our solar system, which give references to websites.
Group activities 1-4: Cards with group tasks written on them (see below); card; paints; colouring pencils; scissors; a computer and CD-ROMs such as *Eyewitness Space and Encarta*; access to the NASA website.

PREPARATION

Prepare sets of cards (enough for one card per group) with the four Group activities written on them (see Group activities 1-4, on page 146) .

BACKGROUND

The universe is everything that exists. It includes many different solar systems and galaxies. A solar system consists of planets and other bodies orbiting a star. A galaxy is a system of stars held together by gravitational attraction. A hundred thousand million galaxies are known to exist. Our star, the Sun, is part of a spiral-shaped galaxy called the 'Milky Way'.

Our solar system consists of all the planets, asteroids and comets that orbit the star we call the Sun. They are arranged in this order: Sun, Mercury, Venus, Earth, Mars, asteroid belt, Jupiter, Saturn, Uranus, Neptune, Pluto. The solar system was formed millions of years ago, when the Sun was born and the planets of the solar system were formed from the material that was left

Differentiation
Support children by giving them a specially prepared worksheet on which they can record the names of the planets in the correct order and filling in missing words about the size of the planets, their temperature and their distance from the Sun.

Extend children by asking them the question: *Why do you think Pluto was the last planet to be discovered?* They could write a story about 'A journey through the solar system'.

over. The Sun was initially surrounded by a rotating disc of gas and dust. The dust came together to form rocks, which joined to form the first planets.

The number of moons (rocky satellites) orbiting each of the planets in our solar system is as follows: Mercury= 0 moons, Venus= 0 moons, Earth =1 moon, Mars =2 moons, Jupiter =16 moons, Saturn =18 moons, Uranus =15 moons, Neptune =8 moons, Pluto =1 moon.

Beyond Pluto's orbit are the remains of the cloud of dust that formed the solar system. This cloud contains many comets. Comets have been described as 'giant dirty snowballs', because they are lumps of ice and rock that move towards the Sun. The ice melts and boils, forming an enormous head and a long tail. As the comet travels, it sheds bits of itself and from Earth, these are seen as showers of light called 'meteors' or 'shooting stars'.

Meteors and meteorites are the same kind of body, but meteorites tend to be larger. They do not have an orbit – they just head towards the Earth, after drifting into its gravitational field. Most are the size of a fist, but some are larger. One landed in Arizona in the USA and produced a crater 1.3km across.

STARTER
Display a poster of the planets in our solar system. Brainstorm what the children already know about these planets.

MAIN ACTIVITY
Show a video that looks at our solar system and beyond. Explain to the children that they will be working in small groups to find out facts about our solar system. Ask them to list where such information could be found. Hopefully they will suggest sources such as books, magazines, television, videos, CD-ROMs and the internet. Show them some magazines or comics about space and the solar system and highlight the fact that these sources give website address links to enable them to find more information. Ask the children to look through the sources in order to find web addresses. Make a list of the websites on the board for the children to choose from. Demonstrate how to find the NASA website, how to use a CD-ROM, and how to print a page off a website or CD-ROM.

Organise the class into groups of three or four. Allocate an activity card to each group, or let them choose. They have to research the information printed on the card, using the internet or a CD-ROM. Each group should try to print out a page and highlight the text to show the key information.

When the groups have completed their activities, they can feed back their findings to the rest of the class. A classroom display, of the children's research, could be created.

GROUP ACTIVITIES
1 The children could find information to answer the following questions: *What is the order of the planets moving away from the Sun? How far are the planets from the Sun? Which is the biggest planet? Which planet is nearest to the Sun? Which planet is furthest away from the Sun? Which planets are larger than the Earth? Which planet is the coldest? Which is the hottest?*
2 The children could find out information about each planet's type of surface, average surface temperature, length of day, type of atmosphere, moons and rings.
3 The children could find out what a particular planet looks like (colour, rings and so on) and then paint a picture or make a 2D model of it, to be hung in the classroom.
4 The children could find out about comets or meteors and meteorites, answering questions such as: *What is a comet? What names have been given to different comets? When have comets been seen? Who was Edmond Halley and what did he do? What are meteorites and meteors?*

ASSESSMENT

Note which children are able to: access an internet site, retrieve relevant information from a website or a CD-ROM and print off the required pages and understand the printed information. These observations could also form part of your ICT assessment.

PLENARY

Ask the children to write out the names of the planets in order and then make up a nonsense memory poem to help them remember the order.

OUTCOMES
● Can name the nine planets of the solar system.
● Know which of the planets have moons.

LINKS
ICT: using CD-ROMs and search engines.

Lesson 5 ▸ Modelling the solar system

Objective
● To know what makes up our Solar system.
● To know the order of the planets in our Solar system.

RESOURCES

A poster showing the planets in our solar system (as for Lesson 4); a cassette or CD player, a recording of *The Planets* by Holst such as *Journey to the Stars* in the *Magical Music Box* series, IRDP); Plasticine®; a grapefruit (or pieces of cardboard); a metre ruler or tape measure; paints; brushes; paper.

MAIN ACTIVITY

Play excerpts from *The Planets*. Before each excerpt, tell the children which planet it is about. After each excerpt, ask the children what words they would use to describe the music. Discuss the fact that people used to believe each planet had a god. The music is meant to evoke the god of the planet and what the planet is like.

Discuss the information from Lesson 4, about the order and size of the planets and their distance from the Sun. Copy the table shown below onto the board or flipchart. Ask the children to make a scale model of our solar system. They can use a grapefruit, or a cardboard disc with a diameter of 11cm, for the Sun, roll a ball of Plasticine, to just 1mm across, for the Earth, and use the information from the table, to make all the other planets to the same scale. They should then hold the Earth at a distance of 12m from the Sun and use the information from the table for the other distances. On this scale, the nearest star would be another grapefruit about 3000km away.

Planet	Me	Ve	Ea	Ma	As	Ju	Sa	Ur	Ne	Pl
Size (mm)	½	1	1	½		11	9	4	4	¼
Distance from the Sun (m)	5	8	12	18		60	110	220	350	460

Other children could paint pictures of the planet gods, using the music they have heard and the words suggested for ideas.

ASSESSMENT

Note which children are able to work out appropriate scales for the different planets, and for their distances from the Sun.

PLENARY

Ask the children to explain their scale models of the solar system to the class. Other children can display and describe their paintings.

OUTCOME

● Can name the nine planets of our solar system.

Lesson 6 ▪ Space travel

Objectives
● To know about space exploration in the past.
● To know about space exploration in the future.

RESOURCES
Starter: A telescope.

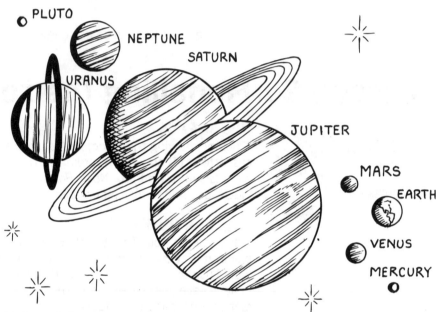

Main activity: Books; magazines and comics, used in Lesson 4.
Group activity: Cards from photocopiable page 159 (also 'Space travel' (red) available on the CD-ROM); computers; encyclopaedia; CD-ROMs.

PREPARATION

Make sets of question cards (one card per group) by copying page 159 onto card and cutting it into sections.

BACKGROUND

Our Sun is a star. It is part of a huge galaxy called the 'Milky Way', which has

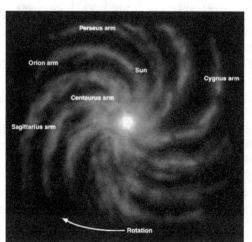

a spiral shape and contains more than a hundred thousand million stars. Our solar system is in one of the Milky Way's spiral arms (see picture below). The nearest galaxy to us is Andromeda. Using modern telescopes, we can see millions of other galaxies. All the galaxies together and the space between them make up the Universe.

The first astronomer to use a telescope was Galileo Gallilei, in seventeenth-century Italy. He discovered Saturn's rings and Jupiter's four large moons. In the last century, space exploration really took off! In 1903, a Russian schoolmaster called Konstantin Tsiolkovskii put forward the first scientific ideas on rocket propulsion. In 1926, an American engineer called Robert Goddard launched the first liquid fuel rocket. Since then, many space travel projects have allowed us to examine our solar system in more detail.

Artificial satellites orbit the Earth and send back information about the weather or point out features such as mineral deposits on the Earth. Navigation satellites help ships or aeroplanes to pin-point their positions. In October 1957, Russia put the first artificial satellite (Sputnik 1) into orbit. This satellite investigated the Earth's atmosphere from space. Sputnik 2, which was launched a month later, contained the first living thing to be sent into space – a dog named Laika.

Space probes are unstaffed spacecraft that investigate and report back information about our solar system. Probe visits began in 1959, with a successful trip to the Moon by Luna 2 from the USA. In 1973, Mariner 10 visited Venus and Mercury. In 1976, Viking 1 and Viking 2 landed on Mars. In 1977, Voyager 1 and Voyager 2 were sent to Jupiter, Saturn, Uranus and Neptune. In 1985, five probes were sent to investigate Comet Halley. 1990 saw the launch of the Ulysses probe which flew over the poles of the Sun and in 1995, the Galileo probe entered Jupiter's atmosphere.

For centuries, humans have dreamed of travelling in space. In 1961, this dream became a reality, when a Russian astronaut called Yuri Gagarin was rocketed into space and orbited around the Earth. On July 20th 1969, the American, Neil Armstrong, became the first person to walk on the Moon. In the 1970s, a Space Shuttle programme was launched. In 1983, Sally Ride became the first American woman in space; in 1991, Helen Sharman became the first British astronaut.

Astronauts can now stay in space stations. These are large satellites orbiting around the Earth, with room on board for people to live and work for months. In the future, space stations may be used as hotels where visitors can stay before travelling further in the Solar system, or before coming back to Earth. The first space station, Salyut, was launched from Russia in 1971. In 1973, the first American space station, Skylab, was launched. In 1983, the first purpose-built space laboratory, Spacelab, was launched. The largest space station, Mir, was launched in 1986.

STARTER

If you have a telescope (or can borrow one), it would be a useful prop to have in order to set the scene for this lesson. Ask the children what they think it is, what it does and what it has been made from. *Have any of the children used one?* Explain that Galileo Galilei was the first astronomer to make and use a telescope for observing the Moon and the planets. Explain what he discovered when he used the telescope (see Background). If any child in the class has a telescope at home, he or she could tell the rest of the class about using a telescope and what can be seen through it.

Now brainstorm what the children know about space travel. Use the board or flipchart to record key words, dates and events. Any space travel enthusiasts among the children may be happy to share their knowledge with the rest of the class.

MAIN ACTIVITY

Ask the children to use the books, magazines and comics from Lesson 4 to find any relevant information they can on the following topics: telescopes, rockets, satellites, space probes, humans in space, space stations. Then ask them to see whether any website addresses are listed that are relevant to these topics. Record the topics and the relevant website addresses on the board.

Explain to the children that they are going to work in groups. Each group will be given a card with a title and a set of questions to answer. They will have to find the information they need, using the Internet or a CD-ROM. Each working group should print out a page and highlight the text to show the key facts.

GROUP ACTIVITY
Distribute the cards from page 159. Give each group a card, or let them choose. The children work to answer each set of questions.

ASSESSMENT
Note which children are able to access an internet site chosen from a list, find relevant information on a website or a CD-ROM and print off the required pages and understand the printed information. These observations could also form part of your ICT assessment.

PLENARY
When the groups have completed their activities, they can feedback their findings to the rest of the class.

List all the ways in which we can explore space. A classroom display could be made of the groups' work.

OUTCOME
● Know about the different methods that are used to explore space.

LINKS
ICT: using CD-ROMs and search engines.

Lesson 7 ■ Science fiction

Objectives
● To think about space exploration in the future.

RESOURCES
A copy of *The War of the Worlds* by HG Wells (Orion); the musical version of *The War of the Worlds*; a CD player (if necessary); a cassette recorder and blank tape; ruled A4 paper; pens; pencils.

MAIN ACTIVITY
Play part of the musical version of 'The War of the Worlds'. Read part of the story to the children. Explain that this is a science fiction novel. In America in the late 1950s, this story was read over the radio as a series. When the first part was read out, many Americans actually thought that it was a news bulletin and that the Earth was being invaded by Martians. Ask: *Why do you think there was such a panic? Do you think this could happen today?* If possible, it would be a good idea to take the children to visit a space exploration gallery such as, the London or Armagh Planetarium, the National Space Centre or you could arrange for a Starlab to visit your school.

The children can work individually or in groups to write their own science fiction stories, based on the information they have obtained from their work in this unit and/or from a visit to a space exploration gallery. They can then read their stories as a radio broadcast. They could also compose their own pieces of music, to provide atmosphere to the story and add sound effects as well. If possible, they should record their 'broadcast' on cassette for other classes to enjoy. They could draw or paint a picture for the cassette inlay card.

Differentiation
This lesson will appeal to children of all abilities. Some children may need help with structuring or writing out their story. Children can be expected to produce a story and a broadcast that is appropriate to their ability.

ASSESSMENT

Note which children used their knowledge and imagination to predict future events in space exploration.

PLENARY

Play some of the children's broadcasts to the class. The story cassettes can be added to the class bookshelf or the school library.

OUTCOME

● Can use scientific knowledge to create a science fiction story.

Lesson 8 ▪ Space exploration

Objectives
● To recognise how quickly space exploration has progressed.

RESOURCES

Main activity: Computers
Group activity: Large pieces of paper; pencils; pens and colouring pencils.

BACKGROUND

Space, or air, travel has advanced rapidly since the beginning of the twentieth century. It was only in 1903 that the first powered aircraft was flown by the Wright brothers and now NASA is launching missions to planets as far as Jupiter and Saturn.

Space exploration accelerated rapidly during the Space Race of the Cold War. Between 1957 and 1969 scientists progressed from launching a satellite into space to enabling Neil Armstrong and Buzz Aldrin to walk on the Moon.

STARTER

Elicit the children's knowledge about space exploration and create a mind-map of some of their ideas, on a board or flipchart.

MAIN ACTIVITY

The children should find answers to the specific questions, using the internet. Examples of websites and possible questions are as follows:

www.kidsastromony.com (for less confident children)
1. When were the first pictures of Mars taken?
2. What did Viking 1 and 2 do in space?
3. Name two NASA shuttles
4. When was Mars Observer launched?
5. When did humans fly the first powered aircraft?
6. When did the first person walk on the moon?

www.astrocentral.co.uk (for more confident children)
7. When was the first satellite launched into Space?
8a. When was the first person sent into Space?
8b. What was his name?
9. Which country carried out 7 and 8?

www.aerospaceguide.net (for more confident children)
10a. What was the first animal to be sent into Space
10b. When was this?
11. When was a monkey sent into Space?
12a. When was the first woman sent into Space?
12b. What was her name?
13. When was the first Space walk?
14. Which planet was first explored in 1972?

Differentiation

More confident learners should be encouraged to add additional information to the timeline, other than the facts gathered via the direct questions listed.

Less confident learners could be organised into groups from the start of the lesson. They could then research two or three questions each and pool their answers for the timeline.

ANSWERS

1. 1964; 2. Orbited and landed on Mars; 3. Challenger and Columbia; 4. 1992; 5. 1903; 6. 1969;
7. 1957; 8a. 1961; 8b. Yuri Gagarin; 9. Russia
10a. A dog; 10b. 1957; 11. 1961; 12a. 1962; 12b. Valentina Tereshkova; 13. 1965; 14. Jupiter.

GROUP ACTIVITY

In groups the children should prepare a poster to include all the milestones of space travel which they have researched. Posters could take the form of a timeline or topic headings, such as 'Space Travel', 'Moon Landings', 'Mars Exploration' and so on. The children should be encouraged to present their research in their own words, rather than simply cutting and pasting material from the websites.

ASSESSMENT

Note which children are able to access an internet site, find relevant information on a website and understand the printed information. These observations could also form part of your ICT assessment.
Note how well groups have completed their posters.

PLENARY

Discuss the results of the children's research. Predict how space exploration will advance in the future. *Will we eventually live in space?*

OUTCOME

● Know the main milestones of space exploration.

LINKS

ICT: accessing information from websites.

Lesson 9 ◖ Assessment

Objectives

● To learning about the Earth, Moon and Sun.
● To assess the children's knowledge about the Earth, Moon and Sun.

RESOURCES ◉

1 Paper; pens; computers; relevant textbooks and software. **2** Photocopiable page 160 (also 'Assessment' (red), available on the CD-ROM).

ASSESSMENT ACTIVITY 1

To review what they have learnt about our solar system the children can devise a quiz (together with the answers). Each child or team could make a list of at least ten questions (together with answers). They can use textbooks, computer software and the internet to help them to generate their questions. Ask the children to pose questions to each other, and help them to judge the appropriateness of the answers. If the class is split into teams, they could compete the quiz over several rounds.

LOOKING FOR LEVELS

The children's questions and answers will reflect their understanding of the content of this unit. The notes on levels in Assessment activity 2 (below) may also be useful here.

ASSESSMENT ACTIVITY 2

Give out copies of page 160 and let the children complete this test individually. You may wish to mark the sheets yourself, or to swap them around the class and let the children mark each other's to encourage discussion of the questions and answers.

ANSWERS

1. Spherical or sphere (1 mark). 'Round' is incorrect. 'Almost spherical' or 'a spheroid' is, strictly speaking, the correct answer.
2. 365¼ days or one year (1 mark).
3. 24 hours or one day (1 mark).
4. The Earth (1 mark). 28 days (1 mark).

Sun   Moon   Earth

5. No (1 mark).
6. For 1 mark, all three must be correctly labelled.
7a. Solar eclipse (1 mark). For 7b, 1 mark for each correct label (2 marks).
8. Sun, Mercury, Venus, Earth, Mars, asteroid belt, Jupiter, Saturn, Uranus, Neptune, Pluto (5 marks, deduct 1 for each error).
9a. Mercury and Venus (2 marks); 9b. Saturn (1 mark); 9c. The Milky Way (1 mark).
(Total possible marks: 20.)

LOOKING FOR LEVELS

All the children should be able to describe the shape of the Earth and say how long it takes the Earth to make one journey around the Sun. They should also know that it takes the Earth 365¼ days to make one complete rotation on its axis, and that the Moon does not spin on its axis. (Questions 1, 2, 3 and 4.)

Most children should know that the Moon orbits around the Earth, and that this takes 28 days. They should also be able to label a diagram to show the relative positions and sizes of the Sun, Moon and Earth, and be able to put the planets in their correct order as you move away from the Sun. (Questions 5, 6, 7, 9.)

Some children should know what happens in a solar eclipse, and what is meant by the terms 'umbra' and 'penumbra'. They should also know which planets have moons and rings and which don't. They should also know that our galaxy is called the Milky Way. (Questions 8 and 10.)

PLENARY

You may wish to go through the answers to the test, with the children, after you have collected in the work for marking.

There may be a question (such as question 8) that many of the children may answer incorrectly. If this is the case, it is advisable to go over the concepts that relate to this question with the class and then ask the children to work in groups, on the problem. You may wish to organise the class into carefully chosen, mixed-ability groups.

On the other hand, there may be a question that the majority of the children answer correctly. In this case, it will be useful to give them an extension question or activity that covers the same concepts. For example, if all the children get question 1 right, you could ask them to answer the following questions: *Look around your school. How many objects can you find that are spheres? What is the largest sphere you can find? What is the smallest sphere you can find? How would you measure a sphere? What units of measure and measuring equipment might you use in order to measure a sphere?*

Sun, Earth and Moon – 1

	Approximate diameter (km)
Sun	1,400,000
Earth	13,000
Moon	3,500

1. How many times greater than the Moon (in diameter) is the Earth?

_____

2. How many times greater than the Earth (in diameter) is the Sun?

_____

3. How many times greater than the Moon (in diameter) is the Sun?

_____

	Approximate distance (km)
Earth–Sun	150,000,000
Earth–Moon	390,000

4. If you were making a small-scale model of the Earth, Moon and Sun, how far apart would you place each object?

_____

_____

_____

Sun, Earth and Moon – 2

■ Keep an account of changes in the shape of the Moon.

1. Look at the Moon every night.

2. Draw the Moon's shape in one of the circles. Colour the bright part of the Moon yellow in each of your pictures. When you cannot see the Moon at all, shade the circle black.

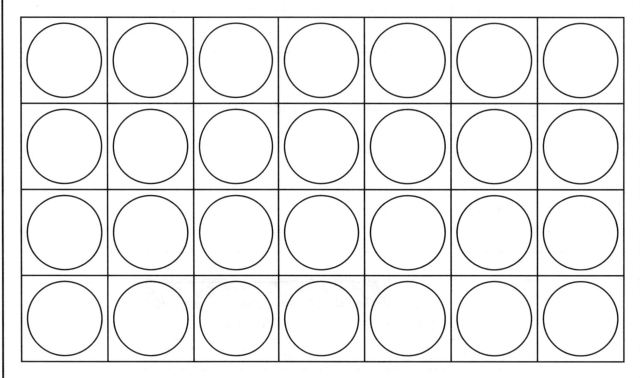

3. Here are some shapes you might see. Find out what they are called.

_____   _____   _____   _____

▲ SCHOLASTIC

Eclipse of the Sun

◀ Label the diagram below with the following words:
Sun, Moon, Earth, umbra, penumbra

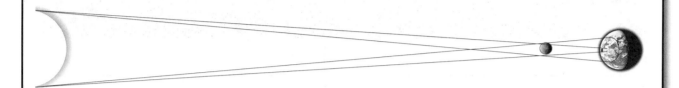

◀ Fill in the missing words:

An eclipse of the Sun (_____ eclipse) happens when the Earth, Moon

and Sun line up in such a way that the Moon blocks the Sun's light from the

_____. A solar eclipse only occurs when the _____ lies

directly between the Earth and the Sun. The Moon's shadow or _____

only covers a small area of the Earth's surface. Anyone standing in this region will

see the Sun totally eclipsed by the Moon.

   Eclipses occur because the Sun and the Moon appear to be the same size in the

Earth's sky. In reality, the Sun is 400 times _____ but because the Sun is

400 times further away, it appears Moon-sized.

   If the Moon were _____ away from the Earth, it would not cast such

a large shadow on the Earth when it passed between the Earth and the Sun. This is

because the Moon is much smaller than the _____.

Illustrations © Tony O'Donnell © Sarah Wimperis

Moon craters

Investigation 1

Our prediction: _____

_____

Height of drop (cm)	Depth of crater (cm)		
	1st drop	2nd drop	3rd drop

Investigation 2

Our prediction: _____

_____

Mass of ball (in grams)	Depth of crater (cm)		
	1st drop	2nd drop	3rd drop

Space travel

Telescopes
Who was the first astronomer to use a telescope?
When was the telescope first used for observing the skies?
What is a telescope made of?
What did Galileo discover by using his telescope?
What is an observatory?
Find out about the Keck telescope.

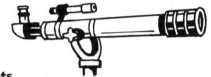

Rockets
What are rockets used for?
Where are rockets launched from?
Find out about Saturn V.
Who was Robert Goddard?

Satellites
What do satellites do?
Find out about Sputnik 1.
Find out about Sputnik 2.

Space probes (1)
What are space probes?
What do space probes do?
Find out about Mariner 2.
Find out about Viking 1 and Viking 2.

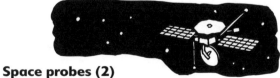

Space probes (2)
Find out about Voyager 1 and Voyager 2.
Find out about the Ulysses probe.
Find out about the Galileo probe.

Humans in space
Why is Yuri Gagarin famous? What nationality was he?
Who was the first person to set foot on the Moon? In what year did it happen?
Who was the first woman in space, and in what year? What nationality was she?
Why is Helen Sharman famous?

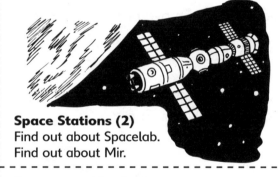

Space stations (1)
What is a space station used for?
Find out about Salyut.
Find out about Skylab.

Space Stations (2)
Find out about Spacelab.
Find out about Mir.

Space travel in the future
Find out about plans for space travel in the future.

Illustrations © Tony O'Donnell © Sarah Wimperis

PHOTOCOPIABLE

Assessment

1. What shape is the Earth?

_____

2. How long does it take the Earth to make one orbit around the Sun?

_____

3. How long does it take for the Earth to make one complete rotation on its axis?

_____

4. What does the Moon orbit around? How long does this take?

_____

_____

5. Does the Sun move around the Earth?

_____

6. Label this diagram using the following words: Earth, Moon, Sun.

7. (a) What is happening in this diagram? _____

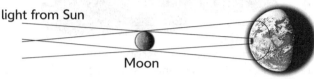

light from Sun

Moon

Earth

(b) Label the umbra and penumbra on the diagram above.

8. The following planets and other bodies are in our solar system: Venus, Earth, Mercury, Pluto, asteroid belt, Neptune, Mars, Uranus, Jupiter, Saturn. List them in the correct order, moving away from the Sun.

_____

_____

_____

_____

9. (a) Which two planets in our solar system do not have moons?

_____

(b) Which planet in our solar system is famous for its rings?

_____

(c) What is the name of our galaxy?

_____

SCHOLASTIC

Illustrations © Tony O'Donnell © Sarah Wimperis

CHAPTER 7 How we see things

Lesson	Objectives	Main activity	Group activities	Plenary	Outcomes
Lesson 1 Shadows	• To know that light travelling from a source can be blocked by an opaque object and that this makes a shadow.	Demonstrate how altering the position of a light source can change the size and shape of a shadow.	Investigate how the position of a light source affects the size and shape of a shadow. Use data about the position of a shadow, on a playground, to infer where the sun might be in the sky.	Discuss how the relative positions of a light source, object and screen affect the shadow. Relate to shadow puppets.	• Can use the terms 'light source', 'shadow' and 'opaque' correctly. • Can make and record observations in an investigation.
Enrichment Lesson 2 Dark boxes	• To know that we see things by light that enters the eye.	Look at pictures in a dark box with and without a torch. Identify the path light takes from the torch to our eye.		Discuss light sources present at night, and the need for light to reflect off things so we can see them.	• Know that in the absence of light, we cannot see. • Know that light from a source is reflected off objects into the eye.
Enrichment Lesson 3 The eye	• To know that the eye contains a lens and a place where images form.	Examine changes in eye pupil size, in different conditions of light. Discuss how the eye forms images on the retina, and how spectacles can help with this.	Make a model eye. Use secondary sources to find out more about why spectacles are worn.	Recap on how the eye adjusts to different light levels and how it focuses. Discuss the importance of sight and use of eye protection.	• Know that the eye can control the amount of light entering it. • Can describe where an image forms in the eye. • Can describe how an optic lens can focus on different objects.
Lesson 4 How we see things	• To know that non-luminous objects can be seen because light which is scattered from, them enters the eye.	Use a torch in a darkened room to demonstrate that when we see an object, light travels from a source to the object and then into the eye.	Draw the path of light in a real context, from a source to an object and then into the eye. Draw the paths of light in invented contexts of objects being seen.	Discuss the path that light takes in various examples.	• Can explain how objects are seen in the presence of a light source.
Lesson 5 Parts of the eye	• To know how our eyes enable us to see. • To know the names and functions of the parts of the eye.	Use a model or diagram of the eye to explain how we see objects around us.	The children draw up their own table and complete it by adding names of the parts of the eye and their functions.	Ask children to identify parts of the eye and explain their functions.	• Can describe how the eye detects light. • Can name the main parts of the eye and describe their functions.
Lesson 6 Mirrors	• To know that mirrors can be used to change the direction in which light is travelling.	Use a mirror to demonstrate the reflection of a light ray. Distinguish between reflection and scattering.	Use mirrors to look at normally concealed places and to look around corners. Draw diagrams to show how they have done this.	Discuss uses of mirrors in everyday life.	• Know that a mirror changes the direction in which light is travelling.
Lesson 7 Reflected light	• To investigate the relationship between the ray of light striking a mirror and the one reflected from it.	Use a torch and mirror to demonstrate that the angle of incidence of a ray of light is equal to the angle of reflection.	Use a torch, mirror and protractor to measure and compare various angles of incidence and reflection. Use a pair of mirrors to see around corners.	Explain how a periscope works, using mirrors set at 45°.	• Can use the angle of incidence of a light ray to predict the angle of reflection from a mirror.
Lesson 8 Reflective surfaces	• To compare the quality of reflection from different surfaces.	Differentiate between reflections and shadows.	The children compare how well different surfaces reflect a beam of light and an image.	Discuss the use of different materials for visibility or concealment.	• Understand that shiny surfaces can be used as mirrors, but dull surfaces cannot. • Understand the use of reflective materials for safety.
Enrichment Lesson 9 Observing reflections	• To know that rays are reflected from surfaces. • To know that flat and curved mirrors reflect light in different ways. • To observe closely.	Exploring reflections of light rays using ray boxes, flat and curved mirrors.		Discussing observations.	• Can recognise that light reflected from a smooth surface produces an image, but light reflected from a rough surface does not. • Can recognise that curved mirrors change the image of the reflection.

Lesson	Objectives	Main activity	Group activities	Plenary	Outcomes
Enrichment Lesson 10 Shadow sizes	• To know that the size of a shadow depends on several factors.	Demonstrate how a shadow changes in size when the screen is moved. Investigate how changing the distance of a light source from an object affects the size of the shadow.		Review the children's findings.	• Can describe how the size of a shadow is affected by: the distance from the light source to the object; the distance from the screen to the object.
Lesson 11 Shadows and reflections	• To know that differences in reflectivity and shadow formation affect how we see our surroundings.	The children map the classroom in terms of reflections and shadows at different times of the day. From this, they decide which areas are best for working and for resting.		Discuss the children's findings and consolidate the vocabulary.	• Can recognise shadows and reflections in their environment. • Can tell the difference between a reflection and a shadow. • Can predict where shadows and reflections will form.
Enrichment Lesson 12 Bending light	• To know that when light rays pass through curved, transparent materials, the paths of the rays are changed. • To make observations and draw conclusions.	Discuss the effect of looking through a curved transparent object.	Investigate the effect that looking through curved and flat transparent objects has on the appearance of a picture or writing. Draw examples of these effects.	Discuss where transparent materials are used and the advantages or disadvantages of using those which change the path of light rays.	• Understand that objects look different through a curved, transparent material because the path of the light rays has been changed. • Can make observations and draw conclusions.
Enrichment Lesson 13 Investigating lenses	• To understand that lenses make light rays change direction. • To decide what evidence to collect. • To choose an appropriate way of presenting results.	Look at convex and concave lenses, and notice differences between them.	Investigate the effects of convex and concave lenses on a light beam. Use a convex lens to form an image on a screen.	Draw conclusions about the effects of convex and concave lenses on light.	• Recognise the ways that light rays are changed by convex and concave lenses. • Know that a convex lens can be used to make an image on a screen. • Can decide on an appropriate way to obtain and record investigation results.
Enrichment Lesson 14 Using lenses	• To know that lenses have a range of applications.	Study a range of optical instruments. Consider what they are used for and locate where the lenses are in each instrument..	Make a water drop microscope and use it to make observational drawings.	Sum up how different optical instruments work. Discuss some unusual uses of lenses.	• Can describe the uses of lenses in a range of optical instruments.
Enrichment Lesson 15 Using a microscope	• To know how to use a microscope correctly.	Demonstration to show the parts of a microscope and how to use it.	Preparing and viewing their own slides.	Discuss the types of objects you would use a microscope to view.	• Can successfully use a microscope to view small details.
Enrichment Lesson 16 Sunlight	• To know that sunlight is made from a range of different-coloured light rays.	Use a prism to split a beam of light. Observe the colours present, and which colours deviated the most and least.	Make a spinner to show seven colours combining to make white. Make a model sky to show how it appears in different colours.	Discuss when and why rainbows are seen, why the sky looks blue and why sunrise and sunset are red in colour.	• Recognise the colours of the spectrum. • Can describe what happens to sunlight when it passes through a prism.

Assessment	Objectives	Activity 1	Activity 2
Lesson 17	• To assess the children's knowledge of how shadows are formed. • To assess the children's knowledge of how we see objects. To assess the children's knowledge of how light is reflected.	The children plan an experiment to show how they could make the same-sized shadow with a football and a tennis ball.	Children answer questions on shadows and reflection.

SC1 SCIENTIFIC ENQUIRY

How does distance affect shadow size?

LEARNING OBJECTIVES AND OUTCOMES
- Measure appropriate distances and sizes.
- Record relevant data in a table.
- Plot a chart and interpret it.

ACTIVITY
Children move an opaque object between a light source and a screen and measure the size of the shadow at different distance from the screen. They convert the data into a chart and use this to develop a conclusion.

LESSON LINKS
This Sc1 activity forms an integral part of Lesson 10, Shadow sizes.

Lesson 1 ▪ Shadows

Objective
- To know that light travelling from a source can be blocked by an opaque object and that this makes a shadow.

Vocabulary
opaque, transparent, shadow, light source

RESOURCES ⊙
Main activity: An opaque shape (not a square or triangle), such as a cut-out of a simple snowflake pattern attached to a piece of string; a lamp; a screen; a metre ruler.
Group activities: 1 A simple card shape, about 5cm²; a lamp; a screen; a metre ruler; paper for recording results; access to a dimly lit area.
2 Photocopiable page 181 (also 'Shadows' (red) available on the CD-ROM).

BACKGROUND
The children should be aware that all light comes from a source and that it travels in straight lines, at high speed. The light is emitted from a source in all directions, not unlike the way that children draw 'sunbeams' coming from the sun (except that the real rays are not separate). They will also know that light can travel through some materials (transparent materials) and not through others (opaque materials).

In order for a shadow to form, light must fall upon an opaque object. The effect of this is that object blocks the light's path and stops it from hitting the surface beyond. The size of a shadow is dependent on the area of the object presented to the light source. A sheet of paper, placed at a right angle to a beam of light, will cast a large shadow but if you turn the paper around, so that it is parallel to the beam of light, the shadow almost disappears.

STARTER
Ask the class about where light comes from, how we see things and how light travels. *What kind of materials can light travel through? What kind of materials can it not travel through? Can you tell me what appears when light is blocked by an opaque object?* (A shadow.) Discuss how in outdoors, the shadow of an object changes in size and shape, during the day. Explain that the class are going to find out more about this.

MAIN ACTIVITY
Reduce the amount of light in the room so that the light from a torch or small lamp can be used to light a small screen such as a flipchart. Ask a child to dangle the opaque shape, in front of the screen, so that a shadow is cast onto the screen. Ask other children in the group to describe the shadow in terms of its shape and size. Now ask the first child to turn the object so that

Differentiation 🔘
Group activity 2
To support children, give them 'Shadows' (green) from the CD-ROM, which includes fewer and less complex questions.

a different shadow is formed. *Why do you think the same object has made a different-shaped shadow?* Move the light source to the left and right and then up and down, to see how the shadow changes shape. It may help the children if one or two of the shadow shapes are drawn, in outline, on the screen as a to reminder of their shape and size. Discuss when the shadows are longest and when they are shortest, paying attention to the angles between the light, the object and the screen. You should find that larger shadows are produced when the opaque object is closer to the light source.

GROUP ACTIVITIES

1 Let the children work in a dimly lit area of the room, investigating how the size and shape of a shadow changes as they move the light source left and right and up and down. They should draw a diagram of their investigation, describe what they have done and record measurements of the distance of the light source from the centre line, the height of the light source above the object and the length of the shadow (see diagram below).

2 Give the children a copy each of page 181. Ask them to infer from the shadows where the sun might be in the sky each time. Longer shadows will form when the sun is lower in the sky (early morning or late evening) and shorter shadows will form when the sun is high in the sky (around midday).

ASSESSMENT

Can the children make 'fair test' measurements to determine the effect of the angle of the light on the size of a shadow? Can they record the results in an appropriate manner?

PLENARY

Discuss how the relative positions of the light, object and screen affect the shadow. Relate this to the way that we sometimes see scary shadows from simple objects, and the shadow theatre of some Asian cultures.

OUTCOMES
- Can use the terms 'light source', 'shadow' and 'opaque' correctly.
- Can make and record observations in an investigation.

LINKS
Art: making a shadow theatre; researching shadow puppets around the world.
PSHE: cultures around the world.

ENRICHMENT
Lesson 2 ▸ Dark boxes

Objective
- To know that we see things by light that enters the eye.

RESOURCES
A closed cardboard box; a heavy cloth (large enough to cover the box); a bright picture cut from a magazine; a torch.

MAIN ACTIVITY
Either as a demonstration or as a group activity, make a 'picture box'. Cut a slit in the side of a closed cardboard box, near the top, long enough to allow a picture to be slid through the box. Make a small hole in the top to shine a torch through, and a small hole in the front to look through. Cover the whole box, except the front, with a heavy cloth to prevent light getting in. The

children should look inside, when the torch is on and then when it is off.

Discuss with the children when they can see the picture, and what it is that makes the picture visible. Draw a diagram on the board showing the path the light takes from the torch to our eyes. Drawing arrows on the light rays, emphasise that the light goes from a light source to the object and then into our eyes.

ASSESSMENT
At the beginning of the Plenary session, ask the children to talk, within their groups, about what they saw when they looked into the box. They should explain how much they expected to be able to see, how much light was available, and where the light was coming from.

PLENARY
Discuss situations where it is easy to see and others where it is difficult, concentrating on the light sources present in different situations. Discuss the light sources available at night, and how much we would be able to see if it really was completely dark. Re-emphasise that we can only see things when light reflects off them.

OUTCOMES
● Know that in the absence of light, we cannot see.
● Know that light from a source is reflected off objects into the eye.

ENRICHMENT
Lesson 3 ▣ The eye

Differentiation
Ask children who need support to identify the light sources in various familiar and unfamiliar situations.

Extend children by asking them to identify the path of light rays in unfamiliar situations, involving reflection to reinforce the knowledge they gained in Year 4.

Objective
● To know that the eye contains a lens and a place where images form.

Vocabulary
cornea, pupil, iris, retina, long sight, short sight

RESOURCES 💿
Main activity: A model or large diagram showing the structure of the eye; mirrors.
Group activities: 1 Photocopiable page 182 (also 'The eye' (red) available on the CD-ROM); scissors; adhesive; colouring pencils. **2** Sources of information about eyes and spectacles (opticians can often provide these).
ICT link: 'The eye' interactive activity, on the CD-ROM.

PREPARATION
If possible, arrange for an optician or a school nurse to talk to the children about how the eyes work and how to look after them.

BACKGROUND
The structure of the human eye can be broken down into three main parts. The light enters the eye through the pupil, a hole that is surrounded by a circular muscle called the iris, before passing through the lens to the retina at the back of the eye. The iris responds automatically to changes in light level, opening or closing the pupil to let in more or less light. This control is needed because the light-sensitive cells of the retina can be damaged by too much light, and so have to be protected by the pupil closing when the light is too bright. Muscles holding the lens in place can contract or relax to make the lens thinner or fatter, changing how much the lens bends light rays passing through it. This is because rays of light from a nearby object have to be bent more to focus on the retina than rays from a more distant object of the same size.

STARTER
Look at a model or large diagram showing the structure of the eye. Help the children to identify the major parts of the eye. Give them mirrors to help them identify some of the same parts in their own eyes: the iris, pupil, eyelid, eyelash and cornea.

MAIN ACTIVITY

Let the children use mirrors to examine their pupils when they have been looking towards a mildly bright light (such as a window), and when they have had their eyes shut. Ask them to describe the change. (The pupil is smaller in bright light.) Explain why this is so, using the model or diagram.

  Discuss why sunglasses are sometimes worn. Draw the attention to the area at the back of the eye and explain that special light-sensitive cells, located in this area, detect light and send signals to the brain. Explain that if you have normal sight, light entering the eye forms a clear image at the back of the eye. If you are long or short-sighted, this image will not be clear unless you wear spectacles: the lenses in the spectacles bend the light so that it forms a clear image at the back of the eye.

GROUP ACTIVITIES

1 Give the children a copy each of page 182 and ask them to construct their own model eye.
2 The children can use secondary sources to learn why spectacles are worn.

ICT LINK 💿

Children can use 'The eye' interactive, on the CD-ROM, to label the parts of an eye.

ASSESSMENT

At the start of the Plenary, ask children to report what they have found out in their research.

PLENARY

Recap on important features of the eye, how it adjusts to different light levels and how it forms an image. Discuss the importance of sight, ways in which eyes can be damaged and situations in which eyes should be protected by dark glasses or protective goggles.

OUTCOMES

- Know that the eye can control the amount of light entering it.
- Can describe where an image forms in the eye.
- Can describe how the optic lens can focus on different objects.

LINKS

PSHE: looking after ourselves.

Lesson 4 ▫ How we see things

RESOURCES 💿

Main activity: A Christmas tree with shiny baubles; tinsel and a string of fairy lights.
Group activities: 1 Plain paper; colouring pencils; rulers. **2** Photocopiable page 183 (also 'How we see things' (red) available on the CD-ROM).

PREPARATION

Before the lesson, check that the Christmas lights are still in working order. Set up the tree and string the lights all around it.

BACKGROUND

It is relatively simple to explain how we see luminous objects (which make their own light). Some of the light coming from the object enters the eye, where the light-sensitive cells (grouped into an area called the 'retina') detect the light and send a message to the brain. (See diagram page 168.)

Differentiation

Group activity 1
Support children by going through the first two examples that they choose with them in order to confirm that they are choosing appropriate objects and marking the paths correctly.

Group activity 2
Support children by giving them 'How we see things' (green), which includes fewer pictures than the core sheet.

Extend children by asking them to label the source of light.

However, the vast majority of the objects that we see are not luminous: they do not give off their own light – so how are we able to see them? Light from a source strikes the object, which then 'scatters' the light (reflects it in all directions). Some of this scattered light enters the eye. Without the light source, the object would have no light 'incident', or light 'falling on it', and so could not be seen. For example, a spotlight may be used to highlight one performer on a stage while, unseen by the audience, the scenery is being changed in the background. If the incident light is well-scattered by a shiny object, the object will appear bright or shiny; conversely, a dull or dark-coloured object will absorb most of the light and so have a vague, unclear appearance.

Whether the object is bright or dark, the light path is always the same: from the source to the object to the eye. Light does not burst forth from our eyes to allow us to see in the dark.

STARTER

Ask the children to explain how we see the lights on a Christmas tree. *Where does the light come from, and where does it go to? Are the lights the only things you can see? If you can see other parts of the tree, are some brighter than others?* The children may see the lights reflected in the baubles. Some of the tree's branches can also be seen, but some branches are brighter than others because they are closer to the light and not in the shadow of other branches.

MAIN ACTIVITY

With the room dimly lit, ask the children to comment on which objects are easy to see and which objects they know are there but are unable to see. Ask: *How might we see these objects more easily?* (We need more light.) Switch on a torch and shine the beam at the children, taking care not to shine it directly into their eyes. *Does this help you to see the object better?* (No.) The children should be able to suggest that the torch should be pointed at the object. Using this example, develop the idea that the light goes from the torch to the object, where it is scattered (reflected) from the object and into our eyes. *Are there parts of the room that the children cannot see from their current positions, even with the torch?* (For example, the far sides of chairs or cupboards.) *Why can't these be seen?* (Either the light cannot reach the object or the light will not be scattered in the direction of their eyes.)

GROUP ACTIVITIES

1 Ask the children to draw some paths that light can take from light sources for example, from a ceiling light to objects in the room or from the sun to parts of the school environment and then to their eyes. Good examples could be redrawn for display (see illustration below).
2 Give the children a copy each of page 183 and ask them to draw the path that light takes when the person in each picture sees the object(s). Remind them that light travels in straight lines, so they should use a ruler to draw the rays of light.

ASSESSMENT

Can the children correctly identify the path that light takes from the source, to the object and to the eye where it is scattered?

PLENARY
Use examples to check that the children understand the path that the light takes when we see an object. Include some examples where there is no light or where the object is a light source.

OUTCOME
● Can explain how objects are seen in the presence of a light source.

LINKS
Unit 3, Lesson 4: adapting to life in the dark.

Lesson 5 ■ Parts of the eye

Objective
● To know how our eyes enable us to see.
● To know the names and functions of the parts of the eye.

RESOURCES
A model or cross-section diagram of the eye (an example is shown below).

MAIN ACTIVITY
Using a model or diagram of the eye, describe how light, from the objects around us, is detected by the eye. Explain the functions of the cornea, iris, pupil, lens, retina and optic nerve. Ask the children to draw up their own table, listing the parts of the eye and their functions.

PLENARY
Choose children to point out parts of the eye on a diagram and explain the function of each. Note which children are able to do this.

OUTCOMES
● Can describe how the eye detects light.
● Can name the main parts of the eye and describe their functions.

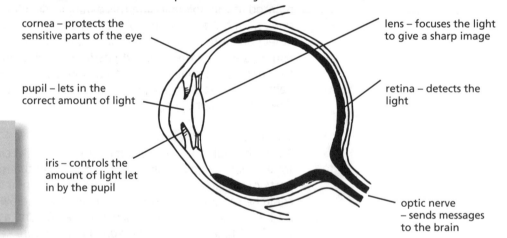

cornea – protects the sensitive parts of the eye

lens – focuses the light to give a sharp image

pupil – lets in the correct amount of light

retina – detects the light

iris – controls the amount of light let in by the pupil

optic nerve – sends messages to the brain

Differentiation
Support children by asking them to play a 'match-up' game with the parts of the eye and their functions from prepared paired cards.

Lesson 6 ■ Mirrors

Objective
● To know that mirrors can be used to change the direction in which light is travelling.

Vocabulary
mirror, reflection

RESOURCES
Main activity: A small torch; a mirror.
Group activity: A safety mirror (one for each group); paper; pencils.

BACKGROUND
Light, from most non-luminous objects, is scattered into our eyes. This means that the light rays that fall, or are 'incident' on an object are reflected in all different directions. The reflective surface of a mirror is so flat and smooth that rays of light that strike it, in an almost parallel manner, are reflected as a series of almost parallel rays. There is no irregular scattering.

This means that light travelling from a source or another object is not 'muddled', and we can see a clear image in the mirror. What we see in the mirror is exactly the same as what we see if we look directly at the object, except that left and right are swapped round (lateral inversion).

STARTER
Remind the children of the path that a ray of light takes when we see a non-luminous object. Show them a mirror and ask them to describe its surface. The idea that it is 'smooth' or 'shiny' should be developed: *What does 'shiny' mean?* The children may be able to comment that it reflects well. Tell them that they are going to look at how the reflection of light, by a mirror and the scattering of light ,by an ordinary object ,are different.

MAIN ACTIVITY
Ask the children what they would do if they were told to 'scatter'. They should say that they would go off in different directions. Reduce the amount of light in the room and shine a small torch across the room so that the children can see the spot of light it forms. Now place the torch on the desk and use a mirror to reflect the light to different parts of the room. If the light is not too strong, you could try reflecting it towards the children. **NB** Light should never be reflected from the sun or another strong light source into anyone's eyes.

Ask: *Is the light being scattered?* (No.) *How do you know this?* (All the light is travelling in one direction.) Explain that this is called 'reflection'. Explain that when mirrors reflect light they change the direction in which the light is travelling. Reflection is different from scattering, because all the rays of light that hit a mirror from a particular direction will travel off in the same direction as each other, whereas scattered rays go off in many different directions.

GROUP ACTIVITY
The children should use mirrors to look at places they do not normally see – for example, inside the waste-paper bin or behind the cupboard.

They should try using mirrors to look around corners. They should draw the positions of the mirror, their eyes and the object they are looking at (see example here of boy looking at the cupboard, using a mirror).

ASSESSMENT
Can the children set the angle of the mirror correctly in order to see around objects?

PLENARY
Discuss some uses of mirrors in our environment such as, make-up and shaving mirrors, security mirrors in shops and dental mirrors. Focus on how these mirrors help us to see in awkward places, or make things clearer by providing an enlarged reflection.

OUTCOME
● Know that a mirror changes the direction in which light is travelling.

LINKS
Maths: reflective symmetry.
Art: light and perspective.

Lesson 7  Reflected light

Objective
● To investigate the relationship between the ray of light striking a mirror and the one reflected from it.

Vocabulary
reflection, incident

RESOURCES 💿

Main activity: A sheet of A3 paper; a torch; a card with a narrow slit; a mirror; a ruler; a pen; a protractor.
Group activities: 1 Photocopiable page 184 (also 'Reflected light' (red) available on the CD-ROM); rulers; pens; protractors. **2** Mirrors on Plasticine® bases (two per group).

BACKGROUND

A ray of light is not scattered from a mirror, but reflected so that it travels in a single, predictable direction. *How can we predict it?* A snooker player knows where a snooker ball will bounce to after it hits a cushion. Similarly, there is a relationship between the angle at which the light hits a mirror (called 'the angle of incidence') and the angle at which it is reflected from the mirror (called 'the angle of reflection'). These two angles are always equal, a fact known as the Law of Reflection (the children do not need to know this name). The two angles are measured from an imaginary line at 90° to the surface of the mirror, called the 'normal'. This law holds for all mirrors, whether plane (flat) or curved.

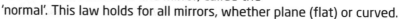

STARTER

Ask the children if there was a pattern to the way they had to angle the mirror in order to see into nooks and crannies in the previous lesson. To develop this idea, stand two children at right angles to each other. Hold the mirror at a point where the sight lines of the two children cross. Align the mirror so that it faces one child, then begin to turn it towards the other child. Ask both children to look at the mirror and say when they can see the other child in it. When they can see each other, the mirror is tilted equally towards each child: there is the same angle on each side. (See diagram, left)

MAIN ACTIVITY

Place a sheet of A3 paper on a desk or the floor so that all the children can see it. Reduce the amount of light in the room. Shine a torch through a narrow slit in a piece of card towards the mirror, as shown on the right (see diagram). Use a metre rule to draw the ray of light going towards the mirror and the ray reflected from the mirror. Use a board protractor to mark a line at 90° to the mirror, then measure the angles from the centre line to the incident ray of light and the reflected ray of light using a protractor. The two angles should be the same (to within 5°).

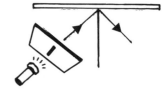

Differentiation 💿
Group activity 1
Support children by giving them 'Reflected light' (green) from the CD-ROM, which includes a cloze sentence for them to complete to explain the conclusion of the experiment. Children may also need assistance with angle measurement.
Group activity 2
Extend children by asking them to record their findings in words and pictures.

GROUP ACTIVITIES

1 Give each child or pair a copy of page 184 to complete. They should use a protractor to measure the angle of each line, then shine the torch along it, draw the reflected ray and measure that angle also. What do they notice about the two angles?
2 Give each group a pair of mirrors. They should place the mirrors over a range of different shapes (as shown in diagram A), then change the angle between the mirrors and observe the effect on the reflections. Secondly, they should put the mirrors facing each other and then turn each mirror 45° in the same direction – can they use this effect to see around corners? (See diagram B.)

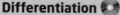

ASSESSMENT

Can the children draw a reflected line from a mirror and measure its angle to the mirror accurately? Can they see a relationship between the angles of incidence and reflection?

PLENARY

Discuss the use of a periscope to see over crowds, walls or the surface of water. Explain why the two mirrors must be set at 45° in order to turn the light by 90°.

OUTCOME

● Can use the angle of incidence of a light ray to predict the angle of reflection from a mirror.

Look here

Lesson 8 ◗ Reflective surfaces

Objective
● To compare the quality of reflection from different surfaces.

RESOURCES

A torch; a selection of different surfaces such as mirrors (clean and dirty); aluminium foil paper (flat and crinkled) and painted surfaces (matt and gloss); paper; writing materials.

MAIN ACTIVITY

Talk about how different surfaces give different qualities of reflection. Make sure the children do not confuse reflections and shadows. Ask them to look at some different surfaces to determine whether the reflection from a torch is clear or dull, and whether it is correctly shaped or distorted. *Can you see your reflection in the materials?* Encourage them to explain their findings in terms of the properties of the materials.

ASSESSMENT

Can the children classify materials in terms of their reflectivity?

Differentiation
Support children by asking them to focus on a limited number of very different materials and say whether they can see a reflection from a torch and their own reflection.
Extend children by asking them to consider reflective materials (such as bicycle reflectors and Scotchlite tape) and relate them to safety at night.

PLENARY

Discuss the benefits of the different types of material: dull materials for camouflage when hiding, highly reflective materials for visibility on roads and so on.

OUTCOMES

● Understand that shiny surfaces can be used as mirrors, but dull surfaces cannot.
● Understand the use of reflective materials for safety.

ENRICHMENT

Lesson 9 ◗ Observing reflections

Objective
● To know that rays are reflected from surfaces.
● To know that flat and curved mirrors reflect light in different ways.
● To observe closely.

RESOURCES

Ray boxes; flat mirrors; curved mirrors; shiny spoons; make-up mirrors.

MAIN ACTIVITY

Let the children use the ray boxes to make single and parallel rays, observing the reflection of those rays and making annotated drawings as they go. Ask them to work through the following sequence of activities: reflections of rough/shiny materials; reflections in a flat mirror; reflections in curved mirrors; set a flat mirror at an angle to the ray and look at the angle of the reflected ray. Circulate and ask the children to describe their observations.

ASSESSMENT
Are the children's observations careful and accurate? Can they describe differences between the way different surfaces and mirrors reflect the light rays?

PLENARY
Ask the children to describe what they observed during each activity and to suggest explanations. Discuss how reflection is the light 'bouncing off' a material and that it works best using shiny surfaces.

OUTCOMES
- Can recognise that light reflected from a smooth surface produces an image, but light reflected from a rough surface does not.
- Can recognise that curved mirrors change the image of the reflection.

ENRICHMENT
Lesson 10 Shadow sizes

Objective
- To know that the size of a shadow depends on several factors.

RESOURCES
An opaque shape (not a square or triangle); such as a cut-out of a simple snowflake pattern; attached to a piece of string; a lamp; a screen; a metre ruler.

MAIN ACTIVITY
Demonstrate how a shadow changes size when the screen on which the shadow is falling is moved, but the positions of the light source and object are not changed.

Let the children work in a dimly lit area of the room, investigating how the size of a shadow changes as they move the light source towards and away from the object. It is important that neither the object nor the screen is moved, since this would change two variables at once. The children should draw a diagram of their experiment (and write a description of it if they can), and record their measurements of the distance, from the screen, to the object, the distance from the light source to the object and the size of the shadow. Make sure they measure a consistent dimension of the shadow to make fair comparisons.

ASSESSMENT
Are the children making accurate measurements and recording them in a sensible manner?

PLENARY
Review the children's results. They should realise that the nearer an object is to the light source, the larger the shadow is.

OUTCOME
- Can describe how the size of a shadow is affected by: the distance from the light source to the object; the distance from the screen to the object.

Differentiation
Some children will need more assistance with the recording of results.
Extend children by asking them compare the relative effects of a 10cm movement of the light and a 10cm movement of the screen. (The former has a greater effect.)

Lesson 11 ◦ Shadows and reflections

Objective
● To know that differences in reflectivity and shadow formation affect how we see our surroundings.

RESOURCES
Paper; drawing materials; pencils; a torch.

MAIN ACTIVITY
Use natural light or a torch to look at how the apparent shape of a volunteer's face can be changed when the position of the face in relation to the light source is changed. Ask the children to draw a map of the classroom, showing where reflections appear and where shadows form at different times of the day. *Is the computer screen difficult to see at certain times of day?* From this, they should be able to say which areas are best for working and resting at different times, and perhaps suggest improvements to the classroom environment or layout. Emphasise the correct vocabulary – for example, distinguish clearly between 'shadows' and 'reflections'.

ASSESSMENT
Can the children use the terms 'reflection' and 'shadow' correctly? Can they identify areas where brighter and dimmer conditions might be more appropriate for the use made of the area?

PLENARY
Discuss the children's results, giving some the opportunity to present their findings. Check that all the children are using the appropriate vocabulary. Consider the children's findings regarding the placement of furniture in the room.

Differentiation
Differentiate by outcome, according to the sophistication of the children's recording.

OUTCOMES
● Can recognise shadows and reflections in their environment.
● Can tell the difference between a reflection and a shadow.
● Can predict where shadows and reflections will form.

ENRICHMENT

Lesson 12 ◦ Bending light

Objectives
● To know that when light rays pass through a curved transparent material, the paths of the rays are changed.
● To make observations and draw conclusions.

Vocabulary
opaque, translucent, transparent, light rays

RESOURCES
Main activity and **Group activities:** A large selection of curved and flat transparent materials such as, glass or plastic optical lenses, sheets of clear plastic or perspex, drinking glasses, glass jars, the plastic stick-on lenses used when towing caravans, plastic rulers and so on; paper; writing and drawing materials.

PREPARATION
Lenses and selections of transparent materials can often be borrowed from secondary schools.

BACKGROUND
Opaque materials (such as wood) do not let any light through. Translucent materials (such as thin paper) let some light through, but we cannot see images clearly through them. Transparent materials (such as glass) allow us to see images through them. Light is refracted (bent) as it goes through any transparent material –this makes pools of water look shallower than they really are and sticks, placed in water, appear to bend. The degree of the bend (or refraction) depends on what the material is and how thick it is.

   In this lesson, the flat sheets of transparent material will cause so little bending of the light (due to refraction) that it will not be noticeable. Any transparent object with a curved surface, with some parts of the material

Differentiation
Group activity 1
Support children by asking them to divide transparent objects into those that make something appear different and those that do not.
Extend children by asking them to relate these properties to the everyday uses of transparent materials (for example, we use flat glass in windows to have a clear view).
Group activity 2
All the children should be able to participate in this activity.

being thicker than others, will act like a lens and bend rays of light. This makes a picture which is viewed through the material appear distorted. The amount of distortion depends on the curvature of the material.

A simple explanation of this effect is that the light is refracted when it enters the material and refracted back again when it leaves the material. If it enters and leaves the material in the same plane (as in a flat sheet of glass), its overall path will not be distorted. But if the plane of the material is different on the two sides (as in a curved piece of glass), the overall path of the light will be changed.

STARTER
Ask the children to try and remember some things they know about light. Make a class list of important points they can remember.

MAIN ACTIVITY
Recap on the definitions of 'opaque', 'translucent' and 'transparent'. Ask the children to name examples of these different types of material. *Do we always see things clearly when we look at them though transparent materials? Why don't they always look 'quite right'?* Explain that sometimes looking at an object through a transparent material makes the light rays change direction and changes the appearance of the object we see. Use a few of the transparent objects to illustrate this, leading into the Group activities.

GROUP ACTIVITIES
1 Warn the children of the dangers of breaking objects – especially those which are made of plastic and glass. Let them investigate a range of different-shaped transparent objects (some curved and some flat) and then draw conclusions about which objects will change the appearance of a picture or writing. They should find that objects with curved surfaces change the path of the light ray, while flat objects do not appear to. Encourage systematic investigation and recording.
2 Ask the children to select one object that they think will change the path of a light ray and one that will not. They should then make accurate drawings of what a piece of writing or picture looks like with and without each of the transparent objects in front of it.

ASSESSMENT
While they are engaged in Group activity 1, ask the children to assess their own investigation for good and bad features. Can they suggest possible improvements?

PLENARY
Ask a representative from each group to tell the class how they planned and carried out their investigation and present their findings. Discuss different places where transparent materials might be used and the advantages and disadvantages of using transparent objects that change the path of light rays (including lenses).

OUTCOMES
● Understand that objects look different through a curved transparent material because the paths of the light rays have been changed.
● Can make observations and draw conclusions.

Lesson 13 ▸ Investigating lenses

RESOURCES ◉

Main activity: A selection of convex and concave lenses with varying curvatures; torches. (Ray boxes can be used, but only if they can be adjusted to give a wide beam.)
Group activities: 1 Photocopiable page 185 (also 'Investigating lenses' (red) available on the CD-ROM); equipment as listed on photocopiable page 186, writing and drawing materials. **2** Convex lenses; torches or ray boxes; cardboard screens; paper clips; Blu-Tack®; paper; writing and drawing materials.

PREPARATION

Check that all torches or ray boxes work (and that you have enough sockets to plug in ray boxes if required). Test your arrangements for providing a dimmed work area. All light experiments give clearer results in darkened conditions. You do not need to black out your classroom; but if you can dim the lighting to the point where a torch beam shows up clearly, you will get better results. You can achieve this either by dimming the whole room or by allowing the children to conduct experiments inside large cardboard boxes turned on their side, with the open side pointing away from any windows.

You can attempt to make your own lenses using water-filled plastic containers, but these give poor results compared with plastic or glass lenses because particles of dust or slight vibrations in the water distort the image. The easiest convex lenses to use are magnifying glasses, which can be obtained with a range of different powers. Alternatively, most secondary schools are willing to lend convex and concave lenses to primary schools, and opticians may supply a range of used lenses from spectacles.

BACKGROUND

All curved transparent materials make light rays change direction. Lenses are transparent materials that have been shaped to alter the direction of light rays in a specifically, designed way. Convex lenses make light rays converge to a point or focus; concave lenses make light rays diverge, making it possible to see a magnified image.

STARTER

Remind the children what they found out about curved, transparent materials in the last lesson. Show them some lenses and ask: *Does anyone know what these are?* Ask them to think of any places where they have seen lenses. Prompt them to think of spectacles, if necessary, but do not worry about any other uses of lenses at this stage. Explain that lenses are shaped so that they make light change direction in special ways. Explain that the class are going to find out what these special ways are.

MAIN ACTIVITY

You should keep this section short, as the Group activities require plenty of time. Pass around some convex and concave lenses. Ask the children to look closely at them and describe any differences that they notice. Emphasise the importance of handling breakable items carefully. Tell the children that lenses can be split into two types: convex (where the sides bulge outwards) and concave (where the sides squash inwards). Say that concave lenses are easy to remember because they have sides like a cave: they cave in. Draw diagrams on the board or flipchart (see below).

Tell the children that they are going to investigate both types of lens to see what they do to light rays. Show them the torches or ray boxes they will be using and any arrangements for fastening screens inside the work area. Explain to them any arrangements you have for making the work area dimmer.

Differentiation
Group activity 1
To support children, give them 'Investigating lenses' (green) from the CD-ROM, which includes fewer questions than the core sheet.

To extend children, give them 'Investigating lenses' (blue), which includes a range of extension questions.

Group activity 2
Extend children by asking them to try to form a different clear image that is larger or smaller than the first one. They will have to change the distance between torch and screen to do this. Ask them to explain to a friend, with diagrams if these will help, what they could do to form a different-sized image.

The groups who have clear images can be asked to make suggestions to help groups whose images are less clear.

GROUP ACTIVITIES

1 Give each child a copy of the instruction sheet (page 185). Allow them time to work in small groups to investigate the effect of putting convex and concave lenses between the torch and the screen on which it is shining. They should find that moving a convex lens towards the screen makes the image smaller, but moving a concave lens towards the screen makes the image larger.

2 Each group should now place a paper clip stuck upright in Blu-Tack® just in front of the torch, and experiment with different positions of the convex lens to make the clearest possible image on the screen. Ask them to draw a diagram showing the positions of the torch, object, lens and image, and to draw or describe the image they get as accurately as possible. They should include details such as size, sharpness and which way up it is. (It will be upside-down.)

ASSESSMENT
Ask the groups to share their diagrams or descriptions in the Plenary session, so that other children can assess how clearly they show the results.

PLENARY
Ask the children to draw conclusions about the effects that convex and concave lenses have on an image on a screen. (Convex lenses make the image smaller, concave lenses make it bigger.) *What does this tell us about the way the lenses affect the beam of light?* (Convex lenses make the beams of light converge or squash together, concave lenses make them diverge or spread out.)

OUTCOMES
● Recognise the ways that light rays are changed by convex or concave lenses.
● Know that a convex lens can be used to make an image on a screen.
● Can decide on an appropriate way to obtain and record investigation results.

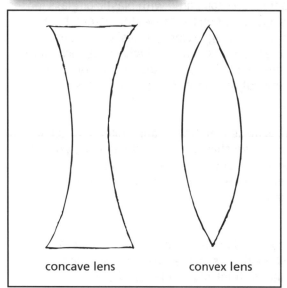

concave lens   convex lens

ENRICHMENT
Lesson 14 Using lenses

Objective
● To know that lenses have a range of applications.

RESOURCES
Books about optical instruments; real optical instruments (as many as possible); microscope slides and eye-droppers; water.

MAIN ACTIVITY
Study a range of optical instruments, using secondary sources and, if possible, real instruments such as a magnifying glass, binoculars, a camera, an overhead projector, a slide projector, a microscope, a periscope or an auriscope. Decide with the children, what each instrument is for – for example, enlarging very small or very distant objects, or making an image on a screen. Try to identify where the lenses in each instrument are. Each child can make a 'water drop microscope' by placing a small drop of water on a microscope slide, then looking through the drop, at small objects, held just

underneath it. They should then draw what they observed.

ASSESSMENT
In the Plenary ask children to feedback on what they learned about a particular optical instrument? Can they explain what it does and how it works?

PLENARY
Sum up some of the children's findings about optical instruments. Decide what type of image each instrument produces: *Is it larger, smaller, the right way up, upside-down?* Discuss some of the less familiar places where lenses can be found, such as endoscopes (for internal examinations), photocopiers, and lighthouses (where a lens is used to produce a narrow beam of light).

OUTCOME
- Can describe the uses of lenses in a range of optical instruments.

Differentiation
Support children by asking them identify the use of some of the instruments and make drawings of objects seen with and without each instrument.
Extend children by asking them to find out about an inventor of one optical instrument – for example, Zacharias Janssen (invented the compound microscope), Galileo (invented the refracting telescope), Kepler (improved Galileo's design) or Daguerre (invented the early camera).

ENRICHMENT
Lesson 15 ▸ Using a microscope

Objectives
- To know how to use a microscope correctly

Vocabulary
microscope, objective lens, focusing wheel, eyepiece, slide, sample, stage

RESOURCES
Starter: OHP showing any image; microscope and slides. There are many types of microscope, some with their own light sources and others with mirrors that must be positioned to reflect light through the hole in the stage and through the sample on the slide. Ensure you are familiar with the your microscope before trying to demonstrate it to the children.
Main activity: Photocopiable page 186; (also 'Using a microscope' (red) available on the CD-ROM)
Group activity: Class set of microscopes and slides; old newspapers, magazines or fabric; sticky tape.

STARTER
Demonstrate the idea of focus using a OHP and transparency with any image. Show the children a focused image and unfocused image. Ask them how the two images are different. Show them how the OHP is focused. Explain that having the lens in the correct place is important to have a clear image.

Show the children a microscope, photocopiable page 186 or the interactive activity from the CD-ROM and talk through the main parts. Explain that the 'stage' is where the object you want to look at goes, the 'objective lens' is nearest the object, the 'eyepiece' is where you look through and that the 'focusing wheel' is used to move the lens (or stage) to obtain a sharp image. Explain that objects that you look at, through a microscope, should be placed on a slide and that a slide is a piece of glass with the sample on. A simple slide can be prepared with a hair or piece of newspaper stuck down with sticky tape. Normally, a thin piece of glass, called a 'cover slip', is used to hold the sample flat and protect it and the objective lens. The children should then complete page 187 from memory.

MAIN ACTIVITY
Demonstrate using a microscope. Place the slide on the stage and position the smallest magnification lens. Whilst watching the lens and stage position (not looking through lens), move lens and stage as close as possible, using the focusing wheel. Look through the lens and move the focusing wheel to separate the stage and lens to obtain a sharp image. If the microscope has other lenses you can repeat in order to view more detailed images.

Differentiation
Less dexterous learners will need assistance in terms of the fine motor skill needed to make the slides. They could look through the microscope at prepared slides and draw what they see.

For more confident learners, a forensic science activity could be set up with the children having to identify the sample of thread or fabric from a crime scene, e.g. 'The headteacher's keys are missing', with those taken from key suspects clothing.

GROUP ACTIVITY

The children can prepare their own slides using newspaper or fabric pieces of various colours. They should be able to see the four colour dots that an image consists of, in the newspaper, or the pieces of cotton thread or fabric edges.

ASSESSMENT

Can the children explain the idea of focus? Can the children explain the stages of setting up a microscope?

PLENARY

Discuss the types of objects that you could view using a microscope. Tell the children that the scientist, Robert Hooke, developed the microscope in order to look at the parts of a plant and that he was the first person to use a microscope to view cells.

OUTCOME

The pupils can successfully use a microscope to view small details.

ENRICHMENT
Lesson 16 ◗ Sunlight

Objective
● To know that sunlight is made from a range of different-coloured light rays.

RESOURCES

Main activity: A prism; a torch or ray box; a white cardboard screen.
Group activities: 1 For each child: card; string; scissors; colouring pencils.
2 For each group: straight-sided glasses; water; milk; teaspoons; torches.

PREPARATION

Practise using a prism to obtain a spectrum. You could use a torch, and mark out the positions you need for the torch and prism which avoids the need to book a sunny day! It is possible to produce a spectrum using a light beam and a glass of water, but this is extremely unreliable. Make sure that the lighting can be dimmed for Group activity 2 (see Preparation in Lesson 12, Bending light). You may wish to provide circles of card, marked into seven equal sections, to help the children make spinners.

BACKGROUND

White light is often said to be made up of seven colours: the bands which are visible in a rainbow. These colours correspond to different wavelengths of light. Sunlight actually forms a continuous spectrum of wavelengths, changing gradually from red, yellow and blue through to violet, but we only give names to the colours we can recognise easily. Some scientists prefer to say that there are only six distinct colours (there is no true 'indigo' band). Each colour has a slightly different wavelength and so is affected differently when passed through transparent materials such as glass or water. All light waves slow down when they travel through glass but red light slows down less than blue light, so is deviated or bent less. Red light is also scattered less than blue light by particles in the atmosphere (see Plenary session).

glass

refracted beam of light

air

original beam of light

The left-hand side of the light beam enters the glass first and is slowed down, causing the beam to change direction – like a car when one wheel goes off the road onto grass.

STARTER

What colour is light? Discuss situations where coloured lights are used, then ask: *What colour is sunlight?* The children will probably suggest that sunlight has no

Vocabulary
prism, spectrum, scatter,
refracted, deviated

colour, but that the sun itself looks yellow. Explain that when light does not seem to have any colour, we call it 'white light'. Tell the children that you are going to show them an experiment to find out whether there are really any colours in sunlight.

MAIN ACTIVITY

Demonstrate how to use a prism to split a beam of bright sunlight (or a torch beam) into the 'seven colours of the rainbow'. Display a large diagram on the board (see illustration) to help the children work out which colour has changed direction – in other words, which colour is closest to the path the light ray would have taken if the prism had not been in the way. Red light changes direction (is deviated) the least; violet light is deviated the most.

Ask the children to invent a mnemonic to help them remember the order of the colours in the spectrum. ('Richard Of York Gave Battle In Vain' is a traditional one that may not be very memorable to children today.)

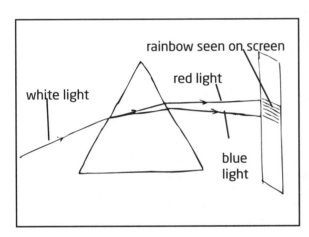

GROUP ACTIVITIES

1 Ask the children to make card spinners divided into seven equal sections (they need to be approximately 51° per section). Ask them to colour each section in a different colour from the rainbow and then put a pencil or loop of string through the centre and spin it. *What colour do you see?* The spinner should look a whitish grey while spinning - thus demonstrating that white light can be made up from a mixture of seven different colours.
2 The children can make a model sky. In the sky, particles of dust and moisture act as minute prisms to scatter the light. This can be modelled using a glass of water and a torch in a darkened room. They should add half a teaspoon of milk to the water. A torch shone at the front of the glass reflects back with a bluish-grey colour, because the blue light is scattered back to us while the red light passes through. A torch viewed through the glass of milky water looks yellowish, like the sun in the daytime. Adding one more teaspoon of milk means the light has to shine through more particles (like the sun shining through a thicker layer of the atmosphere when it is low on the horizon at dawn or dusk). The torch will look pinkish when viewed through the glass, just as the sun does at dawn or dusk. This is because only the red light reaches us: the blue light has been scattered so far that we cannot see it.

ASSESSMENT

Can they predict what they would see if they added more red or more blue to their spinners?

Differentiation
Group activity 1
Extend children by asking them to discuss what might happen if split light from the first prism were shone through a second prism. *Would it matter which way round the second prism was?* (If the second prism were the same way round as the first, it would spread the light further; if it were the opposite way round, the colours would recombine to make white light.)
Group activity 2
All the children should be able to participate in this activity.

PLENARY

Check that all the children know that white light, such as sunlight, is made up from a mixture of colours. Remind them of what happened when light was shone through a prism, and ask them to suggest why we sometimes see rainbows. (Rainbows happen when it is sunny and has been raining, so the bright sunlight is passing through water droplets in the air.) Lead them to the idea that the droplets of water are acting like a prism, splitting the sunlight into its different colours. Link this to the action of lenses (see Lesson 3 ,The eye). Explain that sometimes inexpensive lenses can act like prisms, giving bands of different colours around the edge of the image.

Discuss why a clear sky looks blue. Red and yellow light comes straight to us, from the Sun. The yellow light is brighter and stronger, so the sun looks yellow. Blue light from the sun is so scattered by the particles in the atmosphere that it comes to us from all directions, making all of the sky look blue. At sunrise and sunset, the sun's light travels through so much atmosphere to reach us, that only the red light, which is scattered less, comes through.

OUTCOMES
- Recognise the colours of the spectrum.
- Can describe what happens to sunlight when it passes through a prism.

LINKS
Art: sunrise, sunset and colour mixing.

Lesson 17 ▪ Assessment

Objectives
- To assess the children's knowledge of how shadows are formed.
- To assess the children's knowledge of how we see objects.
- To assess the children's knowledge of how light is reflected.

RESOURCES ◉
Assessment activity 1: Blank A4 paper; pencils; equipment from the experiments with light, in this unit.
Assessment activity 2: Paper; pencils; photocopiable page 187 (also 'Assessment' (red) available on the CD-ROM).

STARTER
You may wish to plan these activities over two sessions, starting each lesson with a quick-fire quiz to revise specific vocabulary.

ASSESSMENT ACTIVITY 1
Ask the children, in groups, to plan an experiment to show how they could make the same-sized shadow with a football and a tennis ball. Do not give out any apparatus at this stage, but let them view what is available. Explain that they will try out their ideas later on, and will be given all the equipment that they have used, to experiment with light.

LOOKING FOR LEVELS
Most children will be able to describe how to make a shadow but some may not be able to describe how they can change a shadow's size. Some children will be able to plan a suitable experiment and explain how they think it will work in terms of the blocking of the light.

ASSESSMENT ACTIVITY 2
Give each child a copy of page 187, to complete individually. You could mark the test yourself or with the class, using answers to promote discussion.

ANSWERS
1.(1 mark for each line.)
2a. Arrow from light to cat to girl's eye (3 marks, -1 for not straight lines, -1 for each arrow with no direction or wrong direction). 2b. Arrow from Sun to car to boy's eye (3 marks, -1 for not straight lines, -1 for each arrow with no direction or wrong direction). 3. Reflection (1 mark). 4. 30° (1 mark). 5. Cooking foil, polished wood, painted wall, freshly cut wood (2 marks, -1 for each error). (Total possible marks = 12.)

LOOKING FOR LEVELS
All the children should gain 5 marks. Many will gain 7 or 8 marks and some may gain 10 marks or more.

PLENARY
Try out the children's plans from Assessment activity 1. In order to create similar-sized shadows, the tennis ball will need to be placed nearer the light source than the football. Relate the findings of the experiment to solar and lunar eclipses (see Enrichment chapter, Lesson 2, Eclipse of the Sun).

Shadows

1. These four diagrams show the shadow from a stick in the ground at different times. Match each shadow to one of the four times listed underneath.

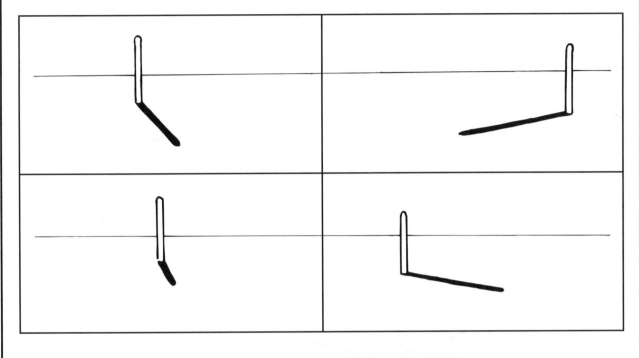

4.00pm   12 noon   7.00am   7.00pm

2. Where is the Sun in the sky when it makes a long shadow?

_____

3. Where is the Sun in the sky when it makes a short shadow?

_____

4. How does the length of your shadow change during the day?

_____

_____

5. Does the time of year make a difference to your shadow?

_____

_____

Illustrations © Tony O'Donnell © Sarah Wimperis

PHOTOCOPIABLE

The eye

◾ Cut out the outline of an eye below and stick it in your book.

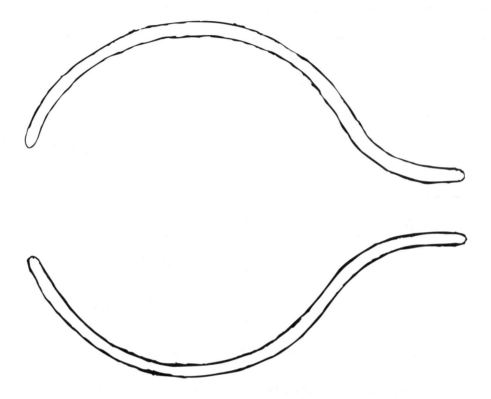

◾ Complete the drawing to show the following features:

cornea   iris   lens   pupil   eyelids

eyelashes   muscles holding the eye in place

◾ Label your diagram correctly.

◾ SCHOLASTIC

Illustrations © Tony O'Donnell © Sarah Wimperis

How we see things

◧ Draw arrows on each diagram to show how the person marked X sees the object(s) in each picture.

Illustrations © Tony O'Donnell © Sarah Wimperis

PHOTOCOPIABLE

Reflected light

Place the mirror here.

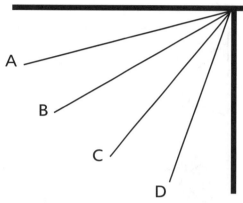

Shine a light along each line.

Mark where light reflects from the mirror here.

■ Measure the angle of each line. Then measure the angle of each ray of reflected light, from the centre line. Record the angle measurements in this table.

Line	Angle of line (degrees)	Angle of reflected light (degrees)
A		
B		
C		
D		

What can you see from your table of results?

_____

_____

■SCHOLASTIC

Investigating lenses

You will need: a torch or ray box, a convex lens, a concave lens, a cardboard screen, a ruler, paper, scissors, adhesive tape, a hole punch.

1. Set up the cardboard screen at one side of your working area.

2. Make a paper cover for the front of your torch:

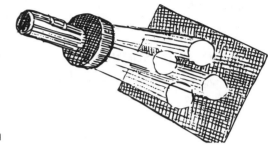

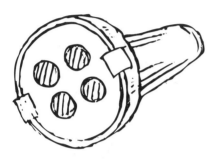

3. Put the torch about 40cm from the screen. Shine it at the middle of the screen. Raise the torch up on books if necessary. Look carefully at the image.

4. Find out what happens if you place the convex lens or the concave lens just in front of the torch.

Questions

1. Describe how the image changes when the lenses are used. Is the change the same for each type of lens?

_____

_____

2. What could you measure to show that the image really has changed?

_____

_____

3. What is the best way of presenting your results to other people?

_____

_____

4. For each type of lens, describe what happens to the image if you move the lens towards the screen (away from the torch).

_____

_____

Using a microscope

■ Label the microscope correctly using the words below:

eyepiece	focusing wheel	objective lens
slide	sample	stage

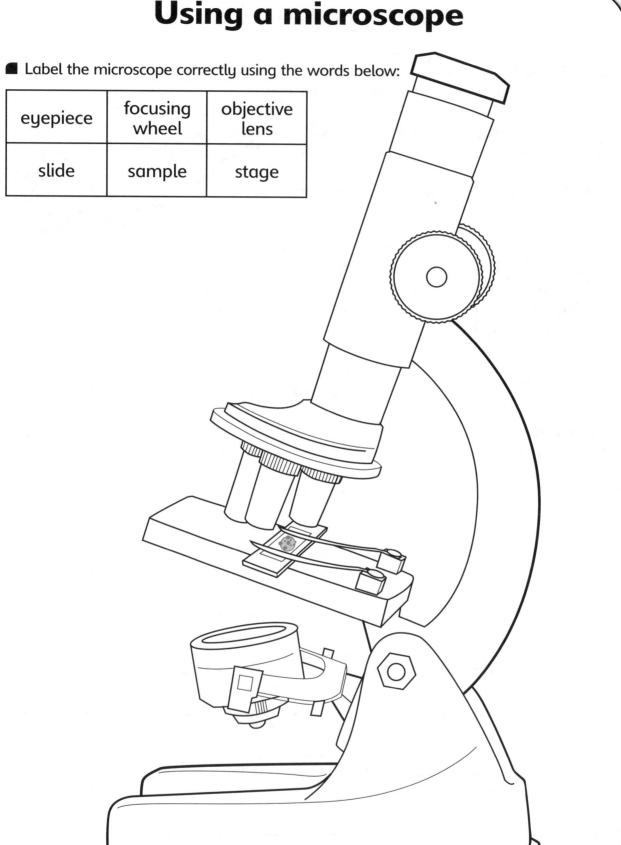

Assessment

1. Draw lines on the diagram to show where the shadow of the ball would be.

2. Draw arrows to show how the object is seen in each picture.

a.

b.

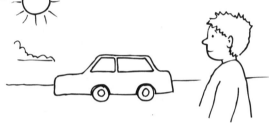

3. Cross out the word in this sentence that is wrong:

When you look in a mirror, you see your own **shadow/reflection**.

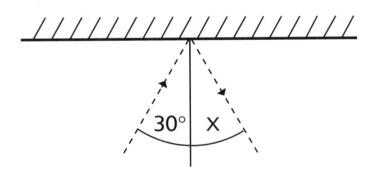

30° X

4. What is the value of X?

5. Re-write the following in order from the most reflective to the dullest:

Polished wood, freshly cut wood, cooking foil, painted wall.

_____, _____, _____, _____,

Illustrations © Tony O'Donnell © Sarah Wimperis

CHAPTER 8 Changing circuits

Lesson	Objectives	Main activity	Group activities	Plenary	Outcomes
Lesson 1 Circuits and bulbs	• To find out how the number of batteries affects the brightness of a bulb.	Demonstrate how the brightness of a bulb depends on the amount of energy from the batteries in the circuit.	Build circuits with varying numbers of batteries and bulbs or motors to observe how the circuit is affected.	Review group work. Discuss power requirements for stronger light sources.	• Can interpret diagrams to set up electrical circuits. • Can make and record observations and analyse results. • Know that more batteries make a bulb brighter or a motor faster.
Lesson 2 Bulbs in a circuit	• To know that having more bulbs in a circuit makes a light dimmer.	The children build circuits with the same number of batteries but different numbers of bulbs, and compare the brightness.		Discuss resistance and its effect on a circuit: the more bulbs, the greater the resistance.	• Know that including more bulbs in a circuit makes all the bulbs dimmer, because they reduce the flow of electricity around the circuit.
Lesson 3 Types of switches	• To know that switches can be placed between parts of a circuit to provide alternative routes for the current to pass along.	Construct circuits and investigate how the switches are arranged to operate the components in each circuit.		Discuss real-life applications of these circuits for the safe or easy use of an appliance.	• Know that different switches can be used to operate a circuit in different ways.
Lesson 4 Switches	• To look at types of switch that could operate a burglar alarm.	Look at diagrams of different types of switch and discuss how they operate.	Build a switch and then write about how it works and where it could be used.	Look at how the switches made during the Group activity could be used in a burglar alarm.	• Can make a simple switch. • Can consider real-life applications of different switches.
Lesson 5 Circuit diagrams	• To learn that electrical circuits and components can be represented by conventional symbols.	Introduce circuit symbols and how they are used to build up a circuit diagram.	Convert circuit drawings into circuit diagrams using conventional symbols. Build real circuits based on circuit diagrams provided.	Consider how specifications for components can be represented in circuit diagrams.	• Know the conventional symbols for circuit components and understand why they are used. • Can draw circuits using symbols. • Can build circuits from diagrams.
Lesson 6 Real-life circuits	• To explain the construction of real-life circuits using their current knowledge of electrical circuits..	Introduce circuit symbols and how they are used to build up a circuit diagram.	The children use secondary sources to prepare a short presentation on electrical safety or energy saving.	Consider how specifications for components can be represented in circuit diagrams.	• Understand how circuits can be used for a range of purposes. • Can explain the uses of different circuit components. • Can describe the dangers associated with electricity. • Can describe how the waste of electrical energy can be reduced.
Enrichment Lesson 7 Burglar alarms	• To design and build a switch which is suitable for an alarm.	Children design and build a switch for use in a burglar alarm.		Use the switches in a circuit. Discuss their operation.	• Can apply knowledge of electric circuits in a practical context.
Enrichment Lesson 8 Electrical dangers	• To recognise dangers associated with electricity. • To know what a 'short circuit' is and why it can be dangerous.	Demonstrate a short circuit. Explain the dangers of short circuits.	Look at a picture of some unsafe uses of electricity. Explain the cause of each danger and its likely effects.	Discuss basic procedures for electrical safety.	• Know how a short circuit occurs. • Know about the dangers associated with a short circuit. • Can compile a list of safe electrical practices.
Enrichment Lesson 9 Testing wires	• To know that the amount of electricity flowing in a circuit is related to the total resistance in the circuit.	Demonstrate that the brightness of a bulb changes when different lengths or types of wire are used.	Observe the effect of using different lengths of wire in a circuit, on a motor's speed of rotation. Record results in a table, draw a graph and analyse the results. Answer questions on a similar experiment.	Reinforce the link between resistance and current.	• Know how the length of a wire affects the electricity flowing in a circuit. • Can carry out an investigation and analyse the results.

Lesson	Objectives	Main activity	Group activities	Plenary	Outcomes
Enrichment Lesson 10 Resistance	• To know that the current in a circuit depends on resistance. • To know that a variable resistor can be used to control the amount of electricity flowing in a circuit.		The children use secondary sources to find out about dimmer switches, volume and speed controllers. Make a display with pictures and descriptions.	Review the children's work and discuss examples of switches and controllers.	• Can describe how a variable resistor affects the flow of electricity through a circuit.

Assessment	Objectives	Activity 1	Activity 2
Lesson 11	• To assess the children's knowledge of ways that a circuit can be changed and the effect that these changes have on components. • To assess the children's ability to recognise circuit symbols and interpret circuit diagrams in order to build circuits. • To assess the children's knowledge that the relative brightness of a bulb is related to the amount of current in the circuit.	Complete a short written test to examine their knowledge of how an electrical current can be varied and how this affects the components in a circuit.	Build four simple circuits and compare the relative brightness of the bulbs. Give reasons for the differences in brightness.

SC1 SCIENTIFIC ENQUIRY

Does the length of a conductor affect the speed of a motor?

LEARNING OBJECTIVES AND OUTCOMES
- Select lengths.
- Build a circuit.
- Measure time taken to lift an object.
- Record results and plot a graph.
- Comment on observations.
- Interpret observations.

ACTIVITY
The children select wire of different lengths. They build a circuit (that includes the test wire) to lift a small mass. Changing the length of wire will result in different times for the mass to be lifted. The children should try to explain why the brightness has changed

LESSON LINKS
This Sc1 activity forms an integral part of Lesson 10, Resistance.

Lesson 1 ▪ Circuits and bulbs

Objective
- To find out how the number of batteries affects the brightness of a bulb.

Vocabulary
battery, flat (battery), bulb, motor, current, circuit, component, flow, potential difference.

RESOURCES 💿
Main activity: A two-cell torch with batteries; one flat battery; two good batteries; a bulb in a holder; two connecting wires.
Group activity: Photocopiable page 201 (also 'Circuits and bulbs' (red) available on the CD-ROM); 15 batteries; six switches; three bulbs (2.5V); three motors (3–4V).

BACKGROUND
For an electric current to flow around a circuit, an electrical supply must be connected within it. Batteries can be used to supply the energy to make an electric current flow. A battery has a 'potential difference' – a difference in electrical energy between the two ends, due to the chemicals inside.

Different chemicals result in higher or lower potential differences, which results in the different voltages labelled on the batteries. Layers of these chemicals can also be placed within a single battery to build up a higher potential difference. If the battery is placed in a circuit, free charged particles in the wire (known as 'electrons') will move around the circuit because of the potential difference. This is the electric current. If a greater number of batteries are used, there is a greater potential difference across them all together, and so a greater current is produced. The potential difference is like a water pump of a fountain: the greater the power of the pump, the faster the water moves around the pipes, and so the greater the height of the fountain.

An electric current can cause different effects, one of which is heating as the current passes through a wire or other conducting material. In a narrow wire, where the electrons have more difficulty passing through (as in a light bulb) this heating effect is greatly increased. Just as a narrow pipe restricts the flow of water likewise, the narrow wire in a bulb resists the electric current. The wire will glow when a sufficiently high current goes through it. The higher the current, the greater the heating effect and hence the more

Differentiation
Group children who need support together and give them the easiest circuits to build. These circuits should not be taken apart once they have been put together. Children with writing difficulties could have a comment started on the sheet for them to complete. The start of a sentence for the concluding paragraph could be particularly useful, for example: In our experiments, we have found out that having _____ batteries makes the bulbs _____. Extend children by asking them to think about the possible effects of having an even greater number of batteries for a single bulb, and what might happen to the wires and the bulb. (Trying this will create enough heat in the filament of the bulb to cause it to melt, 'blowing' the bulb. Can the children think of any further dangers?)

intense the glow. For a low current, a bulb may be seen to glow red hot, while for a greater current it will glow white hot. Thus more batteries means a greater current and a brighter bulb.

Too great a current will 'blow' the bulb, as the amount of electricity flowing through the filament causes a heating effect greater than the filament can take. In effect, you are overloading the filament with passing electrons.

Conversely, having more components (such as bulbs) in a circuit, that use the electric current from a fixed number of batteries, causes a reduction in the rate of flow of electricity (the current). This is due to the wire in each bulb resisting the flow of electricity. If the current is reduced due to increased resistance from additional bulbs, the brightness of each bulb is reduced.

STARTER
Ask the children how they would get a bulb to light up and what equipment they would need. They should be able to list all the appropriate components and tell you that a complete circuit is needed. Ask them what each component of the circuit is for.

MAIN ACTIVITY
Show the children the torch and, if possible, the connections inside. Put in the batteries, making sure that one of the batteries is flat. Shine the torch towards the pupils: it should have a dim light. The children should notice this, but prompt them if necessary. *How could the light be improved?* (By changing the batteries to two good batteries.) Demonstrate this, then remove the batteries and use them to light the bulb in a simple circuit. *What does it mean if a battery is 'flat'?* (It has insufficient energy to make the electricity flow around the circuit.) Explain that with only one good battery in the torch, a small electric current passes through the bulb; two good batteries provide a greater push of energy, giving a higher current, and hence a brighter bulb.

GROUP ACTIVITY
Divide the class into six groups. Give each group a tray containing the apparatus shown on photocopiable page 201. Give each child or group a copy of page 201. Each group should set up the circuits described on the sheet. Ask the children to write a comment under each diagram on the sheet to describe what happens in the circuit. At the end of their experiments, they should make a general comment about what their experiments showed.

ASSESSMENT
Check whether all the children have built their circuits in the same way? Are the components placed in the same order? Does this make a difference? Can the children recognise how the changes they make in their circuits affect the components?

PLENARY
Check the groups' answers on the sheet. They should have found that the higher the battery-to-bulb ratio, the brighter the bulb. Discuss the battery requirements for bigger torches (as used by security guards) and car headlamps. *What power do table lamps need?* (Mains, so 230V.) *How about the lights in concert halls, or the floodlights in football grounds?*

OUTCOMES
● Can interpret diagrams to set up electrical circuits.
● Can make and record observations and analyse results.
● Know that more batteries make a bulb brighter or a motor faster.

Lesson 2 ▪ Bulbs in a circuit

RESOURCES
Batteries; bulbs; connecting wires.

MAIN ACTIVITY
Ask the children to set up circuits with the same number of batteries, but different numbers of bulbs, and to observe whether they become brighter or dimmer. Each child should make and draw two circuits, recording the difference between them and the effect on the bulb(s).

ASSESSMENT
Use the work from the Main activity to assess which children have observed the change in brightness as more bulbs are added to the circuit.

PLENARY
Discuss how the bulbs restrict the flow of electricity through the circuit: the more bulbs there are, the more the flow is restricted and so the less bright each bulb is. Particular circuits to comment on are: one bulb and two batteries; two bulbs and two batteries; two bulbs and four batteries. Where the ratio of bulbs to batteries is relatively low, the bulbs will be brighter.

Where the ratios can be simplified to the same value, the bulbs will be equally bright

Differentiation
Support children by asking them to compare the simplest circuits.

Extend children by asking them to comment on how the energy from the batteries is being used, and compare circuits with matching battery-to-bulb ratios (such as 2:1 and 4:2). They should note that the bulbs are equally bright, as there is the same amount of energy per bulb.

OUTCOME
● Know that including more bulbs in a circuit makes all the bulbs dimmer, because they reduce the flow of electricity around the circuit.

Lesson 3 ▪ Types of switches

Objective
● To know that switches can be placed between parts of a circuit to provide alternative routes for the current to pass along.

RESOURCES
Batteries; bulbs; motors; push switches; two-way switches; rocker switches; wires.

MAIN ACTIVITY
Draw the four circuits shown below on a board or flipchart. Ask the children to construct two of them (see Differentiation) and investigate how the switches are arranged to make the components, in the circuit, operate. Circuit A operates with the rocker switch when it is not pressed, but operates with the push switch only when it is pressed. In circuit B, either switch can be pressed. Circuit C requires both switches to be pressed. Circuit D allows the circuit to be operated from either switch.

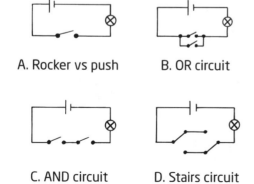

A. Rocker vs push   B. OR circuit

C. AND circuit   D. Stairs circuit

ASSESSMENT
Can the children explain how the switches make the circuits work?

PLENARY
Discuss real-life applications of these circuits for the safe/ easy use of an appliance (A. Push switch – keyboards, remote controls, igniters for gas cookers. Rocker switch – TV on/off, light switches, torch switches. B. For an alarm that can be set off from different places. C. Used where the 'On' switch turns on a machine, only if another switch is activated by a safety device, such as a guard being in place.

D. Used on stairs and in bedrooms where there is a light switch by a door and bed.)

OUTCOME
● Know that different switches can be used to operate a circuit in different ways.

Differentiation
Let children who need support make circuits A and B. Extend children by asking them to make circuits C and D.

Lesson 4 ▸Switches

Objective
● To look at types of switch that could operate a burglar alarm.

Vocabulary
push switch, circuit

RESOURCES 💿
Group activities: Photocopiable page 202 (also 'Switches' (red) available on the CD-ROM); batteries; bulbs; connecting wires; materials for making switches (see photocopiable page 202).

BACKGROUND
A switch has a very important role in a circuit. It provides an easy way of breaking and completing a circuit. Depending on its construction, the switch may only operate for the time that it is pressed or may lock into position until reset.

STARTER
Discuss the difference between the switches which the children would usually find in circuits and a switch that is used for turning on a computer. A computer switch locks into position, whereas the standard 'push switch', in a circuit, only completes the circuit while it is being pressed. Tell the children that they are going to make some switches that work in different ways.

MAIN ACTIVITY
Distribute enough copies of photocopiable page 202, so that every children can see a copy. Go through each switch illustrated and discuss how they might operate. Remind the children that there must be a place to connect a switch within a circuit, with a gap that can be opened and closed, in order to complete and break the circuit.

GROUP ACTIVITY
The children should make one of the switches from the factfile and then write about how it operates and where they could put it in an alarm or another situation.

ASSESSMENT
Can the children build the switch and make it operate within a circuit? Can they give a satisfactory explanation of how the switch completes and breaks a circuit?

PLENARY
Prepare for Lesson 7 by discussing how some of the switches which the children have built, could be used in a burglar alarm (for example, trip wires or alarms on window or door catches).

OUTCOMES
● Can make a simple switch.
● Can consider real-life applications of different switches.

LINKS
PSHE: security at home and school.
Technology: technological projects.

Differentiation
Group activity
You may want to organise the children into mixed ability groups for this activity.

Lesson 5 ▪ Circuit diagrams

Vocabulary
symbol, circuit diagram, component.

RESOURCES
Main activity: A flipchart and marker pen.
Group activities: 1 One copy per child of photocopiable page 203 (also 'Circuit diagrams' (red) available on the CD-ROM); plain paper; pencils; rulers; rubbers. **2** A tray containing bulbs, motors, batteries, wires and switches for each group, photocopiable page 203.
ICT link: 'Circuit diagrams' interactive activity, from the CD-ROM.

PREPARATION
Copy the following circuit symbols (or draw easier or more complex ones, according to the children's ability) onto the flipchart.

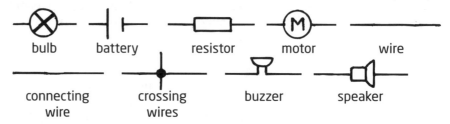

bulb   battery   resistor   motor   wire

connecting wire   crossing wires   buzzer   speaker

BACKGROUND
Scientists require quick methods of recording that leave them time to focus on their experiments. They also need other scientists to understand the work they have done and want technicians to build the circuits that they have designed. To achieve all of this, they use a system of internationally recognised symbols for component parts of a circuit, when drawing electrical circuit diagrams. Each component has a simple symbol that (in most cases!) is difficult to mistake for any other. The common symbols, which children at Key Stage 2/Primary 4–7 need to know, are shown above.

Another convention is that all wires are drawn as straight lines and, where possible, circuits are drawn in rectangular shape. Where wires cross over, to avoid confusing crossing points with joins, the crossing points are drawn as bridges or 'hops' of one wire over another (see diagram above).

STARTER
Select a child and show him or her the name of a component used in an electrical circuit, such as 'battery'. Ask the child to represent that component by drawing it on the flipchart, so that the rest of the class can guess what it is. When a child guesses the component correctly, he or she can be given the name of another component to draw. Carry on for all the components shown above. If the children offer the name of a component that has already been drawn, vary the activity by whispering to the child that they should draw a different type of the same component (for example, an upright square battery rather than a cylinder on its side-). Explain that it is difficult for a scientist to draw components in a way that everybody understands, particularly as there are so many types of motor, bulb, switch and so on. So instead, scientists have come up with a system of symbols.

MAIN ACTIVITY
Using the pictures that the children have drawn, write the name of each component and draw its symbol next to the children's sketches. Now ask a child to come out and draw a circuit containing a battery and a bulb. It is

likely that the child will draw the symbols for these components except for the wires which they may draw as curves. If this is the case then explain that both for neatness and for scientific convention, circuits should be drawn as rectangles.

GROUP ACTIVITIES

1 Give each child a copy of photocopiable page 203. Ask the children to convert the drawings into circuit diagrams, using the correct symbols.

2 Ask the children to convert the circuit drawings on photocopiable page 203 into real circuits, using the components provided.

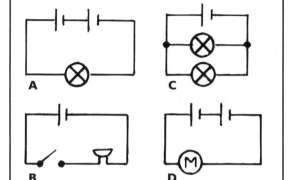

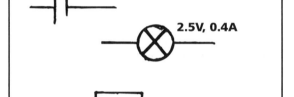

ICT LINK

Children can use the 'Circuit diagrams' interactive to make circuits diagrams.

ASSESSMENT

Note whether the children have completed the sheet correctly.

PLENARY

Show the children a 9V square battery and the more common 1.5V cylindrical battery. *How could scientists show the difference between these on a circuit diagram?* The simple solution is to write the voltage number just above the battery symbol. Specifications for other components (see examples on the right) can also be noted on circuit diagrams.

OUTCOMES

● Know the conventional symbols for circuit components and understand why they are used.
● Can draw circuits using symbols.
● Can build circuits from diagrams.

Lesson 6 ▪ Real-life circuits

Objective
● To explain the construction of real-life circuits using their current knowledge of electrical circuits.

RESOURCES

Photocopiable page 204 (also 'Real-life circuits' (red), available on the CD-ROM) copied onto A3 paper or an OHT; other pictures of real-life circuits (from secondary sources); leaflets about energy saving and electrical dangers.

MAIN ACTIVITY

Discuss the real-life circuits on page 204 (and any other real-life circuit diagrams you have): *What is the power source? What voltage does it have? Where does the current flow? What components have resistance? Why is this resistance useful? How might these components be short-circuited? What safety features does the circuit have?*

Give each group a leaflet on energy saving or electrical safety and ask them to organise a short presentation (perhaps a talk or a play) based on the information.

Differentiation
Support children by highlighting or enlarging part of the circuit diagram to emphasise a few familiar components.

ASSESSMENT

Can the children identify the symbols for 'classroom' components in the car circuit? Do they understand the need for symbol conventions?

PLENARY
The children present their ideas. Discuss any additional or important points as a class.

OUTCOMES
● Understand how circuits can be used for a range of purposes.
● Can explain the uses of different circuit components.
● Can describe the dangers associated with electricity.
● Can describe how the waste of electrical energy can be reduced.

ENRICHMENT
Lesson 7 ▪ Burglar alarms

Objective
● To design and build a switch suitable for an alarm.

RESOURCES
Batteries; bulbs; buzzers; wires; the children's choice of materials for switches.

MAIN ACTIVITY
The children should discuss, design and build their own switch for use in a burglar alarm circuit (for example, a 'pressure pad' design where two pieces of aluminium foil become connected when weight is applied). This may take a number of lessons, and the children may wish to build additional items such as model doors or windows. Remind them that a switch must complete and break a circuit. Once built, insert switches into a simple buzzer circuit to check that they are functioning properly.

ASSESSMENT
Can the children build a switch that works in the way described?

Differentiation
Extend children by asking them to use magnets or more inventive ideas. They could also draw their circuit and describe its operation in writing.

PLENARY
Operate the children's switches in the circuit. Discuss their mode of operation, and where they should be placed to be effective in a burglar alarm system.

OUTCOME
● Can apply knowledge of electric circuits in a practical context.

ENRICHMENT
Lesson 8 ▪ Electrical dangers

Objective
● To recognise dangers associated with electricity.
● To know what a 'short circuit' is and why it can be dangerous.

Vocabulary
short circuit, resistance

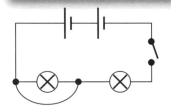

RESOURCES 💿
Main activity: Bulbs; batteries; switches; photocopiable page 205 (also 'Electrical dangers' (red) available on the CD-ROM; plain paper; pencils.

PREPARATION
Build the circuit shown on the right.

BACKGROUND
Electricity flows around a complete circuit, usually to do a useful job such as lighting a bulb or running a motor. However, electricity tends to take the easiest path through a circuit. In order to flow through the components of a circuit, the current encounters resistance due to the construction of these components. For example, it is more difficult for current to pass through the narrow wire in a bulb than through the thick wires that make up the rest of the circuit. If an alternative path, which has a lower resistance, is provided for the electricity to flow along (either deliberately or by accident) then this is the path that the current will take. It will make a 'short circuit' that

bypasses the bulb. The great problem with a short circuit is that often the resistance is so low that a very high current will pass along the wires, causing the wire to heat up to such an extent that it may cause a fire. Short circuits can be extremely dangerous.

Mains electricity plugs have a replaceable fuse inside. A fuse contains a thin piece of wire encased in a ceramic holder that is designed to melt if the current flowing through it is too great. This means that a mains short circuit will 'blow' the fuse and not damage the appliance. It is important, therefore, that the right type of fuse is fitted, so that it does not allow an unsafe level of current to flow (but also, does not blow at a normal level of current).

STARTER
Discuss the children's ideas about the safe use of electricity. Ideas should include not overloading sockets, not mixing water and electricity, not using frayed cables and not poking items into electrical sockets. This discussion should draw on their experiences of electricity at Key Stage 2/Primary 4–7.

MAIN ACTIVITY
Display the circuit you have made. The two bulbs should be lit normally. Connect the two ends of a wire to either side of one of the bulbs. Ask the children to describe what happens. The 'short-circuited' bulb, with the new wire, will be off and the other bulb will be much brighter. Ask the children to describe what has happened to the amount of electricity flowing through the two bulbs. There is no electricity flowing through the short-circuited bulb, whereas the bulb that has become brighter has more electricity flowing through it.

Prompt the children to identify a potential problem with this increase in current. *What has happened to the wire in the brighter bulb? Why is it brighter?* If necessary, explain that the higher current causes a greater heating effect. *Why is this dangerous?* (It could start a fire.) Tell the children that the extra wire that has been attached has caused a short circuit, and that short circuits are dangerous in real life because they can cause fires in the home or the workplace.

GROUP ACTIVITY
Give each child a copy of photocopiable page 205. Ask the children to identify the dangers of electricity on the sheet, and what the risk is to the people in the picture.

ASSESSMENT
Ask individuals to identify the dangers and to describe their solutions.

PLENARY
Go through the children's responses to photocopiable page 205, and discuss their ideas for remedies to the problems. In many cases, this is basic electrical safety procedure; however, some solutions may involve repair work or consulting an electrician - for example, adding extra sockets so that overloading does not occur. Adding extra sockets within the ring main of the house wiring circuit means that less current has to flow through individual wall sockets - instead, the high currents are placed on the ring main, which is designed to cope with them.

OUTCOMES
- Know how a short circuit occurs.
- Know about the dangers associated with a short circuit.
- Can compile a list of safe electrical practices.

LINKS
PSHE: safety in the home, personal responsibility.

ENRICHMENT

Lesson 9 ◾ Testing wires

Objective
● To know that the amount of electricity flowing in a circuit is related to the total resistance in the circuit.

Vocabulary
resistance, resistor, current

RESOURCES ◉
Main activity: Batteries; bulbs; 1m nichrome wire; crocodile clips; connecting wires.
Group activities: 1 Batteries; motors; 1m nichrome wire; crocodile clips; connecting wires; hoists (from construction kits); string; small hanging masses. **2** Photocopiable page 206 (also 'Testing wires' (red) available on the CD-ROM).

PREPARATION
Set up the circuit shown on the right. Use nichrome wire initially, not copper. Some initial experimentation may be required to find out what quantity of wire and batteries give the best results, for a given thickness of wire.

BACKGROUND
The amount of current in a circuit depends on how easily the electricity can flow through the wires and other components in the circuit. The factor that determines how much current flows in the circuit for a given voltage supply is called 'resistance'. The greater the resistance, the lower the current. Resistance depends on the type of material the current is flowing through, and the length and thickness of that material in the circuit. A variable resistor allows the length of a high-resistance material in the circuit to be varied.

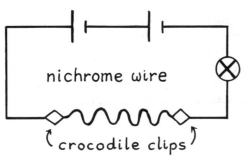

nichrome wire

crocodile clips

STARTER
Ask the class to imagine the corridor outside the classroom just as lunch starts. The corridor is full of people trying to get to one part of the school. *What do you think it would be like trying to get to lunch if the corridor were narrower? Or wider? How does being at the far end of the corridor compare with being halfway down the corridor in terms of the time it takes to get to the dining room?* Tell the children that this is similar to the situation when electricity is trying to pass along a wire. The different widths and lengths of wire are similar to the different sizes of a corridor. The ease with which you can travel through a corridor is like the ease with which electricity can pass along a wire. The factors that would cause a crush in the school corridor are like the factors that cause resistance in an electrical circuit.

MAIN ACTIVITY
Show the class a prepared circuit and demonstrate how randomly moving the connections, up and down the wire, changes how bright the bulb is. Can they suggest a more systematic method for finding out the effect of changing the amount of wire in the circuit? They should suggest comparing the brightness of the bulb for every extra 5cm or 10cm along the wire. In this way, it should be possible to prove that the more wire that is used, the dimmer the bulb will be. Ask the class to explain what is happening to the current in the circuit, based on their observations of the bulb. They should be able to say that when the bulb is dimmer, the current is reduced and should therefore deduce that the greater the length of wire used, the lower the current.

Repeat the experiment with copper wire. This time, no obvious change in brightness should be observed. *What is different about this wire?* Explain that materials which conduct electricity, have differing levels of 'resistance' and copper has a lower resistance then the first wire as it lets electricity flow through more easily. Extend this idea, with some children, explaining that materials which are insulators (non-conductors) have a high resistance.

Differentiation 💿
Support children by giving them 'Testing wires' (green) from the CD-ROM, which includes fewer different lengths of wire and asks them to complete a bar chart rather than a graph.

To extend children, give them 'Testing wires' (blue), which asks them to create a graph/chart of their choice and includes additional questions.

GROUP ACTIVITIES

1 Ask the children to investigate the effect of using different lengths of wire on the speed of rotation of a motor operating a hoist to lift a small mass on a string. They need to set up a circuit using a piece of resistance wire, connected so that results can be taken for five or six different lengths of wire (using the full length of the wire in equal steps). The time taken for the motor to lift the mass a short distance (say 10cm) should be measured each time. Encourage the children to repeat their tests in order to improve the reliability of their results. They should record the results in a table, convert them into a line graph and analyse the data to draw a conclusion.
2 Give each child a copy of page 206 for the children to complete. The answers are: 1. Circuits 1 and 2 or 3 and 4; 2a. Circuit 1; 2b. Circuit 6; 3. Circuits 2, 4, 5 and 6.

ICT LINKS 💿
Results tables and graphs could be prepared using a computer or the graphing tool, from the CD-ROM, could be used create graphs.

ASSESSMENT
Note whether the children can set up an experiment, gather and present data and form a valid conclusion about the from their results. Can they link the pattern in their data to knowledge of current and resistance?

PLENARY
Reinforce the idea that the greater the resistance in a circuit, the lower the current. Reducing the current reduces the speed of a motor or the brightness of a bulb. *Can the children think of a practical application of this knowledge?* This idea leads into Lesson 10.

OUTCOMES
● Know how the length of a wire affects the electricity flowing in a circuit.
● Can carry out an investigation and analyse the results.

ENRICHMENT
Lesson 10 ▪ Resistance

Objective
● To know that the current in a circuit depends on the resistance.
● To know that a variable resistor can be used to control the amount of electricity flowing in a circuit.

RESOURCES
A selection of pictures showing different variable resistors in use, as listed below (try homeware mail order catalogues).

MAIN ACTIVITY
Let the children look at secondary sources to see how dimmer switches, volume controls and speed controllers are used in real life. Ensure they understand that each of these is a 'variable resistor'. *How is high or low resistance created? How does it affect the appliance it is connected to?* The children should use pictures of switches, along with their descriptions of the operation, to make a small display.

PLENARY
Look at the children's work and discuss the examples of switches and controllers. Do the children understand how different amounts of resistance are used to control a circuit?

OUTCOME
● Can describe how a variable resistor affects the flow of electricity through a circuit.

Differentiation
Some children may benefit from seeing real examples of switches and controllers in action.

Lesson 11 ▪Assessment

Objectives
● To assess the children's knowledge of ways that a circuit can be changed and the effect that these changes have on components in the circuit.
● To assess the children's ability to recognise circuit symbols and interpret circuit diagrams in order to build circuits.
● To assess the children's knowledge that the relative brightness of a bulb is related to the amount of current in the circuit.

RESOURCES 💿
Photocopiable page 207 (also 'Assessment' (red) available on the CD-ROM); bulbs; batteries (bulbs and batteries must be identical) wires; paper; pencils.

STARTER
You may prefer to start with a quiz, on the vocabulary, met in this topic.

ASSESSMENT ACTIVITY 1
Give each child a copy of photocopiable page 207 to complete on their own.

ANSWERS
1. Award 2 marks for a simple circuit diagram showing a bulb, battery and switch, with the switch open. Award a further mark for a rectangular shape with straight wires. 2. Award 1 mark for a statement along the lines of: 'A greater number of particles (or a greater current) passes through the filament of the bulb when there are more batteries, and this makes the bulb brighter.' Award another mark for any comment about more energy being supplied. 3. A short circuit is where electricity passes through a wire, avoiding the component that it was meant to pass through in the circuit (1 mark). There is less resistance in the circuit (1 mark), therefore more current and so an increased risk of fire (1 mark). 4. The circuit with the thick short wire (1 mark), because it has the least resistance (1 mark). (Total possible marks = 10.)

LOOKING FOR LEVELS
All children should score at least 3 marks. Most children will achieve 5 or 6 marks. Some children will score 8 or higher.

ASSESSMENT ACTIVITY 2
Draw circuit diagrams for the following on the board or flipchart and ask the children to build them: A. 1 bulb and 1 battery; B. 2 bulbs and 1 battery; C. 1 bulb and 2 batteries; D. 2 bulbs and 2 batteries. The children should write a sentence to describe how the bulbs in circuits B, C and D compare with the bulb in circuit A and give reasons for differences.

ANSWERS
The bulbs in circuits A and D are equally bright because they have the same ratio of batteries to bulbs (or voltage to resistance). In circuit B, the bulbs are dimmer because there is greater resistance in the circuit because of the second bulb. In circuit C, the bulb is brighter because the circuit has the same resistance as in A, but the greater potential difference or electrical push from the batteries gives a higher current.

LOOKING FOR LEVELS
All children should be able to make at least three circuits. Look out for children who are attempting to connect the second battery in reverse.
   Most children will be able to say which bulb was brightest, but only give a vague explanation of why. Some children will say which bulb was the brightest, but give no reason for this other than 'It has more batteries'. Other children will give good descriptions of the flow of electricity in each of the circuits and state reasons for the differences.

PLENARY
Use the answers from these tests to promote discussion of electrical circuits, and how changing different parts of a circuit affects other components within the circuit.

Circuits and bulbs

◤ Set up each circuit as shown below. Write a sentence under each picture to describe what happens in the circuit. Try to compare it with other circuits.

◤ Can you see any pattern in the results? Can you explain this pattern? Write your answer on the back of this sheet.

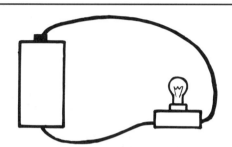

1. One battery and one bulb

_____

_____

2. Two batteries and one bulb

_____

_____

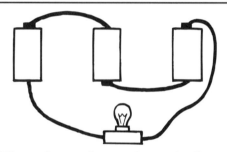

3. Three batteries and one bulb

_____

_____

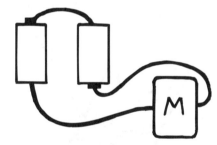

4. Two batteries and one motor

_____

_____

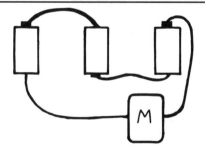

5. Three batteries and one motor

_____

_____

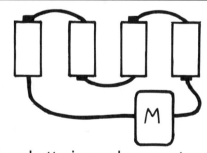

6. Four batteries and one motor

_____

_____

Illustrations © Tony O'Donnell © Sarah Wimperis

Switches

◾ How do these switches work?

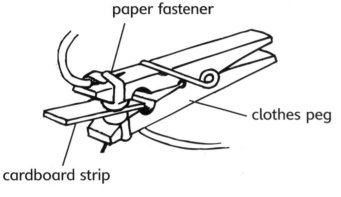

paper fastener

clothes peg

cardboard strip

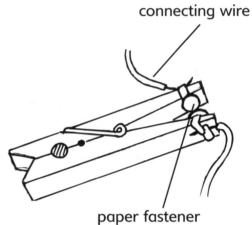

connecting wire

paper fastener

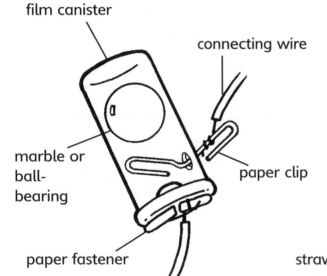

film canister

connecting wire

marble or ball-bearing

paper clip

paper fastener

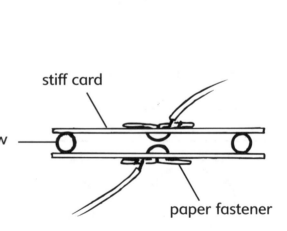

stiff card

straw

paper fastener

◾ Build this circuit to test the switches.

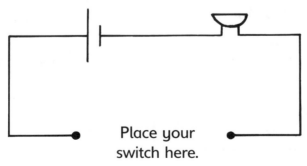

Place your switch here.

Illustrations © Tony O'Donnell © Sarah Wimperis

Circuit diagrams

◧ Use your knowledge of circuit symbols to redraw these circuit pictures as proper circuit diagrams on the right-hand side of the page. Use a pencil, ruler and rubber to make your diagrams neat and to correct any mistakes you might make.

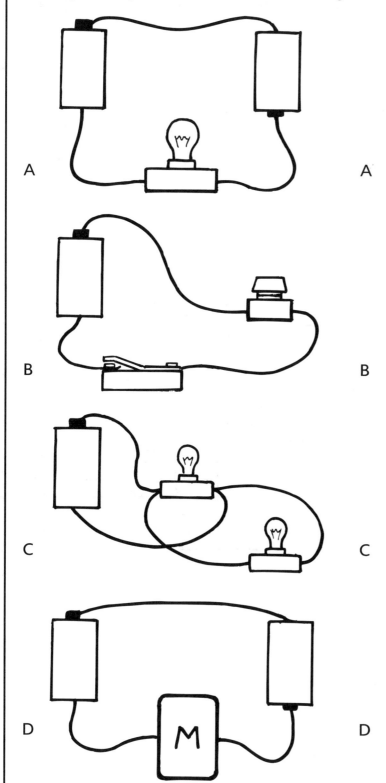

A

A

B

B

C

C

D

D

Illustrations © Tony O'Donnell © Sarah Wimperis

PHOTOCOPIABLE

Real-life circuits

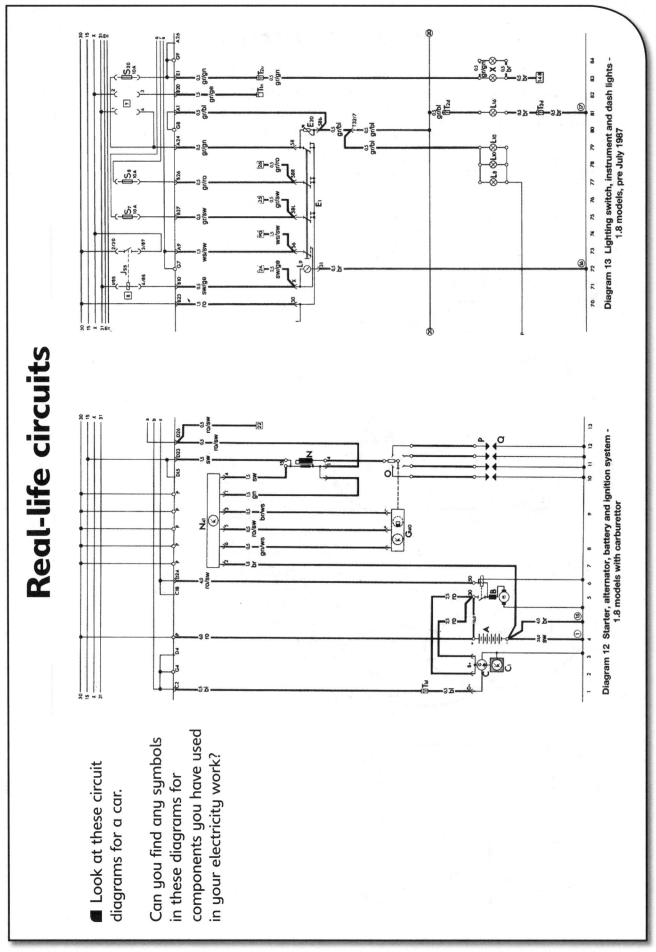

Diagram 13 Lighting switch, instrument and dash lights – 1.8 models, pre July 1987

Diagram 12 Starter, alternator, battery and ignition system – 1.8 models with carburettor

■ Look at these circuit diagrams for a car.

Can you find any symbols in these diagrams for components you have used in your electricity work?

■SCHOLASTIC

Electrical dangers

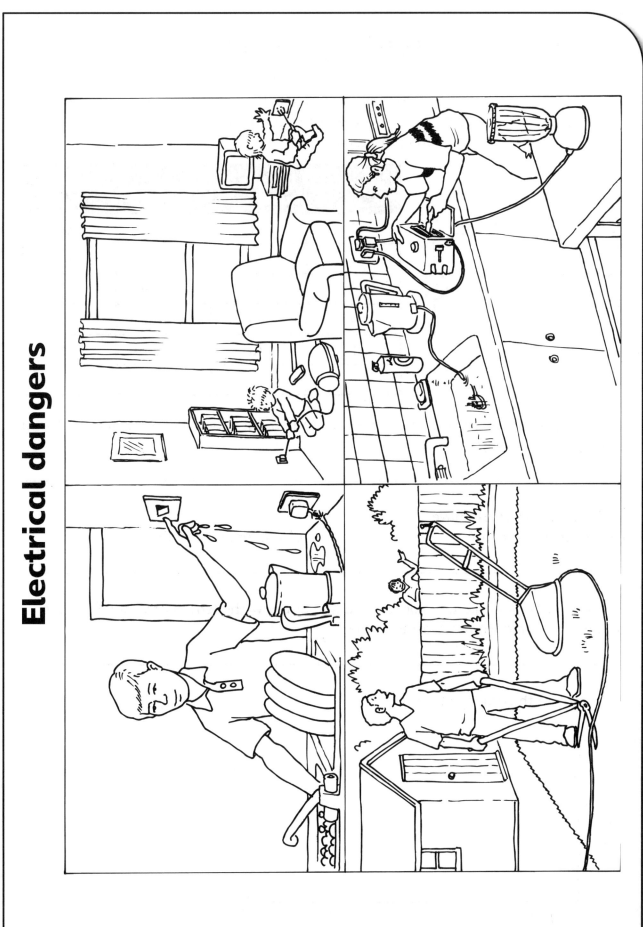

Illustrations © Tony O'Donnell © Sarah Wimperis

PHOTOCOPIABLE

Testing wires

■ Six groups in a class like yours, used the circuit shown below to test different wires by measuring the amount of electricity going around the circuit with each wire in place. Their results are shown in the table.

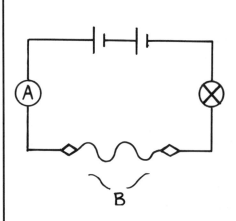

Circuit	Length of wire (cm)	Metal	Reading at A
1	10	copper	5
2	10	nichrome	4
3	20	copper	4.5
4	20	nichrome	2
5	30	nichrome	1.5
6	40	nichrome	1

1. Which pair of results could you compare to find out which metal lets the electricity through more easily?

_____

2. Which circuit would have
(a) the brightest bulb?   (b) the dimmest bulb?

_____   _____

3. Which circuits would you compare to find out how the length of wire affects the amount of electricity that passes through?

_____

4. Complete the graph below.

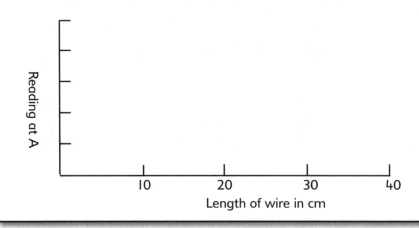

Illustrations © Tony O'Donnell © Sarah Wimperis

Assessment

1. Draw a circuit diagram (with symbols) to show a bulb, a battery and a switch connected so that the bulb will light up when the switch is pressed.

2. Explain why a bulb is brighter if it is powered by two batteries rather than one. Use what you know about electricity flowing through a wire to help you to explain this.

_____

_____

_____

_____

3. What is a 'short circuit'? Why is it dangerous?

_____

_____

_____

_____

4. Which of the following circuits will have the brightest bulb? Explain why you think this.

A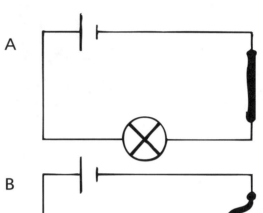

B

C

D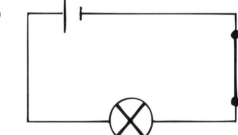

_____

_____

_____

_____

_____

Illustrations © Tony O'Donnell © Sarah Wimperis

SCHOLASTIC

In this series:

ISBN 978-0439-94502-8

ISBN 978-0439-94503-5

ISBN 978-0439-94504-2

ISBN 978-0439-94505-9

ISBN 978-0439-94506-6

ISBN 978-0439-94507-3

ISBN 978-0439-94508-0

To find out more, call: 0845 603 9091
or visit our website www.scholastic.co.uk